Porta Palazzo

CONTEMPORARY ETHNOGRAPHY

Series Editors
Kirin Narayan
Alma Gottlieb

A complete list of books in the series
is available from the publisher.

Porta Palazzo

The Anthropology of an Italian Market

RACHEL E. BLACK

UNIVERSITY OF PENNSYLVANIA PRESS

PHILADELPHIA

Published by
University of Pennsylvania Press
Philadelphia, Pennsylvania 19104-4112
www.upenn.edu/pennpress

Printed in the United States of America on acid-free paper
10 9 8 7 6 5 4 3 2 1

Library of Congress Cataloging-in-Publication Data
Black, Rachel, 1975–
    Porta Palazzo : the anthropology of an Italian market / Rachel E. Black. — 1st ed.
        p.   cm. — (Contemporary ethnography)
    Includes bibliographical references and index.
    ISBN 978-0-8122-4406-9 (alk. paper)
    1. Porta Palazzo (Market : Turin, Italy) 2. Markets—Italy—Turin—Sociological aspects. 3. Grocery trade—Social aspects—Italy—Turin. 4. Grocery shopping—Social aspects—Italy—Turin. 5. Turin (Italy)—Social conditions. 6. Black, Rachel, 1975—Homes and haunts—Italy—Turin. I. Title. II. Series: Contemporary ethnography.
HF5474.I82B535   2012
381'.4564130945121—dc23   2011050014

To my mother, Rebecca, for sharing her love of food, cooking, and gardening. You are a constant inspiration to me.

CONTENTS

FOREWORD

Carlo Petrini

The novelist Giovanni Arpino, like myself a native of Bra in the northwestern Italian region of Piedmont, once wrote that, paradoxically, Turin, the capital of our region, is "the most southern of Italian cities." He was referring to the fact that, as a result of the employment-related internal migration of the 1950s and 1960s, a huge population of the city consisted of people from Calabria, Sicily, Puglia, and so on.

Today I would go farther and argue that, thanks to more recent immigration from North Africa and the Middle East, of all the major European cities not actually on the sea, Turin is the most Mediterranean. I say this largely because it is a city of markets. Most of its quarters hold large, sprawling open-air affairs every day of the week. Historically speaking, I like to think of markets as links between different realities. It was thanks to them that, for centuries, the civilizations that sprang up along the shores of the Mediterranean met and melded. Mediterranean civilization would never have grown as rich and complex as it is without its markets, meeting places but also venues in which goods, culture, and knowledge were and are exchanged.

Today traditional markets not only are of strictly economic importance but also have a clear social and urban significance. Often they are the mirror of the local context in which they are immersed.

The largest of all Turin's markets, known popularly as Porta Palazzo, is held in the city's central and enormous Piazza della Repubblica. It is said to be the largest open air market in Europe—that's just the fruit and vegetable section!—and is encircled at the northern end by the baroque architecture of Filippo Juvarra, not a local but a Sicilian from Messina.

As my good friend the British food and wine writer Matthew Fort has written in his book *Eating Up Italy,* "This was the one that drew the white-collar workers, blue collars, nursing mothers, provisioning grannies, men, women, Ghanaian and Tunisian immigrants and Romanian gypsies, lovers of horsemeat, tripe and lungs, epicures looking for *funghi porcini,* men from Sardinia, Sicily and Calabria who needed the ingredients to recreate the dishes of the villages of their birth. . . . The voices were pitched a plangent, sing-song level. The singers were Algerians and Moroccans, as well as Sardinians, Sicilians and Calabresi."

Large-scale retail logics have influenced the way in which even the most traditional markets work. The supply chain has been standardized and anonymous hypermarkets—nonplaces par excellence—have entered into competition with the urban markets we know and love. In some cases, the new has come out on top. In Paris, for example, Les Halles used to be the liveliest fruit and vegetable market in the city; now it has been replaced by a shopping mall. But open-air markets still haven't been beaten and, at least in Italy, are the places where people go to buy fresh produce. And they will remain so, if they can continue to ensure an alternative to the standardization of taste.

It would be wrong to take the effects of globalization for granted. It may reduce diversity among cultures, but it also promotes diversity inside them. On the minus side, we are witnessing increasing homologation; on the plus side, we are seeing the creation of new diversities. The multiethnic Porta Palazzo market of today is a living symbol of the phenomenon that, regardless of its many contradictions, is becoming a place to understand the reality that surrounds us and to figure out our future—especially at the table.

But enough of the musings of an Italian who has frequented Porta Palazzo since he was a kid. In the book you are about to read—part anthropological investigation, part personal memoir—you will find out what a non-Italian has to say about the place. It is a particular source of pleasure for me that the non-Italian in question is Rachel Black, a Canadian anthropologist who has lectured at the University of Gastronomic Sciences in Pollenzo, near Bra, founded by Slow Food in 2004 to encourage the building of an organic relationship between gastronomy and agriculture. I found her insights profound and stimulating, and I am sure you will too.

Going to Market

The piazza heaved and jostled in front of me. I did not know which way to turn. Warm bodies invaded my space, and elbows jammed into my ribs as I squeezed along the narrow corridor. My eyes searched for a focal point among all the moving shoppers and the stands, something to steady this uneasy shopper. Zucchini and tomatoes were piled in mountainous displays. The shrill voice of vendors burst out close to my ears, their songs like nursery rhymes gone wrong. A pungent stench of rotting meat and pressed citrus attacked my nose. The world was spinning around me, and I feared I would lose my way. I felt as if this huge market would swallow me whole. Intrigued from the start, the first few times I came to the Porta Palazzo market alone I never imagined I could know this complex, bustling place, let alone come to think of this market as my second home.

This fascination with markets is odd coming from someone who had never been a big fan of grocery shopping. Back home in North America, buying food was always part of domestic drudgery, carried out in giant, impersonal supermarkets; these were solitary outings in which I rarely met or talked to a soul, not even in the long check-out lines. In contrast, the markets in Europe were alive with people, heated conversations, amazing produce, and delicious food. Living in Europe, I found that markets offered an entry into the social world of my adopted country. I also began my gastronomic apprenticeship at the market. My interest in markets started from a practical necessity and slowly became a focal point for academic research as I delved below the surface of my everyday experiences.

In 1998, I moved to Lyon, France, to complete my Master's thesis in history. Afterward, I decided to stay on and work for a few years before returning to North America to pursue a doctorate. In 2001, I moved to Turin, Italy, from Lyon to join my fiancé Alberto, a native Torinese. While living in France, I had visited Turin a number of times and was enchanted by the sharp lines of the Alps that marked the skyline on clear, sunny days of spring and the hum and glow of the neon signs on via Roma on rainy days of fall. Initially, I spent my time exploring the city and doing the shopping each morning in the markets. This is where I learned about Piedmontese culture for myself—the food, the dialect, etiquette, and mannerisms. When I was given the opportunity to start a PhD in cultural anthropology at the Università degli Studi di Torino in fall 2001, I jumped at the chance. In 2002, Alberto and I were married; I settled into life in Turin, and my research on markets became a more formalized, structured endeavor.

Before meeting Alberto, I do not think I even knew where Turin was on the map. This northern Italian city lies just south and east of the Alps at the start of the Padan plain. Turin is the capital of the Piedmont region. Despite its historic and economic importance, it is a city that that has often been left off the tourist map and, therefore, has been largely unexplored by outsiders. What I found was a city in full renaissance—Turin had begun preparing for the spotlight of the 2006 Winter Olympics. After my French market experiences and newfound love for shopping al fresco, I was immediately drawn to the city's biggest and liveliest market, Porta Palazzo, fabled to be the largest open-air market in Western Europe. While thousands of kilos of fruits, vegetables, and other foodstuffs are sold here each day, friendships are made, families are reunited, ethnic and cultural tensions are negotiated, and local identities are constructed through the daily workings of the market. Located in Turin's historic center, Porta Palazzo ("palace gate" in Italian) has been one of the city's most important markets since the mid-nineteenth century. For the people living in the areas surrounding the market, it is an integral part of their daily lives. The market shapes the neighborhood as it transforms the immense public square known as Piazza della Repubblica into a commercial and social space, drawing shoppers and vendors from all over the city and surrounding areas. The transient nature of the market and the people who frequent the square make the area a liminal space where illicit activities happen amid the everyday workings of the market. Porta Palazzo is not known as the safest area in the city. It is often referred to as a "popular" neighborhood (in the Italian sense of *popolare*). I chose to study Porta Palazzo because it is in many ways an amplified version of most urban open-air markets in Europe, because of its complexity, and because of the way in which the market has defined the place in which it is located.

For most Europeans, markets are everyday events that are part of the cityscape. From the moment I first set eyes on an open-air market in France and then Italy, I could not help feeling envious of the abundance of food, the aesthetic beauty of most markets, and the people gathered at the street corners or near the market stalls. European marketplaces made me aware of all the things that were missing back home in Canada: fresh produce sold by farmers, someone to suggest a recipe, and a place to meet friends and strangers. I realized that I had always been looking for a place where I could connect with people and food. There is a farmers' market movement in the United States and Canada, which is just beginning to meet people's social and nutritional needs. On one hand, we still have a long way to go, as most markets serve only a small portion of urban populations and market organizers often have to do battle to get permits and find spaces for their markets (Chrzan 2008). Europeans, on the other hand, largely take for granted what they have and have not yet considered the consequences of declining market attendance and the economic shortcomings of local agriculture. Nonetheless, there seems to be a common desire in both Europe and North America to connect with our food, to know where it comes from and how it is grown, and to learn about different culinary cultures. One of the most important and often least discussed parts of this desire to connect is the social aspect of cooking and eating that is integral to markets. The market may be just the place to bring us back to our food, community, and the cultural diversity of food and the acts of cooking and eating. As I began my research, I started to see the Porta Palazzo market as a place that has incredible potential to connect people with their food and in turn to each other.

One of my first questions about markets was, "Has this social aspect always been a part of food shopping?" According to the *Oxford Dictionary of Current English*, a market is the "gathering of people for the purchase and sale of provisions, livestock, etc.; space or building used for this; demand (for commodity and service); place or group providing such demand;

3

conditions as regards, or opportunity for, buying or selling; rate of purchase and sale." This definition places the market on three levels: the physical place organized around the activity of exchange, the gathering of people for the activity of buying and selling, and the abstract economic concept of exchange that in many ways takes us away from the social. At a very basic level, the concept of market is dependent on the social. Open-air markets are driven by the social and urged on by the economic. If we looked at just the economics of markets, there would not be a lot of reason for this form of distribution to continue. Economically speaking, markets are among the least efficient methods of food distribution and retail (List 2009).

Given their economic inefficiency, why do markets still exist in modern European cities? At the market, vendors buy produce at a wholesale market or bring it from their farms in individual vehicles—a costly and disorganized form of transportation. Rather than rationalizing the supply chain through centralization, the open-air market is about individuals who source and transport goods separately. While this model is an outlet for diversity and entrepreneurial independence, it is not the most cost effective way of bringing goods to market. How have these long-standing urban institutions survived in the face of modernization, and what are their economic and social functions in the age of the superstore and the shopping mall? There must be something there of value beyond profit.

Anthropologists have studied open-air markets to understand how economic exchanges are socially and culturally constructed (Geertz 1988; Plattner 1985; Polanyi 1957); however, these institutions deserve renewed attention in the face of drastic changes in food provisioning and eating habits in Europe. Markets need to be studied as important places of sociability in cities, where public spaces are increasingly deserted and inhospitable. Markets can be compared on a social level to plazas and parks, but they also have commercial, nutritional, and culinary functions that are intertwined with the sociability that takes places in the everyday exchanges between market-goers. This ethnographic study of the Porta Palazzo market in Turin, Italy, investigates the way in which social relations are negotiated on many levels through the everyday activities of the market.

I argue that the social life of the market keeps these institutions running. They stand in stark contrast to other forms of provisioning that are largely devoid of social exchanges. This book will investigate the loss of social life in provisioning and how this situation occurred, as well as the repercussions. Since the postwar period, supermarkets have become the dominant venues for provisioning in Italy, and they have played an important part in the creation of consumer society (Humphrey 1998). Western societies place an emphasis on the consumption of goods and value the acquisition of these goods over other achievements and other types of fulfillment. The supermarket is a central site of consumption that has played a part in breaking down the social connections between people while distancing them from the source of their food. If you have ever been to an average supermarket, you will be able to attest that few people converse while shopping or waiting in line for the checkout. There is generally no opportunity to talk to or get to know the people who produced the food you are purchasing, and there are few opportunities to learn anything about this food. Individualism, self-service, and efficiency epitomize the supermarket shopping experience. Local cuisines and diet have been deeply affected by this shift in food provisioning: the number of calories consumed in Italy has steadily increased throughout the second half of the twentieth century.[1] The delocalization of food distribution and provisioning has broken the social relations of food, and the move away from markets has also contributed to the abandonment of public spaces as social places. Going to market gave people a chance to spend time together. The exodus to the supermarket broke down the social fabric created by "marketing." The "delocalizing," or what Anthony Giddens (1991) and Karl Polanyi (1944) call "disembedding," of urban populations and increased mobility due to the accessibility of private transport, namely, automobiles, changed people's sense of community, place, and use of time and space: what has occurred is a "'lifting out' of social relations from local contexts and the rearticulation across indefinite tracts of time-space" (Giddens 1991: 18). Supermarkets have done just this: people no longer shop close to home with their neighbors, and few products they purchase can be considered local. This sort of provisioning fits the pace of modern life, even if there are social trade-offs. Who has time for multiple transactions when buying groceries? Every purchase at the market requires a social and economic exchange, which can be very time consuming. As part of a changing foodscape,[2] markets as viable sources for provisioning have been challenged by the reorganization of daily life and the changing of eating habits. Not many women have the time to shop in the morning or to spend hours preparing two daily meals from scratch. Few studies have taken into consideration how changes in shopping have affected the way people think about food and what they eat. I also argue that these changes are directly linked to shifts in social life and use of urban space.

This seems reason enough for anthropologists to return to markets, this time in the European context. What has changed, and what new findings can this well-trod field provide? Often tied to a bounded conception of their particular field, anthropologists have marginalized or passed over the modern marketplace. In particular, little attention has been given to markets in Europe. With increasing concerns about food production, distribution, and health, the moment is ripe to reconsider the market as a focal point for ethnographic research. The maturing of the field of food studies has placed great emphasis on the production, preparation, and consumption of food, but provisioning is often left out of this research (Beriss and Sutton 2007; Paxson 2008; Stiffler 2002).[3]

The market is not a straightforward object of study, and there are many possible approaches. Anthropologists have developed new ethnographic methods for dealing with complex field sites. It is rare, if not impossible, to find a perfectly bounded field nowadays, and anthropologists have developed excellent techniques for studying connections and relations that are spatially dispersive (Clifford 1997; Falzon 2009; Hannerz 2003); these are perfect for studying markets whose social and trade networks cover great geographic distances. Theodore Bestor's study of the Tsukiji market in Japan is an example of the application of a holistic approach to study a food market (Bestor 1999, 2004). There is a need for more of this type of research with regard to food provisioning—work that looks at food systems and brings together the social, cultural, and economic connections of food and provisioning.

Markets are windows onto many worlds and therefore they are important subjects, but they were long both undermined and overlooked because many anthropologists and journalists represented markets either as picturesque elements of everyday life or as tourist attractions, not as places that can tell us about how people live together. A closer look at the Porta Palazzo market reveals an incredible degree of complexity: in particular, this market is the hub of social relations for minority groups that are increasingly isolated from public spaces and public life. With fewer spaces of sociability in cities, markets provide important meeting points for local residents, the elderly, farmers, tourists, and immigrants. The economic and the social aspects of everyday life drive this meeting place, and what makes this market different from other commercial spaces is its public nature. The combination of social and economic transactions makes the experience of going to market unique: economic exchange facilitates social interaction and creates a space for sociability.

Despite the obvious differences between markets throughout the world, there is something universal about the way in which people from different backgrounds and cultures are brought together for the purpose of exchange, trade, and socializing. Markets are particularly useful sites for studying migrant and transnational populations because they are often the first places in cities to attract such diverse populations. For migrants, the marketplace is often the most familiar institution they encounter in the host country. With so many people from different backgrounds coming together in one place, the negotiation of the use of space can be witnessed on a daily basis; the market is not without its conflicts and moments of tension. These public spaces offer many opportunities for studying diversity and interaction, as well as a unique view of foodways and food choices. Markets offer important sites for exploring the use of public spaces in Western cities beyond parks and the boulevard.

These public institutions have numerous practical functions, including the distribution of reasonably priced food, a place for information exchange, and a meeting point for locals and foreigners. Originally, markets were the city's central outlets for provisioning and the main hubs of exchange between the city and its outlying rural areas. With the rise of the grocery store and the supermarket in the twentieth century, markets took a backseat in the food-retailing panorama. Nonetheless, as the economic importance of these institutions waned, they remained central to local urban life, particularly from a social perspective. The function of markets has changed in many ways over the past century, but their social functions are constant and vital for creating a sense of place and community in cities. Some markets have become sites of leisure, and going to the market is akin to going for a walk in the park or spending time at a community center.

Economic life does not negate social life. I learned from studying markets that the actual exchange of goods for money often facilitates social exchanges. By the sheer number of transactions that people need to engage in to get their shopping done at the market, social interaction of some sort is inevitable. As people wait in line, choose their produce, or pay for their goods, commerce is not the only thing going on. People are discussing their everyday lives together, getting to know one another, even if only on the surface. What types of sociability exist at open-air markets, and what are the conditions for accessing this social world? Not only do economic exchanges facilitate sociability, but many conversations are initiated when talking about food. Observing such interaction has led me to ask how food defines sociability at the market. These are just a few of the initial questions that guided my fieldwork.

Markets are complex spaces of commerce and sociability that often contradict the modern use of public spaces; they are remnants of the past lodged in the hearts of modern cities. At the same time, markets are living institutions rather than static heritage sites, and they exercise important social functions for the neighborhoods in which they are located. Markets are places where people come in contact with each other, places that evoke the senses and often memory. They encourage people to communicate. Markets are places where identities are contested and formed (Venturi, Brown, and Izenour 1977: 9). For all these reasons, markets, in their many forms, continue to be important social places that enrich urban life, give meaning to place, and create social cohesion, despite a trend that points to the diminishing importance of the public sphere as a physical and social space in everyday life.

A Market in Four Parts

Despite spending seven years frequenting and working at the Porta Palazzo market, I felt unable to capture every aspect of the place. It took me some time to find a narrative frame for discussing and analyzing this market—through its complexity, it evaded a straightforward ethnographic description.

Instead of a linear account, I have chosen to focus on specific themes that came out of my fieldwork. In this book, I offer snapshots of the people who work and shop at the markets and the issues they face as they navigate it. These themes will speak to larger social, economic, and political issues in food studies in Italy, the rest of Europe, and North America.

The first part of this book provides a background for the four analytical frames that are introduced in the second part. Chapter 1 gives a general discussion of markets as a field of study. In particular, it looks at some of the techniques I used to carry out my ethnographic research at Porta Palazzo. This chapter is useful for researchers, students, and city planners setting out to study markets. Although focused on the Italian context, I believe that the research methods and questions will serve as a good starting point for those doing research elsewhere. Chapter 2 offers a historical overview of Turin and Porta Palazzo's development as the city expanded. Based on archival research and secondary sources, this historical background is critical for understanding the recent changes that have occurred at the market. Setting the ethnographic scene, chapter 3 gives a description of the Porta Palazzo market as it is today and at the time I was doing my research on markets. The renovation of the market in 2004–2006 is discussed here. This chapter provides a bigger picture of Porta Palazzo, helping to contextualize the more focused snapshots that follow.

The central themes of investigation begin in Chapter 4, which looks at consumption as a form of moral evaluation in the public space of the market. Food often provides a forum for different forms of evaluation; whether looking in a fellow shopper's grocery basket, discussing a recipe, making sexual remarks, or commenting on a person's physical appearance, food is at the center of much of the anxiety-producing banter that goes on at the market. The carnivalesque nature of this unique public space allows for the transgression of normalized gender and social roles, which provides an opportunity for analyzing changing relations between men and women of different ages and social backgrounds. This study uses food as a medium for exploring men's and women's shifting social roles within the family and Italian society as a whole. Through their eating habits and everyday conversations about food and eating, women who work and shop in the market reveal anxiety related to ideal body image. That said, women are not the only people who express their gender identities and anxieties through food; the market is also a space where men can show an interest in gastronomy and build friendships with other men through an exchange of culinary experiences, both sensual and mundane. In Italy, cooking and culinary knowledge can be seen as an expression of masculinity and power. Food also serves as a sexual discourse that allows for the temporary overturning of acceptable gender and socioeconomic relations and is ever present in the vendors' calls that are riddled with innuendoes and off-color comments. While food is the fodder for playful ridicule, it is also the focus for other forms of public humiliation: every day, elderly men and women sift through the refuse left by the market in search of their next meal. The market is a place where food insecurity becomes a public issue that few are willing to face. Food provides a matrix, and the public space of the market provides a venue for individuals and groups to assess and challenge one another and themselves.

Chapter 5 looks at the recent wave of immigration to Italy and the social tensions associated with large-scale in-migration. For newcomers, the market has historically been a point of reference. Like the southern Italians before them, immigrants from Morocco, Romania, Peru, and Nigeria, to name but a few sending countries, appropriate and use the market in their own ways. Often, the market is the first place Italians and immigrants come in contact with each other. On one hand, these encounters can be the first step for both parties to discover the "Other" through the creation of relationships based on personal experience. Such relationships are essential for breaking down problematic stereotypes proliferated by the Italian media. On the other hand, these encounters are not always happy multicultural moments: they can be mired with misunderstandings and are symptomatic of larger social tensions. These interactions are often violent and reveal strained relationships between immigrants and their reluctant hosts.

Chapter 6 looks at Porta Palazzo's fame as a multiethnic center, which has not always been viewed in a positive light; the market area is infamous for illegal trade, petty crime, and drugs. However, the city of Turin and the market administration have recently tried to improve the image of the area by promoting the market as a multicultural commercial space and as a cultural heritage site. The local authorities have represented Porta Palazzo as a place where culinary traditions, both local and foreign, are upheld in the face of global homogenization. Food and cuisine are presented as a potential bridge between Italians and immigrants. Ethnic restaurants, marketing campaigns, and the media are working to make cultural diversity benign and even palatable as they present the Other as a tasty morsel to be consumed. This chapter focuses on how cuisine, food, and culinary discourse can be used as tools for building multiethnic communication and understanding. In particular, the pros and cons of ethnogastronomic tourism are analyzed here.

In Chapter 7, the farmers' market at Porta Palazzo offers an opportunity to explore the construction of local food from the perspective of popular beliefs concerning changing consumption patterns. The *mercato dei contadini* (farmers' market) is separate from the rest of the market, and only farmers are allowed to sell there. This part of the market has a unique culture. In North America and Italy, there has been a great deal of discussion about eating local food: the publication of *The 100-Mile Diet* (Smith and Mackinnon 2007) and initiatives by Slow Food, which started in Italy, are attempts to make people aware of sustainable food production and consumption. Italians have recently coined the term *chilometro zero* for eating local and have their own unique history and relationship to local food production.[4] Farmers' markets are local food at its most immediate: they are points of contact between city dwellers and farm folk and one of the last connections between consumption and production. The meaning of local food is shaped and negotiated by the market itself but also through interactions between farmers and consumers. From a social and linguistic perspective, the *mercato dei contadini* is essential for the exchange of local knowledge concerning language, food, and rural customs. It is a place where local food is constructed, a place where past is present and tradition is adapted and reinvented in the recipes that are discussed. At the farmers' market, the fast pace of city life is slowed down; space is created, time is made for people to relate to each other, and relationships are based on day-in, day-out reputations that are built over time. Most of the shoppers in this area of the market are regulars and have long-standing relationships with the farmers there. Shopping at the *mercato dei contadini* is not something that can be done in a rush; it requires time to talk about the harvest, politics, and gossip.

Although this is book is not meant to be a cookbook, the four main ethnographic chapters (4–7) end with a recipe that has been mentioned or discussed in that chapter. These are recipes that I gathered and adapted during my time in the field. I hope that they will give you a taste of Piedmont and a better understanding of the cuisine that is inspired by the Porta Palazzo market. As I studied the market over an eight-year period, I witnessed a lot of struggles, improvements, and changes. In this book, I have tried to include ethnographic snapshots that portray the vitality of this dynamic place that taught me so much about being an immigrant in Italy, about Italian culture, and, most important, about food.

The Market as a Field

Finding a Place at the Market

The bright orange tram rattles down the tracks and into the belly of the city, Porta Palazzo. I squeeze between the bodies holding tight to seats and handles. My shoes make a thumping sound as they hit the metal step on the way down to the gray street below. As I wander the long horizon created by via Milano, my eyes stop at the tangle of pushcarts and cases of fruit waiting for strong arms to stock them onto the overflowing market stalls. These stands look as if they could tip over at any minute onto innocent customers with their baby prams and rolling market baskets. Which way should I go first? The sheer size of the place, the noise, and the movement are overwhelming: I felt like a little Gulliver in a gastronomic Brobdingnag the first few times I shopped here. At the same time, somewhere in my mind, the Porta Palazzo market has always been everything a market should be: a chaotic, fast-paced spectacle to behold, a place that inspires the spirit and the culinary imagination. Antonio sells me lemons. Giovanna always has a twinkle in her eye and a special deal on fruit for me. I like to cross over corso Regina, the street that separates two sectors of the market, to buy my lettuce and seasonal vegetables from Pietro at the farmers' market. These vendors make me feel special; they make me feel that I belong to this place. They remember my name and where I am from, and they do not mind that I want to know everything about their work, in particular, the food they sell. As I frequent the market more and more, I start to have my routines and favorite places to stop at the beginning and end of my shopping trips—I am becoming a shopper like any other at Porta Pila.

I started full-time fieldwork in the Porta Palazzo market (also affectionately known as Port Pila by locals) in May 2002, which continued for a year and was followed by frequent visits to the market until 2009. The first year I carried out my research as part of my doctoral dissertation at the Università degli Studi di Torino, where I was pursuing a Ph.D. in cultural anthropology. My graduate training offered me the theoretical and philosophical tools for tackling and analyzing fieldwork, but the more practical elements were left a mystery—it was the sink-or-swim school of ethnography. As for ethical research, there was no review board at my university, so I decided to use the guidelines set out by the American Anthropological Association. Despite the lack of institutional structure, I wanted my research to be as ethical as possible. Given this was my first fieldwork experience, I was eager to understand how it was done before entering the field. Fellow graduate students and professors told me that each ethnographer must decide which techniques work best for him or her. Sometimes this required trying things, failing, and then trying something else. Despite a great deal of reading about various field techniques, I was left to my own devices as I headed out into my field, less than a mile down the street from my department.

Initially, I attempted to gather as much information as possible by observing the everyday running of the market and by doing archival research. My observational activities immediately demanded my participation in the goings-on of the market—it was impossible to observe passively, and there was little room to stand still and watch the world go by. The answer seemed obvious to me: my first solution to finding my place at the market was to do my own shopping. Occassionally Alberto, my husband, would accompany me on weekend shopping trips, but generally I went alone. All this shopping worked well as an ethnographic approach because I developed relationships with vendors and had a chance to exchange thoughts and ideas with other shoppers while waiting to be served or waiting for the bus or tram. Needless to say, there were also a number of problems with this type of participation: I was only on one side of the fence. I had no access to the "backstage," the place so much of the vendors' lives inhabited (Goffman 1959). Another consequence of my frequent shopping was an overabundance of groceries: I could only buy and eat so much food. The market took up my mornings, but my afternoons were filled with cooking everything I had purchased. Early on, I learned how to draw out my shopping experience. I wanted to shadow people, but the issue of consent in such a bustling public space seemed almost impossible. On a number of occasions, I shadowed friends and acquaintances on their shopping trips to the market. It was hard to say how much of their behavior changed because of my presence, but these trips offered me a glimpse of what other people's market experiences were like. Each person had his or her favorite stands and vendors who gave deals. Each shopper had a unique mental map of the market and way of navigating this incredible maze. Almost everyone had his or her own market ritual—from a cup of coffee at a specific bar under one of the porticoes or a drink from the public fountain with the bull's head representing the city of Torino. After about a month of doing a lot of shopping, I realized I was going to have to take the next step and cross over to the other side: I needed to find a job in the market to understand the vendor's point of view.

I did not really find my place in the market until I got behind a market stall and climbed onto the vendors' platform. My fieldwork at Porta Palazzo consisted of working with a number of individuals and families from different ethnic backgrounds, as well as doing my daily shopping at the market, for a year. I tried to cover as much of the market as possible. Porta Palazzo is broken up into four main sectors: the big resellers' market, the farmers' market, the fish market, and the clothing market. These are punctuated by several covered pavilions where meat and dairy are sold and a covered market area where house goods such as pots and pans and cleaning supplies are on offer. My research focused on the areas of Porta Palazzo where food is sold in open-air settings, a mammoth task given the size of the retail area and the number of vendors in and around the market square.

At first, I had a difficult time finding a job, and no one wanted to employ me legally. There were a number of practical challenges in finding employment, but I used the flexibility of Italian systems to participate. I began by asking a vendor whom I had befriended, Antonio,[1] if he had any work for me. He looked at me with a dumbfounded expression on his face: this was extremely inappropriate behavior on my part since I was acting outside my prescribed role as his faithful customer. It took Antonio a moment to swallow this idea, but he eventually told me to come back the next day, and he would see what he could do. When I returned, Antonio asked his brother to cover for him at his stand, and he walked me over to meet some friends who had a candy stand. He presented me as someone who was desperately seeking work and in need of money. I tried to intervene and explain that this was not the case, that I was actually doing ethnographic research. "Ethnowhat?" No one paid much attention to what I was saying, but it was agreed that I could come and work two days a week when the stand was busiest on Fridays and Saturdays. Despite feeling I had failed in my ethical duty to explain my activities, I was thrilled to have a chance to stand on the other side of the market stall. As I imagined, this turned out to be a fabulous place from which to study the daily working of the market.

While looking for a job, I started to think about the ethical implications of actually getting a job at the market. How would I communicate clearly what I was doing? Should I accept a salary? If I did, would that be unethical since my main goal was research? If I did not, how would that impact my working relations? Would my experience be less "real"? These are the sorts of questions that whirled around in my mind as I embarked on this new phase of my fieldwork. I certainly was not the first anthropologist who had grappled with making the workplace and apprenticeship part of their fieldwork. Elizabeth Hsu explores the world of apprenticeship and acupuncture in her article "Participant Experience: Learning to Be an Acupuncturist, and Not Becoming One" (2007). Hsu argues that engaging in "participant experience" allowed her to gain practical skills that led to insights that went beyond what could be learned through observation alone. In addition, Hsu feels that that the power relations of the fieldwork experience are shifted when the ethnographer enters into the position of "dependent apprentice" (Hsu 2007: 149). Similarly, I felt that, by taking a paid position as a market vendor, I would have to conduct myself in accordance with the rules of my employer and the market. I would be entering into the inner workings and logic of the market, something that I was not privy to in my position as a shopper. I did not want to be a mere observer. At the same time, I grappled with the ethical issues of being paid for my work: wasn't I already being paid by the university to conduct my research? Was I taking advantage of the situation? Other ethnographers have seen work as an important key to integrating into community life fully. For instance, William Kelleher's study of memory and identity in Northern Ireland (2003) focuses on the mundane activities of everyday life; this includes work. Kelleher not only engaged in community activities such as going to church or having a pint at the pub, but he actually worked in a nationalist glassworks. Although Kelleher also interviewed the management of the factory and did archival research there, his experience as a worker in the glass-cutting shop and then glassblowing factory allowed him to enter into the everyday lives of the workers and lent depth to this rich ethnography (2003: 162). I felt the same way about working in the market, and I knew that my ethnography would only be a one-sided outsider's view if I did not somehow enter into the working life of Porta Palazzo, paid or unpaid.

Antonio helped me land my first job, selling candy with Roberta and Lorenzo, a mother and son from Turin, in the piazzetta Milano. To be honest, I was initially not very interested in this job; I did not see sweets and snacks as "real" food. However, after a few days of work, I quickly realized that I had been extremely lucky to find this job because sweets are very telling of people's relationships to foods seen as luxury items and the way people psychologically justify their sweet tooth over health problems (such as diabetes and a variety of eating disorders). I worked mainly on Saturdays and much more during the busy Easter and Christmas seasons. The better Roberta and Lorenzo got to know me, the more they wanted me to work. It was hard to tell them that I wanted to work with other people to explore the other areas of the market. I could tell that they felt somewhat betrayed and never fully grasped my interest in the market and my need to branch out beyond their candy stand among the flower sellers in piazzetta Milano.

I started to loiter in the farmers' market on my days off from the candy stand. This is how I met Paolo, a cheesemonger from the Susa Valley. He took me under his wing and introduced me to half the farmers' market. I could not have found a more exuberant, forthcoming participant for my research.[2] I ended up working with some younger farmers, Enzo and Pietro mainly, who were friends with Paolo. I was never officially employed there, but I did odd jobs and minded the farmers' stands when they had to fetch their trucks at the end of the day or if they needed a short break. It took a little longer to build trust and a good "working" relationship with the farmers, but these were some of the most meaningful moments I spent at Porta Palazzo. Despite my love for the farmers' market, I still wanted to find out what life in the big market was like. When I did not show up at the farmers' market, people asked me where I had been and why I had not come. They were not impressed when I told them I had been working in the resellers' market: it was as if I had gone to the dark side. I quickly learned that the market is a very territorial place.

I found it hardest to get a job in the resellers' market because the vendors were the most diffident there. This probably has to do with the sheer size of the place; social relations among people working there are more competitive, and there is a lot of turnover in the laborers the vendors employ. In the end, I resorted to going around from stand to stand to see if anyone needed help. I courted one woman for several months; eventually, she consented to let me give her a hand. Giovanna, a woman with roots in Calabria, is a strong character who has kin spread throughout the market. She showed me the ropes with a stern hand and gave me honest advice. However, Giovanna likes to operate alone, and she soon pawned my free labor off on her Moroccan neighbors, with whom she had a love-hate relationship.

Mustafa and his brother "Giorgio" (his adopted Italian name) did not quite know what to make of me at first, but before long they appreciated that I was a hard worker. They had been in Turin for many years and had their very own corner of Porta Palazzo (two stands and another run by a female cousin who was a fresh arrival from Morocco). Mustafa was proud of his success and that he had been able to bring his young bride from Casablanca to live with him in Turin. He invited me over for tea to admire his two-room flat, his imported Moroccan furniture, enormous new fridge, and equally large television blaring news programs in Arabic. Fatima, his wife, did not speak a word of French or Italian, so we smiled at each other and talked with our hands. Working side by side, Mustafa and I got to know each other well. Mustafa's family and the Moroccan community at the market were very welcoming of this Canadian, whom they considered just another French-speaking foreigner like themselves.

The Moroccans were hesitant to give me up, but I pressed on in my journey around the big market. I went on to work in short stints in most of Mustafa's and Giovanna's neighbors' stalls. These included third-generation Torinese vendors; Giovanna's cousins; Tunisians who spoke eloquent French and held bachelor's degrees in economics; and Andrea, an exotic-fruit vendor from Chieri (my initial vendor contact), whose extended family has four stands in the resellers' area. I felt I could have hopped from stand to stand until I covered the whole market if I had more time. Once one person got to know me and could vouch for my character, I was in. The amount of trust I was granted almost immediately was surprising; I had my hands in nearly everyone's cash box after only an hour or two of apprenticeship. If I had made one false move, the entire market would have known.

In addition to the market stalls, I made friends in the bars where I had my many morning coffees and with the waiters who circulated through the market taking vendors' orders. They had the inside scoop on everyone and all market-related gossip. At the farmers' market, I learned to drink hot rum to keep warm and wear thick-soled boots to keep the cold from creeping up into my bones on the coldest mornings. Trying to chase the tingling feeling out of my fingers, I huddled around makeshift stoves with the other vendors until it felt as if my gloves would catch fire. As spring rolled around, the sweat rolled down my arm as I passed clients change under the broiling plastic awning of a fruit stand. I had never felt so exposed to the elements as when I was working at Porta Palazzo, and I found this the most difficult part of the job. After a year, I felt that this chaotic foreign place, which had at first shocked and overwhelmed me, had become a second home. I had worked my way under its hard outer shell.

My fieldwork at Porta Palazzo unfolded in a very organic manner. Over time, I developed a large network of vendor acquaintances, perhaps about forty in total, all over the market. I went on to sell food (in one form or another) at more than fifteen stalls throughout the market. By sweating and freezing next to the people I wanted to understand better, I developed meaningful personal relationships that gave me access to insider information. Although I enjoyed shopping at the market and talking to other shoppers, the most valuable experience I had while studying Porta Palazzo was working as a vendor. This was a delicate research technique that required a great deal of time and patience. Strict hygiene and labor laws imposed by the state, not to mention the tight-knit social order of the market, govern work at the market. I was fortunate to gain the trust and confidence of some remarkable market vendors who opened their world to me. In turn, I paid them back with my hard labor, and our friendship was mutually rewarding.

Defining the Market

As I got to know the market better, I was still unsure how to frame and define this field. Where does the market begin and end? One of the challenges of studying any kind of market is trying to get one's head around the spatial aspect of this dynamic place. Initially, I wanted to draw a clear line around the Porta Palazzo market that coincided with the physical space of the Piazza della Repubblica. As I got to know the market, I realized that this was one of my first misunderstandings about the space in which the market existed. I came to realize that the market is a place where connections are made and that the networks and ties between the market and the rest of the world are innumerable. In turn, these human and relational connections must also be considered spatially. It was nearly impossible to study Porta Palazzo without taking into consideration the links between places: Moroccan traders buy goods that come from Morocco via Paris; fruit vendors buy their wares at the wholesale market where it is trucked in from southern Italy and Spain; farmers bring their produce from their farms located throughout the Piedmont region and beyond; tourists come on buses from Grenoble, France. The market is inherently transnational. One useful way of thinking of a market is as a nodal point of commercial and social relations. For this reason, I opted for a rather abstract conception of the space of the market that went beyond the market square and took into consideration the spatial relations (commercial, imagined, and cultural) necessitated by the act of trading. This is in keeping with the recent development of multisited ethnography, which is particularly well suited for studies of transnationalism and trade (Marcus 1995; Amit 1999; Falzon 2009; Coleman 2009).

This unbounded approach to the market as a field poses specific ethnographic issues. In such a complex space, where does the ethnographer position herself? On my first day at Porta Palazzo, I imagined I would try just to observe people's movements in the market and get a feel for the flow of traffic in the space. I planted myself outside one of the market pavilions and tried to make myself as invisible as possible. This illusion lasted for about one minute. "Chi sei? Che stai facendo?" (Who are you? What are you doing?) asked a smiling Moroccan mint vendor. What was I supposed to say? I told him what I was doing—I was watching the market. This must have sounded ridiculous. He immediately proceeded to ask me a million questions about myself; I had never felt so present and visible. Lesson number one was that my presence had an impact on what I was doing, and I had to do something that would allow me to integrate into this field site. By standing still, I was standing out, and this was one of the challenges of observing and becoming part of the market. At times, visibility had its benefits in that potential participants in my research approached me first. Nonetheless, it also had its drawbacks: was this the everyday life of the market I was in search of, and was I really part of this new environment? At first, I was rather uncomfortable with being "present" but out of place, and I had to overcome feeling shy and awkward. I needed to find an outgoing public part of myself who could talk in Italian to people from all different social, economic, and cultural backgrounds. At that point, I had been living in Italy for about a year, and I still largely spoke Italian like a version of French. I could carry on a basic conversation, but I was struggling to keep up with the graduate seminars at the university. By the time I had completed my fieldwork, I not only could swear like a stevedore, but also could defend my dissertation in Italian with relative competence. In the end, I think working in markets showed me a part of myself I was not aware of; I discovered I could move beyond my personal comfort zone and communicate with all kinds of people. The flexible spaces of the market may have been disorienting at first, but it was eventually this flexibility that allowed me to integrate into this ever-moving, ever-changing place.

In many ways, the market challenged a great deal of what I had read about ethnographic methodology. How was I supposed to interview individuals using a recording device when no one could stop working or shopping for more than a few minutes? Due to the fast pace of the market, I had to adjust my methods to suit the environment. I did not always have time to stop and take notes. I would rush to a quiet place after the day's work was finished or during breaks and quickly write down the key events and my impressions in my field journal. Although many people suggested I use a tape recorder, I generally opted against this because most of the people I was working with reacted negatively. It made them very nervous. I wanted to get as close as I could to these people and their clients; the few times I tried to use a tape recorder, I felt that it created a barrier. Admittedly, recordings are excellent for quoting informants verbatim and picking up on language or phrases that might not have been heard or understood the first time. The market is also a very loud place where it is difficult to record individual conversations because of the cacophony of the background noise. During a number of the semiformal interviews conducted outside the market, I used a tape recorder with the consent of my informants. These interviews usually took place in cafés or private homes, where the atmosphere was less chaotic. The most important thing for me was that my collaborators felt comfortable enough to confide in me: how could difficult questions about family, business, and food be asked without first establishing rapport? Although a French sociologist once encouraged me to conceal my tape recorder, in my mind it was ethically out of the question to hide a recording device since my main goal was to develop a relationship based on trust and good ethical practicies (Marcus 1995: 103–12).

Carrying out visual observations using a camera and a video camera was an equally touchy task at times. I wanted to visually record and analyze the physical characteristics of my field. In some cases, the camera was an excellent way to engage people at the market in conversation (Pink 2001). They wanted to know who I was and what I was doing: this turned out to be a good opportunity for me to introduce myself. However, I noticed that the photos that I took at the beginning of my field experiences and those after I had worked in the markets for a long period were very different. The early photos are impressionistic or sometimes quite posed; the later ones focus on actors and everyday situations that were now familiar. When I look at a photograph of Mustafa, for example, I see him looking into the camera as if he is looking into my eyes; he is searching for me beyond the black box that hides my face. As I went around Porta Palazzo in fall 2003 with a cameraman taking shots of the market for a documentary film I was involved in, I realized how the camera changed everyone's reactions and behavior. While shooting *Quattro canti del mercato* (2006), the film's director Marcello Varaldi helped me understand how even a documentary frames the real world and how the people caught in the frame act out roles of their own construction egged on by the camera. They were playing their market roles for the camera. It became clear that the camera had an incredible power not only to record but also to distort (Ruby 2000). For this reason, I chose not to privilege visual anthropology in my fieldwork because the richness and complexity of the market were often lost in the framing and positioning of the camera. Many photographers and documentary filmmakers had been through the Porta Palazzo market; it was time for a look at the market that went beyond images.[3]

The Social Life of the Market

Integrating into the social life of the market and recording the daily goings-on were certainly some of my most important initial preoccupations. However, once I sat down to begin analyzing and writing about my experience, I was faced with the necessity of pushing myself to think about the relationship between the social and the economic. Can we really consider shopping as sociability? This is a complex question because there are so many kinds of social interactions at the market. It is easy to concede that the exchanges between shoppers fall into the category of sociability. Shoppers are often motivated to socialize by sheer proximity and by the shared experience of being in the market. They socialize for the pleasure of being social, and they can choose not to engage other shoppers in conversation if they so desire. Also, relationships between vendors seem to be motivated largely by a desire for sociability. Vendors often have long-term relationships with one another that sometimes develop into friendships outside the market. That said, these are still social exchanges mitigated by work and often complicated by economic competition. This aspect of economic motivation for social exchanges seems to undermine the definition of sociability, which is largely considered an activity that is not motivated by anything but the desire to have an exchange with another person. But why should economics and monetary exchanges negate the idea of sociability? Are people really paying for sociability when their conversation with a vendor is motivated by a commercial exchange?

Although social and economic life are interconnected, there are really two levels of exchange occurring, and neither can be discounted or separated. I began to consider how economic exchanges facilitated sociability and how the market created a new kind of social situation and a type of unique sociability that was very much part of shopping. Unlike any other food shopping experience, the market is unique because of the numerous transactions that take place during a shopping trip and because of the chaotic physical space in which these exchanges occur.

As I shopped and worked at Porta Palazzo, I was determined to understand why open-air markets and the social life that these institutions foster are different from any other space in the city. To understand better how markets have evolved and changed (or not), it was necessary to understand the history of Turin and the Porta Palazzo market as part of the urban fabric. I started my research in the municipal archives, only a few blocks from the market.

The Evolution of a Market

As I wander around the area surrounding the
market, I can see remnants of the past. There are
ruins of a Roman wall hidden behind market carts,
and someone told me earlier this morning about
an underground system of passageways that lead to
preindustrial "refrigerators." I have yet to explore
these *ghiacciaie* and I feel that I am still only still
skimming the surface of my historical research
about this market and its neighborhood. Each
day at the Archivio Storico della Città di Torino,
the bundles of documents that are delivered up
to me reveal the complexity of this market that
I comb each morning as I try to understand its
inner workings. Yesterday's milk scandals speak
to today's "bird flu" paranoia. The past brings
me closer to what I see now as common themes
emerge, and I begin to see the continuity and
change of this market over time.

—Fieldnotes, February 10, 2002

Torino: A Little History

What comes first: the city or the market? It is not always clear, but historically the development of towns and markets is often linked. Turin is no
exception. Located in the region of Piedmont in northwest Italy, Turin was

founded by the Gauls, and Hannibal sacked this outpost on his famous crossing of the Alps in 218 B.C.E. In 28, Castas Taurinorum was established by Julius Caesar as a military camp at the base of the Alps. Later, the camp developed into a fortified city, which was dedicated to Augustus. The Roman grid structure of the town is still visible in the urban layout of the city center. After the fall of the Roman Empire, the Goths, Lombards, and Franks successively invaded. The strategic position of this settlement along important trade routes beyond the Alps made it a point of passage for many.

Turin became a feudal lordship of the Savoy family under Emperor Frederick II in 1248. The burgeoning city became the capital of the Savoy Duchy during the sixteenth century. Its role as capital of this prosperous duchy helped the city grow and develop as an important center of trade and culture. The city also made its mark politically: Turin-born Savoy king Vittorio Emanuele II was a key player in the unification of Italy. After the events of 1861, Turin became the first capital of Italy, and Vittorio Emanuele was declared king. This privileged position was short-lived when the capital was transferred to Florence in 1865 and finally to Rome in 1871. Nation-building projects that worked hard to evoke the peninsula's Roman past eclipsed Turin as the birthplace of Italy. Today, most have forgotten Turin's moment in the sun.

Although often considered a secondary city, this northern metropolis is historically, architecturally, and culturally fascinating. The markets tell of some of the richest aspects of Turin's development. In the seventeenth century, Turin experienced a period of growth, and the city's markets responded to the new provisioning needs. The markets were grouped by product and spread throughout the city, within the confines of the center. The fruit and vegetable market was held in Piazza San Carlo, the wood and straw markets in Piazza Susina (now Piazza Savoia), the poultry market in Piazza San Giovanni, the fish market in front of San Gregorio (San Rocco) Church, and the wine market in Piazza Carlina (Bianchi 1975: 175–76). In 1755, Benedetto Alfieri reorganized the Piazza delle Erbe market and gradually moved this prosperous market to Porta Palazzo. By the mid-eighteenth century, Turin had not only a central market but also a number of smaller ones.

It was not unusual for a city to have markets divided based on the category of merchandise sold. There was limited open public space within the city's walled confines and no square large enough to accommodate a general market that included all the goods sold in the various markets. Until the late twentieth century, this division made sense on many levels because household purchases were often carried out by a group of people rather than by one person. Various family members, or domestic servants in wealthier households, took charge of different acquisitions. In addition, separation of markets made these distribution points easier to manage for administrators: tax collection was facilitated, and hygiene and congested city streets were easier to control.

Markets have always been important sources of provisioning in Turin, but small, local shops and bodegas were just as important for food supply, social cohesion, and culinary identity. Artisans, such as bakers and butchers, plied their trades and had close social relations with clients in the area. Shopping was generally a local activity that helped create a close-knit social fabric in cities. As Turin developed as a center of industry in the twentieth century, the way people shopped changed to reflect the social and economic shifts of the times.

The large working classes who worked on the Fiat and Lancia production lines still peopled the neighborhood open-air markets in the popular neighborhoods of San Paolo and Mirafiori, with occasional outings to Porta Palazzo. Here people could find reasonably priced food and products from southern Italy. Economically, there were not many other offerings for cheap goods for the growing ranks of workers and their families. Supermarkets did not begin to appear in Italy until much later than in most European countries. Department stores (such as Rinascente and la Standa in via Roma) and supermarkets (Spa in via Garosci) made their debut in Turin in the 1960s. Historian Bruno Maida (2004: 119) underlines that these new types of stores were important settings for conspicuous consumption and social mobility, mainly for the growing middle class. Not everyone could afford to shop in these new retail spaces, certainly not the average Fiat laborer.

While supermarkets remained inaccessible to the majority of Torinese, traditional forms of consumption such as markets kept people connected to their social networks, which often consisted of others from similar backgrounds. Italians from the South who had migrated to work in the factories surrounding the city found compatriots as well as familiar foods. For these people, shopping at markets was a sort of "ritual" activity that helped them cope with large social changes. Slowly the Torinese, regardless of their economic situation, were drawn to the supermarket; social mobility and conspicuous consumption were the main allure of these new commercial spaces. Maida (2004) compares the move from market to supermarket as similar, in a broader social context, to moving from a scale of community to that of society. Giorgio Triani (1996: 18) goes farther, claiming that new places of consumption, such as supermarkets, also played a significant role in the alienation of people from social ties and family and helped create more distant relations with neighbors. Most working-class Torinese still frequented markets for the majority of their shopping to the end of the twentieth century, but the supermarket was winning a growing piece of the market share as economies of scale steadily pushed down prices.

The foodscape of Turin has more or less slowly followed the path of a city moving from an industrial to a postindustrial phase of development. During the 1960s and 1970s, consumers wanted to flaunt their new economic affluence in "theaters" purposely built for these types of public displays. This trend has continued: with shifts in societal and family structures, supermarkets have large distribution and are convenient, while small shops still serve some important needs in local communities. Although they are more expensive compared with other provisioning choices, local shops mainly cater to the elderly who do not have transportation to supermarkets or markets or to people looking for specialty items that are difficult to find. They are convenient for residents who might need to make only a small purchase. In contrast, supermarkets have extended hours, but most of them are located in peripheral areas of the city, requiring a car or a special effort to make an outing to buy groceries. Most families shop at supermarkets once or twice a week. In many ways, local markets are comparable to small neighborhood shops in that they offer an important service as well as a social space. Sadly, small shops are struggling in Turin; they have a hard time competing with supermarkets, and the neighborhoods where they are located are often dormitories that are like ghost towns during the working day.

The last recent development in Torinese provisioning that should be mentioned is the growth of hard discount stores such as Lidal and Eurospin. These box stores offer nonbranded foodstuffs at discount prices and appeal to large and low-income families who often buy in bulk and are attracted by the low prices. Products in these stores are low-quality surplus that shifts from one European country to another. Hard discount stores have taken a small portion of shoppers away from all other forms of "traditional" shopping (small local grocers and markets) in addition to supermarkets (IRES 2001). These stores are often located in periphery areas but not always; in Turin, there are several discount stores in the city center and one not far from Piazza della Repubblica.

Turin's foodscape has drastically mutated over the past century and continues to change. The main trends include a delocalization of food commerce and a move to large-scale distribution focused in the outskirts of the city. This has resulted in less frequent shopping trips, which has had an impact on local cuisine and use of time outside working hours. In the future, shoppers may even increasingly resort to Internet shopping for home provisions, and public spaces of commerce will be transformed yet again. In this shifting urban foodscape, markets have not disappeared, but their functions have changed.

A Historical Gateway to the City

The development of markets and cities is intimately connected; however, while markets can exist without a city, the opposite is unthinkable. Historically, all cities have had markets; indeed, cities formed around markets. A number of groups established markets at predefined places; due to their commercial success, the markets were in many cases the catalyst that initiated the process of urban development. For this reason, markets can often be found at historical crossroads and along important trade and transportation routes. In most cases, cities are centers for local or international trade: the greater the population and flow of trade, the larger the markets. Fernand Braudel remarks in *The Structure of Everyday Life* that "every town, wherever it may be, must primarily be a market. Without a market, a town is inconceivable. A market, on the contrary, can be situated outside a village, even on a site on the open road or at a crossroads, without giving rise to a town. But a town needs to be rooted in and nourished by the people and land surrounding it" (1981: 501). The founding of markets often corresponded with population changes and urban expansion; when new neighborhoods were built, new markets appeared to serve the population's provisioning needs (Bromley 1998: 1317). Markets create central nodes in the commercial and social fabric of the city. In all cases, marketplaces became important central places in cities throughout the world.

Markets, and in turn cities, put themselves on the map through their connections outside their limits. Historically, markets have drawn people and goods from surrounding areas as well as distant places into the city and provided essential points of contact with the outside world. This was one of the most important functions of the market: it brought people from outside the city inside. It also facilitated economic as well as social exchanges between city dwellers and rural folk, between people from different cultures from near and far:

> The market square was a crossroads, and if it was the focus of community, it was also the point of intersection of different cultures. The variety of commodities, buyers and spectators was necessarily linked to the variety of economic and political connections between villages, regions and nation-states. (Stallybrass and White 1986: 36)

Markets in France are still referred to as *marchés forains* (foreign markets), and the vendors are called *forains* (foreigners) because, in the past, they would have all been from outside the city.

People from elsewhere were not the only things foreign at the market: as Pep Angli notes, Mediterranean agriculture was transformed by the introduction of new crops, such as tomatoes and potatoes, from the Americas, Asia, and the Middle East. In turn, the introduction of these plants changed not only the landscape but also the eating habits of the people in the Mediterranean (Angli 2004: 238). Alfred Crosby's *Columbian Exchange* (1972) is an in-depth exploration of the cultural and biological impact of the exchanges that took place between Europe and the Americas, including the introduction of new plants to Europe. When these new foods, such as the tomato and potato, were brought to Europe, markets were one of the first places where they were introduced as they slowly became integrated into local diets. Market vendors explained to their curious clients how to prepare these novel fruits and vegetables, and would have sung their praises as part of their spiel. In this case, the market had an educational role: it was a place where new products were distributed and discussed and where shoppers could learn how to prepare them. Markets have historically been central places for goods and people.

But where exactly were these central places first situated in the urban landscape? We imagine them colorfully laid out in the town square or near a large church. Yes, this was often the case. However, there is another answer: markets were established just outside the city gates. Historically, nearly all European cities taxed goods once they entered the gates of the city. To avoid this taxation, a great deal of trade happened just outside these points of entrance. This is not say that there were no markets inside walled cities like Turin; nonetheless, it was fairly common for a shady, less-regulated type of trade to develop along the urban periphery. This is the case with the market outside the palace gates of the royal city of the Savoy family. However, in the past, a lack of mobility constrained city dwellers to doing their shopping within a relatively small radius of their homes—in many ways a captive clientele. Markets can also be traditionally found near waterways and main roadways that facilitated transportation of goods and people. These places of trade were often found in liminal spaces.

The Porta Palazzo market was no exception: the area now referred to as Porta Palazzo has always been geographically marginal in relation to the city center and socially marginal due to the transient and sometimes undesirable character of its inhabitants and visitors. Located just outside one of the city's main gates, Porta di San Michele, at an important crossroad that leads to Milan, the area has always been well trafficked. The Porta Palazzo area became a place of industry and trade because of its location near the city and its proximity to the Dora River. While thriving and bustling, Porta Palazzo is a transitional area, with people and goods in constant movement and change.

Consequently, Porta Palazzo has historically been known as the gathering place of transient people and undesirable trades. In growing cities in Europe, it was common to find illicit activities (illegal trade, prostitution) and undesirable trades (tanning and animal slaughter) at the fringes of urban settlements (Lee 2008). City dwellers see these workplaces as unhealthy and associate them with disease. In fact, the area known as Borgo Dora (often grouped as part of the Porta Palazzo neighborhood) was home to the municipal slaughterhouse and grain mills, the *molassi*. The mills in the Borgo Dora area dated to 1492 and played an essential role in providing flour and grain to the city's inhabitants. A system of canals provided water for the mills from the Dora; until the 1940s the canals were a unique feature of this neighborhood. Although the close proximity of food production and processing was certainly advantageous for Turin, the municipal government deemed the area a health risk. In 1869, as the city expanded, the slaughterhouses were moved to a site closer to the city limits on corso Vittorio Emanuele because the Borgo Dora location was no longer considered sanitary or large enough to meet the city's growing need for food.[1] All these marginal, unhygienic activities permanently marked the historical memory of the Torinese; for this reason, Porta Palazzo and Borgo Dora have never been able fully to shake their reputations as polluted, peripheral areas.

How could a market flourish in such an area? At second glance, it may not seem so odd. There is a perfectly logical reason for the development of a major market in this location: as mentioned earlier, commercial activities often spontaneously occurred at city gates because vendors and buyers could avoid taxation by selling and buying goods before they entered the city. The presence of Roman ruins, an amphitheater, and the Palatine Gate attests to the fact that this site has long been a place of trade, transportation, and communication. A square was eventually formed to serve the purpose of trade, as well as to control access into the city. In 1699 Porta Palazzo (the Palace Gate), also known as Porta Vittoria, was completed. A square was planned in front of the San Michele Church, specifically as a place of trade. In keeping with the logic of municipal administration, if you cannot plan an institution, you can at least contain and try to control it. If there was going to be a market outside the city gate, the city might as well acknowledge its presence, tax the goods, and try to create better conditions for trade.

With this desire to create a better planned urban space, architect Filippo Juvarra at the end of the seventeenth century reenvisioned the area surrounding the gate and created a square enclosed by porticoes.[2] This particular type of architecture, mixing built forms with public spaces, is indicative of Mediterranean conceptions of space (Calabi 2004: 127). The porticoes took into consideration the less than hospitable northern climate of Turin and offered shelter from rain in the winter and harsh sun in the summer. These contained public spaces foster commerce, giving passersby a comfortable place to window shop and gather.

After Napoleon's conquest of Piedmont in the 1800s (Duggan 1994: 93), the French razed Turin's walls. At this point, the city was connected with outlying areas and could easily expand (CICSENE 1997: 65). The Napoleonic government drew up a *plan d'embellissement* (beautification plan). These were the first renderings of the piazza that was to become the heart of Porta Palazzo: a tree-lined square where two important boulevards would intersect.[3] The piazza was eventually constructed through a series of town planning schemes overseen by architect Gaetano Lombardi. Initially, the form of the square was developed based on architectural aesthetics, rather than a functional purpose. The intersection of two main arteries, via Milano and corso Giulio Cesare, created four equal quadrants. The current Piazza della Repubblica is still the same basic structure despite changes to the various bordering buildings and those eventually constructed in the square. For hygiene reasons, the market in front of the town hall in Piazza delle Erbe was moved to just outside the palace gate in 1835. Piazza Emanuele Filiberto (the square's original name) was completed in 1837 and became the largest square in the city. At this point, Porta Palazzo in its current form effectively came into being. City officials moved the market in front of city hall, which had served as the main provisioning point at the heart of the city, and joined it with the unofficial market that the municipality had turned a blind eye to for so long. This shift in municipal market organization was an important change to the city's physical and social structure—the city was expanding outward, and food provisioning was moving from the center.

Through the nineteenth century, Porta Palazzo's importance as a marketplace grew, attracting vendors from the regions surrounding Turin and shoppers from the entire city and outlying areas. Also for this reason, it is hard to think of Porta Palazzo as merely a local market: it has always been a major intersection of people from the entire city and for those coming and going. The ambulant vendors added to the transient nature of the neighborhood. Its functions as a market, a meeting place and a neighborhood have always made Porta Palazzo a "popular" neighborhood (in the Italian sense of the term *popolare*), attracting low-income groups and migrants. The social and economic makeup of this area has never placed it in a positive light in the eyes of most Torinese and the municipal authorities. The chaotic nature of market activities, the heaps of waste created by the market, and the masses of people the market draws create an environment and atmosphere that can be described as the polar opposite of the well-ordered bourgeois neighborhood. Porta Palazzo and Borgo Dora's poor reputations as lower-class neighborhoods eventually led to a half-century of decay and the present struggle to breathe new life into one of the richest neighborhoods (at least from a cultural perspective) of Turin.

Was this decline of the market and its surrounding area unique to Porta Palazzo? Historically, did the chaotic nature of certain markets eventually lead to their decline, or was it central to their existence? There is no simple answer to these questions. The markets of Rome and the Halles de Paris were certainly victims of decay and changing politics of food distribution (Thompson 1997). Despite its unruly nature, the Porta Palazzo market persists and maintains its original chaotic nature.

Controlling the Market

The market is a sort of contained chaos. The location of markets often corresponds to the positioning of political power: in that way, institutional power is transferred to urban structures (Malerba 1997: 17). One of the first steps to understanding the market's placement and organization is to investigate its past. I began my research by doing a historical survey of European markets to try to better understand developments at Porta Palazzo. Social and political control emerged as overarching themes.

After the fall of the Roman Empire, retail selling went through a period of decline. This was largely due to a decrease in population (of both consumers and producers) and the dangerous nature of selling goods in public spaces. Merchants feared being robbed. For this reason, most trading took place inside monasteries and on church property or within the walled confines of castles, where vendors paid for a space to sell their goods (Jah 2004: 223). Typically in the Middle Ages the Church watched over the public space of the market. Here we can see the origins of modern market

Figure 1. Piazza delle Erbe, Giovanni Tommaso Borgonio in Theatrum Statuum Regiae. Celsitudinis Sabaudiae Ducis, I, Amstellodami, Blaeu, 1682. ASCT, Collezione Simeom, N.1, tav. 17. Courtesy of the Archivio Storico della Città di Torino.

administration: the group that controls the market space requests a user's fee and, in return, offers a "secure" commercial space. Hannerz (1980: 85) reminds us that the extent of political rulers' protection and regulation over markets should not be underestimated. The paternalistic stance of municipal governments reaches back to this original function of protection.

The European economy began to grow again between the ninth and eleventh centuries, which, in turn, caused an increase in the population, trade, and markets (Malerba 1997: 20–21). In addition, since most "fairs" in the Middle Ages were associated with religious festivities, they took place in front of the church (22). The square around the church, much like the forum before it, was an important place for religion, social life, and commerce. Slowly, a shift occurred away from the Church toward the municipality and then the State, and along with this change, the positioning of markets near the city hall became common: in these locations, the authority of the State could keep a close eye on and impose taxes and regulations. This change occurred as municipalities consolidated their power and took on the central role of governing markets, food provisioning, and safety. The symbolic and often political power of the Church and the State has always had a place at the market: it would seem that trade in Europe, specifically in public spaces, could not exist without the presence of a higher moral power. In England, many market squares still have market crosses that, as Schmiechen and Carls point out, are "a silent reminder that the marketplace had historically been the center of peace and the rule of law" (1999: 4). It could also be said that access to food and fair dealings in trade have a moral side, and, as the powers of municipalities grew along with their paternalistic stance, cities began to take care of the well-being of their citizens. Any good government knows that well-fed citizens are happier and more peaceful politically. In this case, the health of the body politic has very much to do with the health of the physical bodies of citizens.

At times, the physical bodies of citizens were also used to display political and administrative power in the public sphere. In England, public punishment was frequently carried out in the center of the market square, where the pillory, a ducking stool, and a whipping post were located (Schmiechen and Carls 1999: 4). Michel Foucault (1995: 48–49) underlines the importance of the public ritual of punishment and how its public nature gave power back to the sovereign whose laws had been disrespected. Once again, the market was a place of political power, this time from the public enforcement of laws and spectacle of punishment. Citizens' bodies were not only controlled positively through access to food at the market, but there were also negative impositions of power on the body in the form of punishment in the marketplace, attesting to its importance as a place for public authorities to display power and maintain public order in the face of the intrinsically chaotic nature of the market. Still today, the brisk arrest of irregular foreigners and petty thieves is carried out with a certain ceremony: the police march the "prisoners" through the market while masses of bystanders observe the spectacle. This serves the age-old purpose of reinforcing the symbolic and military power of the State over this public space.

Order and authority in the marketplace have generally been signs of good government and civic well-being. In Borgonio's seventeenth-century etching shown in Figure 1, the market in Piazza delle Erbe in Turin, city hall is given a prominent place; it looms large in the background over the busy market. In fact, the town hall and the municipal tower (a strong symbol of civic power) dwarf the perspective of the market and the people in the image, reinforcing the importance of the municipality in the running of this everyday institution. The placement of the market stalls in orderly rows can be seen as a depiction of good government. Helen Tangires (2002) notes in her study of nineteenth-century American markets that they were the measure of the success of the local government. Historians often use market records as an indication of the social and economic health of a city. A well-run market meant that people had access to a good food supply and were more likely to be in good health. In addition, it also meant economic prosperity and that local government was capable of managing complex civic institutions. The need to secure a constant supply of food was among the most pressing concerns for most municipalities. The other main troubles city officials needed to combat were fraud and food tampering, which were not uncommon practices. Sometimes the municipality needed to deal with economic crisis through price fixing to ensure a food supply that was accessible to all, particularly in times of war or following poor harvests and other natural disasters (Helstosky 2004). These were not popular policies with farmers, but they helped avoid urban uprisings.

Food and civic unrest have always been deeply linked: markets became the theaters in which political power was sometimes challenged but then confirmed through bread riots or the rationing out of food (S. Kaplan 1996). During World War II, citizens received rations from a municipal distribution point at Porta Palazzo near the farmers' market, evidencing that, even during times of rationing and scarcity, markets remained distribution points for the little food that was available. At present, scarcity and the rising price of food have brought market squares into public focus as the center for tensions concerning everything from political corruption to food access issues.[4]

In the past, another important (and often contentious) element of the market was the weigh scale. Most markets in Europe had communal scales that were used by all merchants and buyers. It was the city's duty to make sure that the scale was in good working order and that people were not being defrauded through faulty measures. In this case, the State acted as a mediator in everyone's interests. This was also another way in which the city created income through taxes: all goods that were weighed were in turn taxed. When vendors began to use individual scales, the municipality had to regulate these scales as well, a much trickier task, in order to protect citizens. To some degree, at this point municipal authorities lost direct control over the majority of transactions and had to find new means for policing and collecting taxes.

The market administrators were also responsible for the hygiene of the market. By the eighteenth century, preoccupations about health and disease caused European markets to move from a rather rudimentary and informal form of vending to a highly controlled and regulated commercial activity (Stanziani 2005). Foodstuffs were sold from tables or stands that were raised off the ground. Stands and pavilions were constructed to shelter goods from the elements (sun, dust, rain) and created a more organized market environment. Hygiene, in the sense of what is considered dirty, contaminated, or inedible, is largely constructed by social and cultural norms that dictate what is or is not edible (Douglas 2002). Hygiene norms are not static, and the popularization and implementation of new scientific understandings about public hygiene have had a great impact on modern provisioning institutions, both markets and supermarkets. Many markets have been shaped, destroyed, or renovated due to concerns related to hygiene. Dominant cultural or social groups often impose these hygiene norms.[5]

Moving beyond the scale of microbes and germs, it may be easier to control physical bodies than political bodies. For this reason, markets are hard to control in other ways. These public spaces have nearly always been places where politics are discussed and where politicians come to campaign. Still today in Europe, politicians come to address the public and hand out leaflets before elections. In the political imagination, markets have always been popular public spaces par excellence. The market square continues to act as a public forum: market-goers discuss politics and current events among themselves or with vendors, who often carry their political feuds with other vendors into the discourse of their vendors' calls. Politics often plays a central role in sociability in these public places. What other public spaces still bring together such an important cross-section of a city's population? What places allow for open discussion of just about any topic?

Architecture and built spaces of the market are another issue that relates to the physical and social control of the market square. Perhaps the biggest change to the structure of markets took place in Europe in the nineteenth century. During this period, new technologies for building with steel created a novel type of architecture that became popular in Western Europe for public structures such as markets, train stations, and exhibition halls. Some of the best-known examples of these structures included the Eiffel Tower, the Halles de Paris, and London's Crystal Palace, to name but a few. The high ceiling supported by cast iron pillars created an airy feeling that also helped ventilation, which at the time was thought to make an important contribution to hygiene. The Tettoia dell'Orologio and the Tettoia dei Casalinghi in the Piazza della Repubblica are cast iron structures that are part of this tradition and some of the best examples in the industrial city of Turin.

This new type of architecture was popular because it created large open spaces well adapted to housing markets. Cast-iron structures became monuments to the Industrial Revolution and the modernity and technology of nineteenth-century Europe in England, France, Italy, and Spain. During the nineteenth century, there was a strong push by many municipal governments to move open-air markets into these new types of buildings: covered markets were easier to control and regulate, and they were more hygienic and "modern" (Schmiechen and Carls 1999). The relocating of open-air markets to covered structures was a trend that continued well into the twentieth century. The sale of food in outdoor public spaces was being forbidden in many countries for reasons attributed to changing notions of hygiene. By moving markets indoors, municipal governments were trying to cast off the past and public activities associated with disorder. Commerce, in the age of modernity, was to be orderly, efficient, and hygienic. In its efforts to appear on the cutting edge of this move toward the modern, Turin wanted to have a market that reflected these values.

In Victorian England, market halls became monuments to public order. As Schmiechen and Carls explain in their thorough study of the British market hall, the government saw markets as part of a larger social project: "Social and moral reformers believed that social behavior could be better controlled if public buying and selling moved off the streets and into a single building. Indeed, the rearrangement of the public marketplace is a good example of how architects, working for local government, sought to redefine human interaction in public spaces" (1999: x). This regulation of human interaction included a separation of social classes and large groups that could pose a potential threat to municipal authorities. This tendency to use built spaces to control public behavior was perhaps most pronounced in Victorian architecture, but issues of moral control and public markets were not unique to England. Thompson delineates in "Urban Renovation, Moral Regeneration: Domesticating the Halles in Second-Empire Paris" (1997) how nineteenth-century public officials in Paris were also concerned with taming the marketplace and making it a morally upstanding place through the imposition of structured built environments.

Despite this nineteenth-century penchant for containing and controlling markets, these institutions persisted in a somewhat chaotic fashion. For instance, covered pavilions were surrounded by temporary and semipermanent stands attached to the outer structure of the building. The Porta Palazzo market is a good example of this hybrid development, with its four permanent pavilions (built between 1836 and 2006), semipermanent shops, and movable stands. The human desire to carry out commerce in open public spaces was stronger than the moralizing of the ruling classes. This is particularly true in Mediterranean countries, where the climate encourages open-air markets and the use of streets and squares for social and economic activities.

Most municipalities have carried out policies of containment rather than total control over markets: despite the desire and necessity to regulate markets, these institutions continually subvert control from above in one way or another. Notwithstanding strict hygiene regulations and increased policing of European markets, traditional forms of commerce and attitudes have persisted. Markets somehow continue to defy modernity. According to de la Pradelle (1996: 19), markets miraculously carry on traditional forms of commerce in the shadow of modern forms of big distribution.

The Growing City, the Expanding Marketplace

In contemporary history, Turin is most famous as an industrial capital of Italy, home to Fiat and other large industries that put Italy on the economic map in the twentieth century. During this period of industrial expansion, the city's population grew most drastically. The first wave of migration began in the 1930s when workers came to the city from the surrounding countryside. This movement of people was largely stimulated by changes in agricultural structures: farms were now smaller holdings, and less labor was required (Fofi 1964; Pugliese 2002). The city and industrial wages beckoned. Under Fascism (1922–43), this type of migration slowed due to the imposition of a law against urbanization in 1939 that forbade people from moving to provincial capitals and industrial areas without first having a means of sustaining themselves (Fofi 1964). Although this law was not abolished until 1960, there was still a great deal of illegal migration into cities from the countryside (Pugliese 2002). During this period, migrants would often return to the nearby countryside to participate in the harvest and other agricultural activities that required a great deal of labor. The seasonal nature of work could still be felt even in the Torinese factories since a large portion of the work force was drawn from the surrounding countryside.

The second wave of migration in Turin was directly related to the "economic miracle" and the rise of Fiat and automobile manufacturing, which would become one of Italy's most important industries. Turin was essentially a one-company town: Fiat used its influence to shape the city for the rest of the century. Migrants who swarmed into the city in the 1950s and 1960s mainly came from the Veneto area and the south of Italy. This massive migration created a great deal of tension in Turin. First, the influx of migrants happened on a large scale and with a rapidity that alarmed many Torinese, who felt they were being overrun by newcomers. Second, cultural differences between northerners and southerners were felt deeply: most migrants came from the countryside and had a decidedly lower standard of living and literacy compared with those of the local inhabitants. Although these migrants were Italian nationals, they suffered discrimination at the hands of the locals and often lived and worked in difficult conditions: for example, signs posted on bar doors prohibited the entrance of *napoli* (a pejorative Italian term for southerner that makes reference to the southern city of Naples), and landlords would not rent flats to people from the South, despite the terrible housing shortage. Linguistic differences also posed challenges—Italian was not usually a common language as both northerners and southerners spoke local dialects. Rapid social and economic changes left their mark on Turin and the Torinese in this period. Vanessa Maher (1996) argues that the impact of migration in the 1950s and 1960s has had an important influence on the present migration situation, which has evoked the painful memory of the past. Previous discrimination against southern migration has greatly shaped the perception and treatment of current foreign migrants and immigrants (Sacchi and Viazzo 2003).

In the past and in current waves of migration, Porta Palazzo has been one of the most important gateways to the city. Not only was it a physical gate to start with, but it has historically been a receiving area for migrants. There were migrants from the Piedmontese countryside at the turn of the twentieth century, and then southern Italian migrants from the 1950s to the 1970s (Fofi 1975; Castronovo and D'Orsi 1987; Pugliese 2002). San Salvario and Porta Palazzo are the two areas that have traditionally attracted migrants since the nineteenth century (CICSENE 1997). Porta Palazzo has always been a nodal point for migration, where information is exchanged, contacts are made, and work can be found; all these activities strengthen the networks that encourage chain migration (Huag 2008; Portes and Sensenbrenner 1993). Porta Palazzo became so well known outside the city in the 1960s that it was reported that, in certain villages and towns in the south of Italy and Sicily, Porta Palazzo was synonymous for Turin and northern Italy (Maida 2004). This was one of the few places where migrants felt at home: there were familiar faces, people spoke in dialect, there was food from home, and socializing in the square was acceptable and usual public behavior. In other areas of the city, southerners were less welcome; sometimes they were discriminated against and discouraged from settling in the area.

Porta Palazzo became a home away from home for many newcomers. Slowly, migrants from the South began to have a real impact on the market and the surrounding area. In fact, commercial activities were one of the best ways to assimilate socially and economically into this new city, culture, and society. Southerners rented and eventually bought stalls at the market and opened businesses in the area that were often related to food, underlining the importance of food in the maintenance of identity and cultural practices (Caplan 1997; Castellanos and Bergstresser 2006). Many of the people I worked with at Porta Palazzo told me that, if a Calabrian went to shop at Porta Palazzo in the 1960s, he or she could find all of the comforts of home, which had not been available at the market prior to the 1950s. Lemons, tomatoes, mozzarella, and capers are just some of the ingredients brought to Turin by southerners.[6] Eventually, these ingredients also became familiar to the Torinese, and they began to eat a number of southern dishes and even include many of these ingredients in their own "traditional" cuisine.

Food was not only being transported from southern Italy, but southerners were sending food home to the South (Teti 1999: 97). While I was working at a sweets stand at the market, Roberta, the owner, explained to me how the 1960s and 1970s had been the golden years of her business: "The *meridionali* (southerners) would send large bags of chocolates and sweets in the post, or before leaving Turin to go home for holidays, they would buy large quantities to take with them. They wanted to show that they had arrived, that they had money and could afford little luxuries."[7] Food became a status symbol, a way to show success to those back home. Since the sixteenth century, sugar and chocolate have historically been signs of affluence and power (Mintz 1985).

Often food is the first stepping-stone in the cultural exchanges that occur when two groups meet. Like the physical presence of migrants, the initial impact is met with resistance, but slowly the two begin to coexist and sometimes even mingle (Goody 1982). The Piedmontese began to eat dishes from the South, and the southerners slowly adapted to Piedmontese food. In time, Porta Palazzo, which had been a stronghold of rural Piedmontese culture, became a place also associated with southern Italian culture, particularly cuisine. This would not be the last time that the Porta Palazzo market would act as a melting pot, bringing different cultures together around food.

When a new wave of migration began in the 1980s, Porta Palazzo was once again a receiving area. A report published by CICSENE in 1996 notes that, from the early 1990s, although the city's population was in decline, that of Porta Palazzo was increasing. This was largely due to the availability and low cost of housing that attracted migrants. The social-cultural changes in the area's population led to a general decline in the state of buildings and also the sense of security of the area's inhabitants (CICSENE 2002). Presently, Porta Palazzo has one of the highest percentages of non-European migrant residents for all neighborhoods in the city, not including illegal migrants who are nearly impossible to quantify.[8] According the official statistics, the main migrant groups in Turin at present are Romanians (50,434), Moroccans (18,010), Peruvians (7,231), Albanians (5,488), and Chinese (4,601) (Ufficio Statistica Comune di Torino 2009). The number of Romanians has doubled since Romania entered the European Union in 2007. It is important to consider the number of unrecorded illegal immigrants; in particular, sub-Saharan Africans make up a large portion of the immigrant population that does not appear on the official census. High incidents of human trafficking make this group particularly vulnerable to prostitution and exploitation on the black market for labor (Aghatise 2004).

The current situation in Turin and at Porta Palazzo between migrants and Italians is highly tense, and encounters can be unpleasant, even violent at times. This is also related to the problem of the petty illegal drug trade that occurs in and around the market (mainly after business hours in the evening) and also on the side streets off the piazza. This has not helped the area's reputation—illegality, drugs, and violence at Porta Palazzo have become associated with foreign migrants, although the drug trade existed prior to the influx of foreigners and many Italians are at the center of this illegal activity (Maher 1996: 166). The local press has encouraged and inflamed this image (CICSENE 1997). Once again, Porta Palazzo finds itself in a marginal position. The market in this case has not helped the area's image: markets are chaotic and associated with dirt and disorder. In fact, digestion and dirt are both tropes Italians frequently use to talk about migration (Edwards, Occhipinti, and Ryan 2000; Maher 1996). Common statements I heard included: "It's hard to swallow all these migrants coming to our country" and "Migrants are dirty." For this reason, food and the market are not seen in a positive light. The flip side is that food and cuisine can also offer one of the first points of contact between individuals, which can lead to a more humanized understanding of the migration process and cultural diversity.

One of the first things all migrant groups brought with them to Porta

Palazzo was their culinary culture. Food also serves as a pretext for communication and sociability. In the window of the Asian market on corso Regina, there are numerous notices for work, services, and other snippets of information written in Mandarin and Cantonese. Senegalese men stand in front of the African market in via delle Orfane a few blocks off the market square. Going shopping is an important social moment for migrants that aids in creating community, networking, and feeling more at home in the host country. A plethora of "ethnic" groceries and restaurants have popped up around the market square. In addition, the number of vendors' licenses held by foreigners for the Porta Palazzo market has substantially increased. In 1997, foreigners held only five licenses, whereas by 2001 there were eighty-one (thirty-two held by Moroccans and fifteen by Tunisians) (CICSENE 2002). The presence of ethnic businesses, immigrant vendors (legal and illegal), and groups of foreign shoppers has made migrants very visible at Porta Palazzo. Some Italians I spoke with expressed the feeling that the market was slowly being taken over by foreigners (often compared to the "invasion" of southerners in the 1960s). The sense of fear and the feeling of having one's neighborhood overrun by foreigners have also occurred in San Salvario, the other main receiving area for foreign migrants, near the city's main train station, where tensions between Italians and migrants run high (Maritano 2000a, b). In reality, the number of foreign license holders at Porta Palazzo was only 7.1 percent of the total in 2001 when I started my fieldwork, although this number is growing and many foreigners work or rent stands with licenses held by Italians.

Although it is often referred to as one of the most multiethnic neighborhoods of Turin, Porta Palazzo is far from a peaceful global village, and growing pains related to migration are being felt once again in Turin with the recent waves of migration. The conflict and everyday reality of migration are lived out each day in the market, as Italians and newcomers struggle and compete to make a living and provide their families with food.

A Neighborhood, a Square, and a Market

> Rachel—Where does Porta Palazzo begin and end?
> I am having a really hard time understanding this.
> Federico—It's hard to say . . . Marrakesh? The
> Langa? Really, Porta Palazzo is the name of the
> neighborhood, the square, and the market; but it is
> a place that is connected to the rest of the world.
> Rachel—How am I going to study this thing called
> Porta Palazzo!
>
> —Fieldnotes, May 20, 2002

Porta Palazzo is one of the largest open-air markets in Western Europe, 51,300 square meters, with 4,991 square meters used for commercial activity during the market. It is not entirely open-air: it has several permanent pavilions and covered areas. On an average day, 756 licensed mobile vendors set up their stands (13 percent of the city's ambulant vending licenses), on Saturdays, 796.[1] Of these mobile vendors, 350 sell nonfood items (clothing, flowers, housewares, etc.), 366 sell produce, and producers run 100 of these. In addition, the market has 24 stalls assigned to vendors who attend Porta Palazzo on a rotational basis. There are another 159 vendors in the three covered pavilions. These figures include all kinds of vendors (mainly clothing and food), but do not take into consideration the numerous illegal vendors who occupy the peripheral spaces of the market and central positions after market hours. The market operates from Monday to Friday from early in the morning (approximately 8 a.m. to 1 p.m.) and has longer hours on Saturday (8 a.m. to 6 p.m.). An estimated 100,000 people visit the market each week. The square, Piazza della Repubblica, is a space in constant movement: stalls are set up in the middle of the night, used until the afternoon, and disassembled; rubbish is put in massive piles and hauled off by trucks; then the piazza is scoured by street-cleaning machines. A seemingly endless flow of people moves through this massive urban space, from sanitary workers and drug dealers to shoppers and vendors. The social and economic functions of the square change depending on the time of day. Although the built structures of the market (the covered pavilions, streets, and the part of the square created by surrounding buildings and arcades) act as a container and provide some spatial boundaries, the physical structure of the Piazza is constantly being adapted, changed, and reconceived through its market functions and by the people who use this space to work, socialize, and play.

A Map of the Market

Defining and navigating the market are subjective processes. Each shopper, vendor, police officer, and tourist develops his or her own mental map of the market based on personal experience. Points of reference might include familiar faces, a specific smell, or a number on the paving stones at the end of the square. Everyone's experience and spatial conception of the market is different; this is my attempt to give an overview of the Porta Palazzo market to help orient the ethnography that follows.

The aerial view of the market alludes to a spatial order that is constantly challenged. Piazza della Repubblica is an octagon that is broken up into quadrants. The piazza is bisected by via Milano, which becomes corso Giulio Cesare (as it runs southwest to northeast), and corso Regina. The market is made more efficient through this partitioning of space—shoppers can focus on what they want to buy and go directly to the specific area that concerns them, rather than having to go through the entire market. This layout is one of the things that make shopping at Porta Palazzo market so different from other neighborhood markets in Turin. Most markets in the city are a mix of foodstuff, clothing, flowers and plants, and household products; there is little or no division of goods sold at the stands. It is possible to find a table full of ladies' underwear next to a stall selling lettuce. The separate sectors at Porta Palazzo make the area somewhat easier to police and manage, if we take into consideration the Foucauldian concept that breaking down public space makes individual bodies easier to control (Foucault 1995: 143).

The northern quadrant was largely under construction during my fieldwork, but it now houses a covered pavilion designed by Italian star architect Massimiliano Fuksas. Born in Rome, Fuksas has become well known for his striking designs that are part of the urban landscape in cities such as Vienna and Strasbourg. He has also been an advisor to the Institut Français d'Architecture and was director of the Venice Biennale in 2000. It is common to find Fuksas's buildings highlighted on architectural tours of Europe. The structure designed by Fuksas at Porta Palazzo has been dubbed "Palafuksas." Originally, it was meant to replace the outdated covered clothing market; however, most vendors decided not to return once the structure was completed, and the building did not pass code for public use as a market space. Many safety issues remained unresolved until very recently.

The new pavilion initially housed temporary exhibitions and special events. Urban planners hoped the building's architectural importance would help bring a wave of renewal to the area. However, in 2009, several years after the completion of the Palafuksas, most people I asked found it difficult to say whether it had raised the status of the piazza. Many have called Palafuksas Porta Palazzo's albatross. The market trudged on for thirteen years despite the worksite, and then the unusable structure took up nearly a quarter of the area; in the remaining open-air spaces around the Palafuksas, there are a number of clothing and shoe vendors, their haphazard, largely improvised stalls and cheap merchandise in sharp contrast to the modern architecture of the new building. The Palafuksas remained barricaded behind building site fences and did not play any role in the daily activities of those who came to Porta Palazzo to shop. Most people saw it merely as an obstacle.

As this book goes to press, this building has finally been opened and used in part for its initial function—a clothing market. The inauguration of the "Centro Palatino" (still referred to by all as Palafuksas) took place on March 25, 2011. Much to the chagrin of the architect, the building has been turned into a shopping mall for all intents and purposes.[2] There are glassed-in storefronts, escalators, and a dining area, all with the feel of a modern mall. The new *centro commerciale* attempts to bring back some of Porta Palazzo's old glamor: once known for cutting-edge fashions, it had become a place to buy cheap, foreign-made clothing and shoes. As the Centro Palatino website advertises, the new market is intended to be the *centro di moda* (fashion center).[3] With thirty-four shops and a restaurant with a panoramic view of the square, it remains to be seen how this new addition will integrate with the rest of the market activities.

The smaller roads that connect to this area of the market lead to Borgo Dora and the Saturday Balôn flea market. This area has been the central focus of urban renewal projects. I saw many improvements to buildings and street surfaces while doing my research; these were mainly part of the Gate project (see later in this chapter). Unlike the Quadrilatero Romano south of the market square, gentrification has been very slow: the area has largely remained a low-rent neighborhood that attracts immigrants from all over the world.

Moving east across via Milano, the Mercato dell'Orologio-Alimentare IV (Figure 2; named for the large clock on the front of this elegant cast-iron building constructed in 1916) dominates this quadrant of the square. This large, enclosed pavilion is home to numerous butchers, bread resellers, cafés, and vendors selling everything from dairy and deli goods to pet food and beauty supplies. This part of the market is closest to a modern shopping mall because of the variety of services and goods under one roof. Along the corso Giulio Cesare side of the market, there is a covered area, the Tettoia dei Casalinghi, where mainly small household items are sold; in front of the pavilion and down the other side are a number of vendors selling clothing. Behind the pavilion is a covered area that houses the farmers' market (see Chapter 7).

The majority of the fruit and vegetable stands are located on the south side of the square (Figure 3). The vendors' stalls spread out over a large part of the open-air area; their colorful green, red, and white striped awnings have become a symbol of Porta Palazzo. Uninitiated shoppers easily get lost in the tight alleyways created by the stands. In contrast to the farmers' market, the vendors here are resellers: they buy their goods from a central

Figure 2. Mercato dell'Orologio-Alimentare IV seen from corso Regina.
Photo by Rachel Black.

wholesale market (CAAT, Centro Agroalimentare di Torino) just outside
Turin and bring these goods to market. From the pride expressed by these
vendors, it is sometimes difficult to imagine they did not grow the fruits
and vegetables themselves. Often vendors have a deep cultural connection
to food items representative of southern Italian cuisine (such as hot red peppers and certain types of chicory), which makes the selling of these foods a
little more personal and connected to Italian culture from regions outside
Piedmont.

The organization of this area is complex and challenging: it defies the
logic and efficiency of modern food retailing for a number of reasons. First,
the resellers have storage spaces around the square, often in the deep underground *ghiacciaie* (ice houses) that served as cooling units prior to modern
refrigeration.[4] Second, restocking the stalls is an art that requires careful
collaboration between the sellers and their *facchini* (porters). Last, I always
found it curious that two stalls selling nearly the same goods could be competitive. If you follow classic economic theory, you would think that intense

Figure 3. Inside the labyrinth of the resellers' area of the market. Photo by Rachel Black.

competition would create the best prices. This is not always the case, and often vendors collude to fix prices, including dropping prices as the market day progresses. What I learned from frequenting and working in the market was that personal relations and reputation are just as important, if not more so, than price. Often economic theory leaves out human relations that include fidelity, rapport, and the reciprocal bonds created by gifts.

Although it takes up most of the surface area, the resellers' open-air market is not the only commercial activity in this quadrant of the market: this slice of Porta Palazzo is also home to the Mercato V Alimentare (built in 1836), another covered market very similar to the covered pavilion described above in the eastern quadrant of the square. Again, this covered market is home to many butchers, deli stands, and a bar. When I went back to Porta Palazzo in 2006, the Mercato V pavilion was under renovation, and all the vendors had been moved to a square to the east behind the market. When I left Turin in 2008, it was nearing completion and the disgruntled vendors had weathered the storm, although many claimed that the long process had caused them incredible financial hardship. The process of renewal at Porta Palazzo has not been without its grumbling and strife. In 2009, the Mercato V had been restored to its former glory, and I had a hard time imagining it was the building I had first seen with flaking paint and shutters hanging half off the second floor. It certainly is one of the glories of the square, and the bright, new white paint has not taken away any of its nineteenth-century charm.

Not all parts of the market are in the square: some hidden architectural jewels in and around the area play a role in the goings-on in the piazza. The Gate offices (the organization that coordinates many of the renewal projects) were located in the historic Galleria Umberto I to the south (Figure 4).[5] The area is also home to one of the city's largest police stations, behind the Roman gate to the city and other archaeological ruins from the Augusta Taurinorum (the name of the original Roman settlement). It is interesting to note that this area southwest of corso Regina, the Quadrilatero Romano, has managed to find new life in urban renewal and is home to designer boutiques, fashionable apartments, and trendy restaurants that spill out onto pedestrian streets, while the neighborhood known as Borgo Dora on the other side of the market square is still plagued with social and economic issues despite major physical and architectural renovations.

The diversity of Piazza della Repubblica and its surrounding neighborhoods never ceases to amaze me. Crossing via Milano, one finds this last quadrant of the market in the west corner of the piazza. Here there is another large covered pavilion, the 1836 Mercato II, which houses the fish market. On top of the fish market sits the local police station responsible for regulating the market and adjacent areas. From this bird's eye perspective, the officers can conveniently see nearly the entire piazza. This surveillance gives a certain panopticon feeling to the area and establishes a relationship of power of the municipal forces over the square. Besides the fish market with its pungent smells and loud, playful vendors, who largely escape the attempts of the imposed order directly above their heads, the rest of the quadrant is home to a clothing market that wraps right around the fish market and fills up the rest of the square, creating another covered maze of hanging trousers, the latest denim knockoffs, and frilly pink children's clothes at very reasonable prices. Where via Milano widens at the southwest side of the square, piazzetta Milano, there are additional clothing vendors, a couple of

Figure 4. Galleria Umberto I, just off Piazza della Repubblica. Photo by
Rachel Black.

flower stalls, and the candy stand where I found my first employment in this
special area of the market.

Not all the square is used specifically for commercial activity. In the space
between the area of the stands and the road, trucks with stock are parked,
and produce and rubbish are discarded in large heaps. There are often people sitting on the railings along the road watching, resting, and socializing

or selling phone cards. Sometimes there are elderly people sifting through the refuse, salvaging produce. All kinds of marginal activities take place in these peripheries around the main market area.

This short description of Piazza della Repubblica is certainly influenced by my own lived experience of the market. What I have focused on and the things I have omitted are also part of my mental map of the market. Market-goers usually have their own "maps" of the market and select focal points that serve their social and provisioning needs. Their map will also depend on how often they shop or frequent the market and the relationships they create with vendors and others in the piazza. In each area of the market, there is a different atmosphere and dynamic between the vendors and the clients, and going to market is a subjective, personal experience.

Porta Palazzo as a Sensory Experience

Each sector of the market has its unique sights, smells, and sounds. Going to the market is an experience that makes an impression on all the senses. When "mapping" the space of the market, I tried to take into consideration the total sensory experience of the place. Porta Palazzo is an urban space with a heavy impact on eyes, ears, and nose: the colors of the awnings and produce are dazzling; the vendors cry out trying to capture the attention of potential customers; the smell of freshly baked bread, capers, and anchovies mixes with a subtle undertone of rotting fruit. The sensory experience of the market changes with the seasons as temperatures change along with the goods on sale. Unlike supermarkets, where sensory experience is controlled right down to the smell, open-air markets produce both pleasing and repelling scents, at times simultaneously. While I was making my observations outside the Mercato V near the trash compactor, parked in a small courtyard, I was overwhelmed by the stench of garbage, rotting fruit, and urine. At the same time, the strong pleasing smell of pecorino cheese wafted from a nearby cheese stand. In part, it is this contrast of smells that makes the market experience quite intense. These sensory contradictions are part of "being there," and this form of retailing has largely escaped the hygienic rationale of modern food retailing.

Sensory perceptions of space are also intense at Porta Palazzo. The awning-covered market stalls in the resellers' section are set in a tight grid in the space that surrounds the permanent pavilion of the Mercato V Alimentare. When navigating through this area, it is difficult to get by other shoppers. People often bump into each other, and vendors carrying stock struggle to get to their stands. I have watched women with baby carriages fight a path through the crowd and old women struggle with heavy bags along the tightly packed corridors. There is constant movement in this area of the market: customers mill about between stalls; young men run back and forth from trucks parked on the outskirts of the area, restocking the stands; and vendors stand shouting out the prices of their goods and the bargains of the day from within their U-shaped stalls. Personal space is at a premium, and a feeling of claustrophobia is not uncommon among those new to the place.

The visual impact of the open-air market where the resellers are located is striking. A multitude of colors catch the eye as one strolls down the aisles. Unlike the farmers' market, there is not much seasonal change in colors here: since the resellers buy fruits and vegetables at the wholesale market, produce comes from all over Italy and the world. In addition to the rainbow of produce, colorful awnings cover each stand, providing protection from the elements but also lending to the festive atmosphere of the place—blue, green, and red light is cast on the stands, enhancing the appearance of the produce. As part of the renewal project that is underway, there has been a proposal to standardize the colors of the awnings in accordance with the type of produce being sold. Many people who enjoy the colorful visual element of the market have opposed this move. It will be interesting to see whether the plan will be carried out and, if so, what impact it will have on the market experience. A number of shoppers I interviewed mentioned how they liked the improvised appearance of the market; the wild display of colors was part of the charm and experience of going to market. One elderly gentleman told me, "The colors are all part of the display." A young mother said, "If I wanted organized, I would go to Auchan."[6] Once again, the carnivalesque market stands in contrast to the rational and orderly nature of the supermarket.

Shopping at an open-air market is an unforgettable and unique sensory experience. It is perhaps the sensory aspects and the temporal nature of a market that set it apart from any other retail activity and contribute to its emotional impact. When the market began to undergo renovations while I was in the field, everyone worried that this process would leave the piazza sterilized and that shopping there would not be so different from pushing a shopping cart down the aisles of a supermarket. Fortunately, it takes more than some fresh paint and some new paving stones to alter the unique sensory experience that is Porta Palazzo.

A Market Under Repair

The market's new paint was a long time coming. By the late 1980s, the Porta Palazzo market had seen better days. The crumbling façades and broken-down buildings gave only a glimpse of the area's former vitality and prosperity. The local newspapers regularly reported on robberies, drug busts, and violent crimes in the area. They frequently tied this to the presence of immigrants. Cheap, ramshackle housing and poorly lit workshops added to the overall rundown feeling. If you asked most Torinese in 1995 what they thought of the area, they would tell you that Porta Palazzo had been the heart of the city with a vibrant market and working neighborhood but that it was now one of the worst places to live in the city.

In 1996, the City of Turin presented a project called "The Gate—Living Not Leaving" to the European Union as part of the European Innovation Actions Fund for Regional Development.[7] The goal of this pilot project was to improve living and working conditions in the Porta Palazzo area. In 1998, the Comitato Progetto Porta Palazzo (Porta Palazzo Project Committee) was formed as a nonprofit organization to manage this urban-renewal program, funded by the EU, City of Turin, and Italian Ministry of Public Works. The European phase of the Gate Project ended in 2001, but Turin pledged its support to continue the initiatives that had been started. In 2002, the Gate became a local development agency largely funded by the city. The Gate not only was responsible for architectural interventions and administration but ran and still runs a number of social programs and has been involved in numerous cultural events, from outdoor film screenings to food festivals. The projects organized and run by the Gate have been wide reaching in an attempt to address both brick-and-mortar issues and the social challenges of being an important receiving area for immigration. Social projects under the aegis of the Gate ranged from setting up an office to help foreigners deal with Italian bureaucracy in starting a business to applying for legal immigrant status. Urban-planning projects included building an underpass beneath Porta Palazzo to ease the flow of traffic through the market, resurfacing roads, helping fund the refinishing of building façades, and valorizing the hidden historical aspects of the area (for example, creating a symbolic trace of the former waterways that punctuated Borgo Dora by laying a blue stripe into the pavement of these areas).

Perhaps the most radical project carried out by the Gate was the underpass under corso Giulio Cesare. This has reduced traffic congestion through the square. Unfortunately, the underpass only has two lanes and has created its own congestion problems, causing some people to bypass the square altogether. On the positive side, the reduced traffic in the square makes it easier for shoppers and porters to cross from one area of the market to the next. The roadways are dedicated to public transport, which has certainly made it easier to get to the market from all over the city. In a moment of public support, the mayor of Turin even promised to do his shopping with a shopping cart at the newly accessible Porta Palazzo market to demonstrate the improvements to citizens.

In 1999, the Gate organized an international architectural and planning competition to renovate the market square. These projects included novel equipment for covering the stalls, designs for new stalls, lighting, electrical outlets, and up-to-date hygiene and waste disposal systems. The judging panel was made up of city officials, European experts in urban planning, and local citizens chosen by the Gate. The competition was run in a very efficient and seemingly democratic manner; however, when it came time to choose and announce a winner, the Gate staff was forced to announce that the competition was null and void due to a complaint to TAR Piemonte by participants.[8] On further investigation, it was apparent that there were also political motivations for not carrying out the design competition to its end. The details remain undisclosed.

While I was doing my fieldwork in 2003, the city began to make plans for the renovation of Piazza della Repubblica using its own engineers. Initially, the municipality tried to create an open forum before defining its project. Its attempts immediately ran into major resistance from people who worked at the market. At a meeting I attended on April 10, 2003, vendors and representatives of the city in charge of the initiative were present, but rather than a productive dialogue, shouting matches broke out and ended only when municipal officials left the meeting early, escorted by the police for their own protection. The following week a strike was held at the market: most vendors did not set up their stands, and those who did were physically threatened by strikers until they took the stalls down. A rally was held in the square, and the vendors marched to the doors of city hall demanding an audience with the mayor, who eventually agreed to receive representatives from the angry crowd. The protest made it clear that the discontent was general but had many factions, with leaders out to represent very personal economic interests. The strike did not resolve many issues, but it did make the public aware of the territorial battle being fought at the Porta Palazzo market. Under all the shouting, the main issues appeared to be general lack of trust in the city administration and a desire to maintain the status quo and personal positions within the physical structure of the market. This is when I started to realize how difficult it was to build consensus in a place like Porta Palazzo. It seemed to me that the city's job was going to be nearly impossible when it came to reorganizing and renovating the market.

Although opinions were solicited, first by the Gate in focus group studies and then by the city in public meetings, I heard no common voice or desire at the market: everyone was looking out for his or her own interests, and this incident proved that there is little desire to cooperate or make any type of sacrifice for the common good. Silvio was worried about having to give up the prime location of his stand to make corridors wider and easier to navigate for customers and vendors. Giorgio did not want to have to park his van at a lot off the square because he would have to hire someone to carry his vegetables to his stand and watch over his merchandise. Everyone was concerned about the temporary move of the market while the work was being carried out: it meant a loss of business for all, even if only temporarily. No one wanted to give an inch, even if it would have made the market a better place in the end. The market vendors did not have much long-term vision or sense of civic unity. The result was a limited project that helped the market meet European standards for public vending of foodstuffs.

The Gate and the City of Turin carried out an urban renewal project for the Porta Palazzo market to bring it up to European hygiene standards and prepare the city for 2006 Winter Olympic Games (the work was actually completed in April 2006). This time there was to be no design competition and only limited public consultation. The market vendors were up in arms over this decision, and a number of incidents and civil protests ensued following the announcement.

In 2004, the city began the 15-million-euro renovation project, which included resurfacing and upgrading the paving of the market square.[9] Moving all the vendors out of the open-air market areas to temporary positions along corso Regina and the neighboring squares caused numerous protests from vendors and a few shoppers who could not find their regular stands. In 2005–2006, market-goers and vendors constantly lamented the state of the market. Some vendors were afraid their regular clientele would not find them in the chaos of the move, while others were afraid of losing their hard-earned positions in the square. Some shoppers seemed confused and put out by the temporary changes. The vendors fought to gain each inch they had, and they screamed and kicked to be put back in the exact place they had been before. The number one topic of conversation and debate was the move and renovation. Another concern I heard expressed by many was that the market would lose its authenticity and feel with its new clean and orderly paving. Never in my life had I heard people talk so much about the ground they stood on. When the market returned to its regular position in the square in 2006, I went to talk to customers and vendors to see how they felt about the changes. I quickly noted that fears of the demise of the market had faded and the new paved surface was generally accepted as superior to the previous stones. There were only a few who pined for the past, and people joked about no longer having to shuffle over discarded lettuce to avoid potentially fatal falls.

The renovation of the market was carried out in several phases due to the logistics of moving such a massive market. The main improvements included resurfacing the market area and new lighting, electrical outlets, and water supply. The covered markets also underwent restoration inside and out, but this occurred after 2006 and was not completed until 2009. This construction also required the vendors there to be displaced to temporary structures in a nearby square. When all was said and done, most businesses survived, and nearly all vendors and customers agreed that Porta Palazzo was a better place because of the changes.

Although funding is now reduced and it largely depends on money from the City of Turin, the Gate office stands watch over the market. This office acts as an incubator of social and cultural projects that take place in the Piazza della Repubblica (from multicultural soccer games to language lessons and exchanges for Italians and foreigners). The office and its employees have become an unofficial point of reference for mediating conflicts at the market and in the neighborhood. The Gate is also an important reference for the municipality as local politicians try to keep their finger on the pulse of one of the most volatile areas of the city. Elda Tessore, director of the Gate during its European funding phase, has moved on to city hall, where she is a councilor. Her long-time protégé and Gate employee Luca Cianfriglia took her place. This changing of the guard assured the continuity of the work being carried out at the Gate and created an even stronger link with city hall.

As can be said of most urban planning projects, it is hard to measure the success of the Gate project in concrete terms. However, it is undeniable that many physical and social transformations have taken place at Porta Palazzo since 1996, and that the Gate was key in initiating these changes. From a structural and architectural perspective, the overall goal of the project has been achieved: the areas surrounding the market and the market itself have not been sanitized while necessary upgrades were made to the square. Thanks to this initiative, much of the important architectural heritage of the area has been preserved from a crumbling fate. Despite a few grumbling voices from those who frequent and work in the market, Piazza della Repubblica is cleaner, easier to use, and a safer place to work, shop, and live. Thanks to many of the social and cultural projects initiated by the Gate, the people who live and work in the area are starting to have a better understanding of one another.

When I went back to the Gate in September 2009 to follow up on the projects the office had shepherded forward at Porta Palazzo and to check on the current state of affairs, I remarked on the change of outlook the staff expressed concerning the design and execution of urban projects. After more than ten years of dealing with the challenges and complexities of the piazza and its surrounding neighborhoods, the Gate staff seemed tired and somewhat disillusioned. As one of the early staffers, Luca Cianfriglia has seen just about everything at Porta Palazzo as it has gone through many changes; he told me how the Gate staff had found it impossible to build consensus among the many actors who lived, worked in, and frequented Porta Palazzo. Individual interests and those of small factions constantly blocked projects that required a larger vision. I left thinking that maybe the Gate staff lacked perspective—maybe these workers were just too much in the thick of it each day for so many years. Perhaps they did not see all they had accomplished. On further reflection, I was also left puzzling through larger questions about human nature, economics, and civil society. I knew I needed to unpack these through my own experiences and ethnographic research at the Porta Palazzo market, and fortunately I had this book as an outlet for my reflections.

Is Porta Palazzo a Diamond in the Rough or a Thorn in the Side?

CICSENE, an independent agency that was employed to assess the impact of the Gate project, reported that Porta Palazzo experienced a decline of 7.8 percent in license authorizations from 1991 to 2000, compared to 8.5 percent for Turin as a whole (CICSENE 2002). Few new licenses were granted, but a large number changed hands, indicative of a generational shift and the increasing presence of immigrants at the market. Compared to many other markets in Turin, Porta Palazzo was relatively successful. I also discovered that much of the doom and gloom I kept hearing from vendors was a front hiding success, which could potentially draw the dangerous attention of envious neighbors. Some anthropologists would say that the vendors at "Porta Pila" were just trying to ward off *malocchio* (the evil eye) (Herzfeld 1981, 1984; Galt 1982; Dundes 1982).[10]

The Torinese, even those who do not frequent the market, see Porta Palazzo (despite its problems) as the epitome of an open-air market and central to Piedmontese culture. Like many markets in Europe, Porta Palazzo is a popular tourist attraction, but without being altered by tourism. Porta Palazzo is not just a special place for foreigners; it is a "magical" place in the minds of the Torinese. Many of the older Torinese I interviewed had childhood memories of the abundance of the market after the meager years of World War II and the harsh food rationing.

Citizens and politicians deemed the living cultural heritage of the Porta Palazzo market so important that local officials and interest groups decided it needed protection and promotion. In 2006, the Emporium Association was created to highlight the cultural significance of major European markets, and Porta Palazzo was nominated as one of the founding markets.[11] Although the association is largely symbolic and political, it could possibly play a role in securing a functional future for these historic markets. With many renewal projects completed, Porta Palazzo continues to negotiate its place in the city through a grander past, an exotic present, and an uncertain future.

Early in my fieldwork I went to see Luca, then a young architect working at the Gate Project offices, and he showed me an aerial image of the Porta Palazzo market (Figure 5). The market area stands out as a pregnant bulge in the urban structure. It looks ready to burst out into the surrounding streets. Its geometric forms hardly hide something organic, something beyond the restraint of urban structures—chaos seems just barely controlled and contained. Looking at the market from above, I was struck by its immensity and the fact this is all public space dedicated to commercial and social activity that anyone can be part of. This was a new perspective that I took to my everyday view from the ground; it helped me conceive of the spatial structure and importance of the marketplace. It was no longer just a maze of bodies and fruit stands: Porta Palazzo was now easier to imagine as a central gathering place in the city. This seemed particularly important since Turin, the home of Fiat, has developed into a city that privileges the automobile and fast-paced living. How many other social spaces like this exist in Turin on such a large scale? As I searched the city, I came to the conclusion that there were no other places in the city quite like Porta Palazzo.

Although the physical space of the market may seem disorderly or illogical to the average shopper, Porta Palazzo's built structure has been shaped by the development of the city and urban expansion. It is an expression of the historical layering of different conceptions of public space, urban aesthetics, and conceptions of the movement of people in the city. Porta

Figure 5. Aerial view of the Porta Palazzo market circa 1998. Photo by
Giovanni Fontana.

Palazzo has developed over time into one of the largest and most vital public spaces in Turin. As I looked at the market square from above, I could not help thinking of the way the official mapping of the city and the mental maps of the city dwellers intersect, conflict, and create new forms through lived experience. The history of this neighborhood, a gateway to the city, reveals much about its current situation and helped me understand the role of the market in bringing vitality to the city of Turin.

Fare la spesa: Shopping, Morality, and Anxiety at the Market

While waiting in front of Antonio's fruit stand, I looked over to see what the woman next to me was buying. She caught me glancing and shot me back a glare: "Che cosa stai guardando?" (What are you looking at?). Trying to defuse the tension of the situation, I smiled and replied, "I was only looking for inspiration for tonight's supper." I imagined this woman thought I was going to criticize her choices. We began to talk about the drudgery of cooking two meals a day, our husbands' expectations, and how eating at home was different in Canada compared to Italy. After just a few minutes of casual conversation, we had told each other something about our domestic experiences and what we felt was expected of us as women in the societies in which we lived. I walked away from Antonio's shaking my head amazed at how much can be shared between strangers and learned through this mundane, everyday act of grocery shopping.

—Fieldnotes, March 23, 2003

Perhaps you do not think of the tedious act of grocery shopping as a tension-filled or anxiety-producing activity; however, for many people, it is a minefield through which the shopper must navigate gender stereotypes, body image issues, class identity, and financial insecurity. While shopping and working at the Porta Palazzo market, I witnessed and took part in many situations, like the one above, that showed me some of the unexpected aspects of doing the shopping. This chapter explores some of these anxiety-producing issues and how shoppers at Porta Palazzo negotiate these often uncomfortable encounters and social situations. Food is frequently associated with the private sphere, and when it is brought into the public space of the market, it brings with it many private concerns for both individuals and the various social groups who frequent Porta Palazzo. The market square offers a place for shoppers, vendors, and passersby to make comparisons and sometimes engage one another both playfully and aggressively. In particular, shopping and consumption become forms of moral evaluation in the public space of the market. The ethnographic examples in this chapter look at the intersections between consumption, private life, and the public sphere.

The Market as a Gendered Field

I had my own anxieties and apprehensions about operating in the chaotic public space of the market when I went into the field: I wanted this to be a good study, I wanted the people at the market to trust me, and I desperately wanted to fit in. Finding a place at the market was certainly one of the first challenges I faced. Once I knew where I could stand (literally and figuratively), I quickly realized the importance of understanding who I was to the people around me. First and foremost, I was a woman, and it became apparent to me how gendered the market was as a field. Being a woman in an outwardly male-dominated field had positive and negative effects on my research. I felt very conscious of being a woman and how this affected my understanding of my field environment, my access to information, and how I presented myself. Prior to this fieldwork experience, gender was not something I gave much thought to in my everyday life. Perhaps I even took on what has been referred to as the asexual pose when first approaching the field (Markowitz and Ashkenazi 1999; Probyn 1993). I was very focused on discovering the gender dynamics of people working and frequenting markets, and in doing so I asked myself questions. Did mostly women do the shopping? Who controlled the money in a household? Did women do most of the cooking? Why were almost all the butchers at the market men? However, when I entered the field, questions of gender took on a new turn, and I was constantly reminded that I was a woman: "Sei una bella ragazza!" (You're a beautiful girl!) or "Dove sta il tuo marito? Lui sa che sei qui?" (Where is your husband? Does he know you're here?). At first, I was rather shocked and put off by these catcalls and comments; to me this sort of language was loaded with meaning, and I took it all quite seriously as either a proposition or an affront. Initially, I felt that walking the length of the market was a bit like running the gauntlet. I did not like having to confront sexual tensions and my own sexuality each day. I can even remember lying in bed dreading having to put up with the day's questioning about my marital status or comments on the size of my backside. I felt psychologically unprepared for dealing with issues of gender and sexuality at such a personal level. During my fieldwork, gender and sexuality became a heavy daily weight, and I knew I had to find some way to turn this factor around and make it a positive aspect of my research. I was inspired by Les Back's comment on gendered participation: "It is not a matter of trying to 'overcome' the effects which the gender of the researcher has on a particular field situation, but to explore how the participant observer's gender identity becomes intertwined with the process of knowing" (1993: 218).

I certainly felt that my gender determined and limited what I could know first hand. For example, I knew I could not hang around on street corners with the Moroccan boys selling mint and try to understand their world fully. They would never accept me as an insider, and I would always be treated in a culturally prescribed manner. At the same time, I was surprised that this was not always true. When I worked with Mustafa and Giorgio they really did not care if I was a woman or a donkey: I was labor. On the other hand, being a woman also had its advantages: I had relatively easy access to the lives and inner circles of other women. I felt that being a woman made me less of a threat to many of my informants. However, my age, gender, and marital status were something found threatening or inviting depending on the status of the person I was dealing with. At many markets in Italy, the sexual discourse is overt, and men freely expressed their sexual opinions and desires. Each party was expected to act according to predefined gender roles: the man publicly expressed his sexual interest; as a woman, I was expected to state my refutation publicly or retort in order to protect my respectability (Butler 1990). Not until I had made a place for myself at the market could I begin to play the game of subverting gender roles. As I became more familiar with daily life at the market, I realized there was room for me to throw back my own opinions and engage in playful banter that I was too prudish and shy to do at first.

Just as much as the ethnographer is trying to place informants into categories (intentionally or inadvertently), the people she works with are trying to place the ethnographer into their own culturally constructed categories, particularly when it comes to gender and life stage (Markowitz and Ashkenazi 1999: 162). One of the first questions most people I worked with in the market in Italy asked me was if I was married. When I told them I was, it put me in a different social category, and I was excluded as a possible match for male relatives and friends. At the same time, I was seen as less of a threat in the "competition" to find a husband (something my Italian informants placed a lot of importance on for a woman my age, mid-twenties). The next questions were "What does your husband think of your working at the market?" and "Where is your husband, and does he know you are here?" My informants used my responses to judge what kind of wife and, in turn, what kind of person I was and what sort of family I was from: was I going shopping so I could make my husband supper, and was my husband coming to pick me up? It became clear to me that the people I was working with really were judging me, and that this was part of the process of rejecting or accepting me into their worlds. They were trying to fit me into a category familiar to them. This is not unusual, and many anthropologists have talked about their experiences of being placed in or having to conform to gender identities that are not their own in order to operate in other cultures (Bell 1993; Gregory 1984; Mann 1976; Probyn 1993; Whitehead and Conaway 1986). Even though I did not place much importance on my marital status as a defining factor of my identity, it was essential in the creation of my social status in the field. It was a type of membership I shared with many of my female informants, and they liked to use it as a topic of conversation that could bring us closer together.

The commercial exchanges that happen at the market may seem at first to preclude personal relations, but quite the opposite is true. The intensity and frequency of transactions make the market experience particularly personal for those who work and shop there. At the beginning of my fieldwork, I was uncomfortable sharing parts of my personal life with the people I was working with, but I also wanted to be honest, and I quickly realized that I did not have much choice. If I wanted to ask personal questions about these people and get to know them in more than a superficial way, I was going to have to divulge a little information about myself. While doing research in Turin, I often felt as if I were taking the field home with me or that it would follow me home. The points of "entry" and "exit" were not well defined (Bacchiddu 2004; Gupta and Ferguson 1997: 11; Hall 2009). How and where do you draw the line between your personal life and your fieldwork? This is something each ethnographer has to decide for him or herself. As Markowitz and Ashkenazi (1999: 162) eloquently put it, "Intimacy is what all anthropologists desire in the field and also what they fear the most—that nebulous line between being 'in' and going native, retaining objectivity and an autonomous sense of self versus doing and feeling as informants do and thereby losing part of the self in the process." This is certainly a sensation that many an ethnographer has felt. As I carted my brimming basket through the market, it was often hard not to invite someone home for a meal.

Although the market as a field sometimes reminded me of a village, with its intimacy and familiarity, there were also many differences that made the familiar seem alien and initially unknowable. The fact that it was a place in constant flux from sunrise to sunset required me to adopt special techniques and considerations when approaching the field. Depending on the flow of people and the density of the crowd, I needed to choose whether I would try to participate in shopping or take refuge and observe from a more tranquil position behind a friend's market stand. When vendors I knew were feuding, I had to figure out how to take the most neutral stance possible and not alienate myself from a group by taking sides. While I wanted all the gossip, I did not want to be a gossip. Each day was a negotiation of complex human relationships and a heaving mass of hungry people.

While working at the market, I could not help but reflect on and observe the ways men and women talked about their relations and challenged well-confirmed gender roles and identities as they did their shopping at Porta Palazzo. As I watched people choose their produce and carry their bags, through these simple everyday acts it became clear that relations of gender and power are culturally constructed, deeply affected by life stage and economics. I hoped that my observations and personal experiences would lead me to better understand changing gender roles in Italian society and the ways in which people expressed their gender identities and social anxieties through buying, talking about, and eating food.

Changing Gender Relations

Pietro and I were stocking his stand in the farmers' market. It had been a slow day. The farmers were complaining about the lack of business and wringing their hands with worry. Just before lunch, around 1 p.m., a few well-dressed women came hurrying through the market.[1] One woman approached our stand, started to ask for lettuce, and wanted to know if we had any eggs left. She also began to complain about never having enough time to do the shopping:

> This is my lunch break [in a tense tone that expressed her distress]. I used to work closer to the market over by the Police Station and it was quite convenient. Now I work on the other side of town and I still come over here with the car because the produce is so much better and the prices are good. When am I supposed to have time to shop, cook, clean, and see my family? I go to work at 7 a.m. and return home at 7 p.m. at night. I am exhausted, but I don't have much choice, do I? [as she rifles through her wallet preparing to pay][2]

This woman was not alone in her feeling of not having enough time for both household duties and work outside the home. Numerous customers expressed this same frustration: they wanted to go to the market during the week, but their working hours and childcare duties would not allow them to do so. Unfortunately, the inflexible hours of the market (Monday to Friday from approximately 8 a.m. to 1 p.m. and Saturday from 8 a.m. to 6 p.m.) do not take into consideration the hours people work. To me, this seemed to be the number one reason for the drop in business, at least among Italians, at open-air markets over at least the past fifteen years. I was always perplexed at why Turin has not tried experimenting with hours outside the regular workday. This may be due to rigid mentalities, local regulations, associations, and strong union groups within the market.[3] There have been a few experiments with Sunday markets: in the summer, there is a farmers' market in the historic Piazza delle Erbe in front of the city hall. Although these markets do draw a different crowd from the daily market, Sunday in Italy is still generally considered a sacred day when people do not work.[4] The people who come to the Sunday markets are generally willing to pay higher prices for organic produce purchased directly from the farmer. They buy speciality items such as honey, cheese, and salami; rarely are they shopping for everyday items. For these shoppers, the Sunday market is a treat, a leisure activity rather than a necessity.

Silvana, a female shopper I interviewed at a friend's house, said that she had Thursday mornings off, so she took that time to go to the market. She was lucky enough to have a managerial job and could take the liberty of arranging her working hours. Silvana told me she would like to go to the market more often because she thought the products were better quality than those in most supermarkets. She also mentioned that she enjoyed the banter between customer and vendor and the personal exchange that goes on while she does her shopping. She knows many of the vendors by name and feels that they have a good relationship; they give her the best of what they have to offer. For Silvana, who lives in Borgaro, the half-hour drive to Porta Palazzo was worth her efforts because of the choice and quality of the products as well as the friendly atmosphere of the market.

Unlike Silvana, not many women who work outside the home in Italy have the liberty of dictating their working hours. The large number of women who have joined the workforce is a recent phenomenon in urban Italian society and one that is presently causing a great deal of tension in gender relations (Saraceno 2004). Women are still expected to keep house as if they were housewives, completely dedicated to the home and family, while having to work long hours outside the home (Rossi 1993; Hochschild 1989, 1997).

As Carole Counihan underlines, this is largely due to Italian men's unwillingness to contribute to household tasks, such as cleaning and cooking: "in the 1970s Italy moved toward formal public equity, but male privilege persisted in the household" (2004: 165). However, she also notes that this attitude is changing and men are becoming more involved in household duties and parenting (172). In many ways, provisioning falls outside these gendered tasks, and at times men can be found doing the shopping; however, they are usually accompanied by their partners, and this may be an activity that takes place uniquely on weekends. My conversations with women in the marketplace and in their homes revealed that women often feel anxious about fulfilling roles as working people, mothers, and wives. In *Garlic and Oil: Food and Politics in Italy*, Carol Helstosky notes, "Italian food habits changed most dramatically in response to shifts in societal and family structures (smaller families, women working outside the home, more varied leisure patterns)" (2004: 148). I could see this trend at the market, where middle-aged Italian women were often a scarce group during the week.

Many Italians have not stopped eating three-course meals in the home at least once a day, and women are most often the ones called on to prepare these laborious meals that require a great deal of provisioning. This partly explains the rise in consumption of prepared and frozen foods (Helstosky 2004) and the decline in regular provisioning for fresh food: there is simply less time available for the activity of grocery shopping. Also for this reason, working families shop at supermarkets, which have flexible hours and frozen foods (Harper and Faccioli 2009). Helstosky also remarks that Italians are increasingly eating outside the home and that eating at restaurants is now becoming a regular activity, whereas it used to be infrequent and reserved for special occasions. This move to eating outside the home can be seen in two ways. First, not having to shop for and prepare meals certainly eases women's domestic workload and allows for more leisure time. Second, when meals are not prepared in the home, there is a shift in domestic gender relations. Not cooking at home means that women no longer control the household budget that was once used for provisioning. At the same time, having their own earnings from work outside the home offsets this shift. However, women no longer control the distribution and quality of the food at the table. The domestic dinner table is a very different place from the restaurant table: at the restaurant, people can choose what they would like to eat and they are served by someone outside the family, while eating at home helps build family ties and aids in the reproduction of family hierarchy and gender roles that are played out through the distribution and sharing of food. Eating more frequently outside the home has a number of repercussions that range from personal choices about food to the distribution of gender roles to the cohesiveness of the family.

In general, Italians stay in family homes longer than other European adults. Chiara Saraceno's (2004) study of statistics sheds light on the current state of the Italian family. Saraceno reveals that most Italians delay leaving home and that marriage, the traditional passage to adulthood, is occurring later than before.[5] Although learning to cook is often done under the apprenticeship of mothers in Italy, it is not until a daughter leaves to start a family of her own that she really begins to cook on her own. Mothers tend to hold strongly onto their roles as family cooks and often see their daughters' attempts to move in on this role as an affront to their position in the family. Daughters generally have minor roles, if any, in the kitchen. Most sons are not required to participate in preparation of meals in the Italian household and are actually forbidden to get involved in food preparation. In many middle-class families, young women are even discouraged by their mothers from learning to cook, in the hope that they will focus on salaried activities. One twenty-eight-year-old woman, Silvia, a recent university graduate still living at home, told me that her mother would not let her cook meals on her own, discouraged her from cooking, and pushed her to study so she could get a good job and earn good money. Silvia told me that her mother hoped Silvia would have an easier life than she had. The ironic outcome of leaving home late is that young Italians are not acquiring the same level of culinary skills as in the past. This is perhaps also a factor in the increased consumption of prepared foods, eating out, and the simplification of many culinary traditions. There is a lot of talk about food, but sometimes there is not much cooking.

Market Banter and the Sexualized Discourses of Exchange

Another area where there is a lot of talk and little action is sex. Talking about sex at the market is a way in which people at the market diffuse social tensions and anxieties about gender by turning the usual power relations on their heads. The atmosphere of markets, bazaars, and fairs has been compared to that of a carnival: there is something festive as well as disorienting in the disorder and chaos of markets and fairs. As historian Robert Darnton explains, "During carnival the common people suspended the normal rules of behaviour and ceremoniously reversed the social order or turned it upside down in riotous procession . . . a time when young people tested social boundaries by limited outbursts of deviance, before being reassimilated in the world of order, submission, and Lentine seriousness" (1984: 83). This same overturning of social order can be seen on a smaller scale at markets on a daily basis.

One day while working next to Giovanna at her fruit stand, I listened to thinly disguised sexual remarks, lewd comments, and insults that lacked the veil of any kind of witty delivery.

Giovanna: "Come here young man. I have something special just for you but you have to come here first."
Old man: "What good fortune could bring me such a gift?"

Giovanna [leaning over her stand toward the man, emphasizing her bust]: "You see these grapes. I know you will get great pleasure when you eat them. I promise you" [she says in her low husky voice].

The old man stands gazing at Giovanna's chest. His wife gives him a shove with her elbow, and they move along the aisle. I wondered how these people could get away with this kind of verbal exchange, which would certainly have been considered provocative in any other context. According to the Russian scholar Mikhail Bakhtin, writing of markets in Renaissance France,

Abuses, curses, profanities and improprieties are the unofficial elements of speech. . . . Such speech forms, liberated from norms,

hierarchies and prohibitions of established idiom, become themselves a peculiar argot and create a special collectivity, a group of
people initiated in familiar intercourse, who are frank and free in
expressing themselves verbally. The marketplace crowd was such a
collectivity, especially the festive, carnivalesque crowd at the fair.
(1968: 187–88)

As historians Stallybrass and White (1986: 28) underline, Bakhtin was
also remarking on the fact that, historically, markets and fairs often fell outside local official hierarchy and fell into the language of the popular festivity.
In addition, open-air markets do not have the social constraints of a public
building. Space and time are essential to the carnivalesque atmosphere of
markets, and the creation of space free of structures evokes a festive feeling,
even outside holidays. The instability of roles, the constant renegotiation of
the place, of spectator, and of spectacle make room for "symbolic acts of a
self-consciously political kind" (1986: 42).

Within the context of the Porta Palazzo market, the instability of gender and social identities is often expressed through exchanges between
vendors, as well as between vendors and clients. The most obvious form
of the exchange at the market is verbal, and vendors' calls are essential
to communication, competition, and creation of the carnivalesque atmosphere of the market. Jacqueline Lindenfeld's (1990) study of speech
and sociability in French urban markets reveals that vendor calls are a
form of performance that establish "clear dominance patterns among the
marketplace protagonists" and serve to draw an imaginary line between
sellers and buyers (1990: 68–69). However, these lines are usually renego-
tiations of social hierarchy. For example, one morning when I was working at Mustafa's stand in the center of the market, I heard a nearby vendor
call to a well-dressed, middle-aged Italian woman: "Hey lady, come and
touch my round tomatoes. They are red and bursting. I am sure you don't
have any like this at home." The woman to whom this call was addressed
casually turned to the vendor and asked if he had a special price for her,
and the vendor replied, "Of course, all the lovely ladies know I have the
best goods, and since you are a bit of sunshine in my day, I will make a
very good price for you." The customer seemed impervious to the sexual

banter, she was willing to play along, and the vendor seemed pleased that he had made a sale and expressed his sense of virility through his goods in front of his competition. Performance is essential to these exchanges. As Lindenfeld notes, there are frequent sexual overtones in market banter, and often customers do not seem to mind, but they frequently do not respond. However, if a customer initiates a joke or playful insults, vendors nearly always join in with humorous talk (119). This also holds true for same-sex exchanges at the market stall. Vendors try to put themselves in an advantageous situation that will also follow through into the economic exchange that they hope will ensue after the banter.

In addition to the verbally dominant position that most vendors take in relation to clients, who are often from social classes above them, in the resellers' area at Porta Palazzo vendors are physically placed in a position of power, standing on a platform that allows them to look down at their goods and their customers. The gesture of receiving your purchase, which is handed down to you, and the act of paying, handing the money up to the vendor, can also be seen as symbolic physical positioning that creates a temporary form of dominance of vendor over client. It should be the clients who ultimately control the transaction because it is their decision in the end if they want to buy. I often experienced the spellbinding power of some vendors, as I walked away from their stand with too many onions for which I had paid far too much, perplexed at the lightning-fast transaction that had just taken place. A smile still came to my face.

Vendor spiels and banter are not all about male dominance over females. As Giovanna's "come on" above demonstrates, female vendors also use their charms to sell their goods, handing out compliments to men, in particular, to older men. Women vendors also try to attain a position of power through sexual discourses that play on traditional gender roles, although frequently appropriating them for their own ends. On another trip to the market in the autumn, I heard a female vendor selling porcini mushrooms yell out, "Come here, and I'll cut it open. I'll cut it for you!" to a passing man who did not blink an eye. This woman's vendor call was odd because it was both trying to show the quality of her goods, showing there were no worms in those mushrooms, but it also took the form of a potential sexual threat. The fact that she was brandishing a knife seemed to affirm that she was a potential menace, and the inherent phallic nature of the mushrooms did not help either. This was not necessarily the best sales technique, but context seemed to be everything, and a couple approached her stand and asked for a demonstration. They were pleased with the quality of the porcini and made their purchase.

It should also be added that there is frequently a homosexual discourse in vendor calls and exchanges between male vendors. These calls are not usually addressed at anyone in particular, and if they are, it is normally between male vendors who frequently stake out their territory with humorous sexual banter that often acts as a confirmation of their heterosexual identities. However, in southern Italian language and local dialects, there is frequent reference to the homosexual male that makes him an accepted part of the sexual and linguistic landscape. Although homosexuality is outwardly abhorred, there is an inner acceptance and attraction at the same time. The Neapolitan *femminielli* ("man-women," generally prostitutes) are part of the local sexual landscape in Naples (Atlas 2002). Public expressions of homosexuality both challenge masculinity and, through expressing dominance over other males, affirm virility.

Often the fruits and vegetables on sale play an essential role in the sexual banter that takes place at the market. Many types of produce have forms that evoke sexual organs or have linguistic double meaning, but they also serve as linguistic supplements that allow for a public discourse of sexuality that would otherwise be considered too lewd for public offer. In this case, food in its raw form becomes fodder for sexual appetites that remain largely verbal. Market sociability allows for the open expression of all sexual possibilities. Consider this tropical fruit vendor: "Take a look at this beautiful banana. It won't go all soft like his [pointing to a vendor down the aisle] when you get it home."

This sexual banter takes place partly to get the attention of potential customers but also because, at a large market like Porta Palazzo, the vendors and their clients generally remain anonymous. Interestingly, in the farmers' market section of Porta Palazzo, there is less, if any, sexual sales banter. This is a smaller area of the market, and there are more regular shoppers who have long-term relations with the specific vendors they frequent. The farmers do not have as much competition or need to differentiate themselves since the goods they are selling and their displays are generally unique. This is one of the reasons the atmosphere at the *mercato dei contadini* is so different from the rest of the market.

Paolo's Stand: Cheese, Sex, and Alcohol

At the farmers' market, alcohol can sometimes be central to sexually charged discussion, but these sorts of conversations usually take place between people who already know one another. Different forms of drinking take place between various groups at the market and in different spaces. Alcohol consumption is nearly always male-dominated and is generally a social activity. The conversations I heard and took part in over drinks at the farmers' market often pertained to sex, and more generally they contested and confirmed gender roles and norms. Paolo's cheese stand in the farmers' market was a central hub for this sort of banter.

The "Saturday crowd" at Paolo's stand would talk about all sorts of things. In particular, virility and the quality and authenticity of food were common themes. It is hard to say if these two subjects were related, but often they overlapped, whether consciously or unconsciously. Paolo was aware of his ability to attract people at the market and often talked about it in sexual terms. He told me that he knew that women were attracted to him, as well as men, hetero- and homosexual. I sometimes reminded Paolo that the quality of his cheeses was part of the attraction. He was not bothered by homosexual men and often talked about helping out Luigi, a troubled transgendered flower vendor across the way. He said he was often flattered by gay men and did not see their advances as a challenge to his masculinity. However, Paolo lamented the fact that he did not have a serious relationship with a woman. There were constant remarks about the physical appearance of female clients, and Paolo would often replay conversations with these women, who, he was convinced, were using their cheese purchases as a pretext for making advances. Granted, Paolo also used cheese as a means of seduction—serving samples, offering a glass of wine, and engaging in culinary conversation as a form of small talk with female clients. In this way, food and sex were intertwined; cheese was the first means of seduction; even if things did not get farther than that, Paolo never stopped trying.

Paolo's mainly male entourage discussed their conquests and evaluated the women who shopped at the stand, but they also exchanged recipes, talked about their favorite dishes to be made with cheeses from Paolo's selection, and pondered the perfect wine to accompany a particularly sharp pecorino (sheep's milk cheese). Recipes and language varied in sophistication but were extremely inclusive. Unemployed manual laborers, retired Fiat workers, opera singers, filmmakers, doctoral students, and illegal immigrants all participated in these conversations: everyone had something to contribute, at least consistently on the culinary front. Often recipe exchanges would be followed by a collection of the ingredients from the surrounding market, followed by dividing up the goods and recapping the cooking procedures. The oral acquisition of culinary knowledge was at its finest here: nothing was ever written down.

The following weekend, the Saturday crowd would gather to discuss how the recipes had turned out, and new recipes would be exchanged. However, it should be mentioned that often these recipes never got cooked, at least not by the men gathered around Paolo's stand. Sometimes these men would take home their acquired ingredients for mothers, girlfriends, and wives to prepare. A few of these men cooked, but others just liked to talk about food. I felt like a privileged member of the group since I was female and enjoyed access to this male world. I tried to understand this penchant for culinary talk. In some ways, I felt that these men were trying to use their knowledge of cooking to impress others (men and women) and show that they had a certain level of appreciation for food. Culinary knowledge is something that is highly regarded in Italian culture, and it is quite common to hear people having a heated debate about the preparation of *vitel tonné*.[6] As David Sutton (2001: 21) states, the handling of food through preparation and shopping "is an opportunity to show one's intelligence and skill." Here it is important to note that the actual act of cooking was not necessary in this display; it was enough to have knowledge and to vaunt it publicly. The behavior and culinary talk of Paolo and his friends seemed very similar to the types of food discourses discussed by Jonathan Deutsch in his study of fire hall cooking: men negotiate new gender scripts through their food-related discourses, and this type of talk and activity "suggests that the relationship between gender and cooking is complicated by particular contexts where people construct their work identities and their domestic lives" (2005: 112). The public nature of food talk was not particularly anxiety producing for this group of men because it was punctuated with affirmations of virility, discourse of mastery, and specialized culinary knowledge.

It also occurred to me that these men were treading on ground, that of the kitchen, which was traditionally and stereotypically female. Perhaps they were attempting to appropriate this domain, or maybe they were actually challenging traditional Italian gender roles through a culinary discourse. They affirmed their masculinity by having disregard for any taboo attached to activities that are generally seen by Italian society as female. On further investigation, my analysis yielded some exceptions that went beyond gender stereotypes and helped explain these male culinary discourses and performances. For example, through the creation of a profession, men have controlled and raised the prestige of an activity, cooking, normally seen as a mundane female chore when it comes to the everyday preparation of meals in the home (Trubek 2000; Ortner 1974; Swinbank 2002). The professional chef has come to be seen as a male role in Italian society. Men's gastronomic societies, *txokos*, in the Basque region of Spain are another example that confirms European men's place in the kitchen. Andreas Hess argues these exclusive societies in which men cook and eat together are essential to male social bonding (2007). Unlike Deutsch's firemen, Paolo's group were operating within European gender scripts that place men squarely in the middle of culinary mastery as holders of this knowledge (Sobal 2005). Food remained the initial and constant social bond between the individuals in the group of men who gathered around Paolo's stand.

Food was not the only focal point for discussion and reason to spend time chatting: alcohol was an important element in sociability. "Andiamo a bere qualcosa insieme al bar" (let's go have a drink at the bar together) or "Passa un attimo con noi, prendi un bicchiere di vino" (spend a moment with us, have a glass of wine with us) were phrases I heard often; drinking was a pretext for spending time together talking, and it helped form a bond between the drinkers (Douglas 1987; Wilson 2005). Drinking defined group exclusion and inclusion. Although I am not much for drinking before lunch or outside meals, I learned to drink to keep company. It felt like drinking was a test, and to be included in the group, I felt had to drink. At the same time, I knew I was breaking with northern Italian gender norms: you will not find many Italian women drinking in public among men. This was not necessarily a bad thing; I was a foreigner and could get away with quite a lot of unusual behavior (Whitehead and Conaway 1986; Warren and Hackney 2000). Of course, the men made remarks about my being a woman and asked after my love life, but at the same time, I was not easily categorized and perhaps dismissed as a woman because of my unusual behavior.

Social drinking was much more common in the farmers' market compared to the reseller's market, where I only occasionally saw people have *caffè corretto* (coffee usually with a dash of *grappa* or perhaps some other strong alcohol). This could be due in part to different cultures of drink, a different pace of work, and a more laidback social atmosphere at the farmers' market. There was more time for talking at the market, and most people had known each other from childhood when they started to go to the market with their parents. There is not the same sense of competition here, which helps create a sense of community. Not everyone drank, but Paolo's group often imbibed when it was bitter cold or sweltering hot. I learned to drink to stay warm. On chilly winter mornings, I could feel the cold creep up my legs, and hot rum was one way of keeping one step ahead of the cold. Drinking was both social and weather-induced. Alcohol also loosens the lips, and as people sat around drinking, their views became more and more opinionated. This led to heated debates, but all taken in the context of camaraderie. Unlike food or sex, alcohol was not explicitly discussed; it seemed to be more of a backdrop and was not something to take notice of, although on occasion some made appreciative remarks about the wine. In *contadino* (rural/farm) culture in Italy, it was not unusual for workers to take a flask of wine out into the field or even be served wine at the cafeteria in factories. An important source of calories, wine was considered food until the 1970s and early 1980s (Grivetti 1996).

Social drinking at the farmers' market was seen as part of a *contadino* tradition and was further normalized by its proximity to antisocial alcoholism. There were a number of regular alcoholics who would come and drink their cheap wine and beer in and around the market. They generally kept to themselves and only made a spectacle when slumping over in front of moving delivery trucks or defecating in public areas. A form of public drinking was acceptable because social interactions were still under control, while the latter was seen as antisocial and out of control because of the lack of respect for social norms. This said, the market attracts drinkers of all kinds; another two groups who came to the farmers' market to drink, particularly on Saturdays, were the Rom and Romanian communities. The Rom often made a picnic at the end of the market and asked the farmers for any "leftovers." The women removed the bottle tops with their teeth, the children chased pigeons, and the men joked and laughed loudly in groups. Romanians are another group who use the area around the farmers' market as a public drinking and social space. Sometimes there were up to twenty or thirty Romanians, adult men and women, who gathered on Saturday afternoon after they had done their shopping. They would buy beer inside the covered market or at shops off the piazza and spend several hours catching up with friends and family. Most Italians frowned on the behavior of these immigrant groups, despite the fact that they were seldom disruptive.

For Italians, those who are not alcoholics generally do not drink in public spaces and usually not outside meals. Even bars in Italy are not alcohol-oriented like pubs in Britain or bars in North America. Although this trend is changing, drinking is rarely done in excess and is often associated with meals and the private sphere. As in France, drinking in public spaces, other than bars and designated areas, is not seen in a positive light. Nonetheless, drinking at work, under stress and for social reasons, is permissible in many cases. Food could also factor in here since snacks were usually served with drinks on these informal occasions at the farmers' market. As Mary Douglas notes in *Constructive Drinking* (1987: 8), the world is socially constructed and so is drinking. Drinks give structure to sociability, which may differ between cultural groups. This is apparent at the Porta Palazzo farmers' market, where I witnessed these culture variations of public drinking that often centered on masculinity and *contadino* culture. Drinking could either create social cohesion or could become an anxiety-producing activity when it took place outside cultural norms.

Anxious Shoppers: Sweetness, the Body, and the Public Nature of Consumption

If shopping for dinner were not anxiety-producing enough, there is a whole other set of worries to be negotiated when buying nonessential food items. One of my first jobs at the market was with a Torinese family at its sweets stand. While working alongside Roberta and Lorenzo, I got to know the shoppers who frequented the stand. I realized the importance many women placed on being frugal and managing money, but also the place of pleasure and indulgence that seemed to slip outside the grasps of economic rationality. Mostly women came to the sweets stand, and they made a bigger production out of buying this little extra than they did buying fruits and vegetables. Customers often took the time to talk to me about weakness and indulgence. This was contrasted by comments on what good buys they had searched out in the rest of the market and what wholesome meals they cooked. As one elderly female customer told me,

> Yes, I think I will treat myself to some chocolates today. Well, it is nearly Easter. My grandchildren will be coming by, and it would be nice to have some sweets for them. I know I shouldn't really eat too many sweets, but I cook such healthy meals and it's always nice to have a little something once in a while. (elderly female Italian customer)

Many women felt a need to justify their purchases of sweets, most certainly a gastronomic and an economic indulgence. The shopper above makes a point of underlining the health issues and the fact that it was a festive season, which allowed for special behavior toward foods that might otherwise be forbidden or seen as unhealthy. This was not uncommon: many customers felt it necessary to validate their "unhealthy" purchases by balancing out their caloric consumption with wholesome accounts of family meals and "wiser" purchases made at the market that day. Others admitted their weakness for sweets and declared their guilt when it came to unhealthy eating. All in all, this was a predominant theme among our female customers. Women seemed to feel that they had to be the guardians of their family's health, and in buying sweets they had to justify their diversion from this role. I challenged my own assumptions about the role of sweets in the household and also took into consideration what role these foods played in family relations.

One customer told me that holidays just would not be the same without heaping bowls of chocolates for guests and children. Sweets are attached to the idea of celebration, particularly for children. Another middle-aged client told me that she gave her sons sweets when they did well at school: children are rewarded for good behavior with sugary treats that break from everyday foods. In most cases, it seemed to be the mother or the grandmother who controlled the distribution of sugar. In this case, sugar really is psychological power in the family and between generations. It also plays a big part in food memories: "I always remember the cut glass bowl of candies that my grandmother kept by the front door. They were fruit jellies that came in a shiny wrapper. Whenever I eat one of those candies today, it brings me back to visits with my grandmother." Many shoppers shared with me their Proustian memories associated with specific types of candies that we sold at our stand.

It was not all teary-eyed memories and positive associations when it came to buying candy and snacks. Women in particular seemed to struggle as they faced the mounds of sweets. In many conversations I had with female customers, they expressed anxiety about not conforming or living up to images of the female body portrayed by the Italian media. It was as if we were catching them in the very act of defiance or self-indulgence. Some tried to cover up their weakness for sweets. One extremely overweight woman, as she ordered over a kilo of sweets, told me: "They're for my children." I glimpsed her putting her hand in the bag as she walked away. Children often served as decoys for the adult sweet tooth. There were also people who justified their purchase as a matter of merit. Margaret Wilson, in her short essay "Indulgence," describes similar scenes at a café in Seattle: she finds that individuals are constantly negotiating lines between indulgence and restraint through their food choices (2005: 155). Although the Italian situation is very different from the endemic obesity in the United States, Italians are getting increasingly heavy, and the much-vaunted Mediterranean diet is largely a thing of the past. As Italians get heavier, feelings of guilt are focused more and more on eating and food.

The regulars at Lorenzo and Roberta's market stall also brought forth other health issues; for example, there was a die-hard group of diabetics who could not kick their sugary habits. Luckily, we sold sugar-free candies that seemed to serve as a sufficiently acceptable placebo without having to get these "addicts" to sign waivers. The diabetic embodied the extreme of self-restraint, indulgence, and health risks associated with an unhealthy diet. When I looked into the eyes of a customer I knew was diabetic and handed him or her a bag of chocolate-covered cherries, I felt a sense of deep irresponsibility, and I desperately wanted to make the buyer promise these treats were for someone else.

Food desires seemed to be stronger than health concerns, and weakness toward this "sin" was negotiated publicly with constant excuses and the occasional confession. The public nature of the act of shopping was very important for many customers: it was an exciting and happy moment, but it was sometimes also a moment of public admission of a private problem, a cause for anxiety. This was compounded by a growing awareness of body image in Italy; media images endorse the slim female body (and now the muscular male body) as the only desirable body type. The well-rounded *mama* figure is no longer the appealing shape for aging women, who are becoming ever-more body conscious.

The body was not the only anxiety-causing subject for female shoppers at the sweets stand; this superfluous purchase required justification in the face of increasingly slim family budgets:

[wringing her hands and smiling] I got such a good deal on these zucchini, and pears are in season. I bought a kilo for 1.50 euros. Isn't that a great price? I guess I can buy some more sweets. (middle-aged female Italian customer shopping on her own)

This shopper placed a clear emphasis on budget and money. She carefully controlled the money she was in charge of for household provisioning in order to allow herself the occasional small luxury. Italian women are often put in charge of their husbands' salaries so that they can carry out the everyday family activities such as shopping for food, clothes, and supplies for the household (Counihan 2004: 105). As the shopper above demonstrates, women use their buying power not only to nourish their families but to fulfill their food desires. After I had interviewed many female Italian shoppers, it became clear that the woman's objective was to *fare economia* (be frugal); by making savings for the household, she was seen as a good female role model and an outstanding mother.

Some shoppers felt it difficult to stay within their budgets: the temptation of buying extras like candy was one challenge, and the sense of obligation created through market exchanges was another. Frequently, market vendors will give shoppers a gift. This might be a few extra strawberries, a handful of herbs, or a lemon. The gift might also take the form of advice, a recipe, or extra time taken to explain the products. The vendor usually makes a show of the gift, and the shopper profusely gushes thanks, sometimes by purchasing more than that person needs or set out to buy. This gift is meant to create a bond of obligation that ties the two actors together (Mauss 1950). In a market with so many stalls selling nearly the same items, this is very important. While the gift creates a bond that is generally to the vendor's advantage, the submissive shopper can find this exchange anxiety producing. When I interviewed shoppers and asked them about gifts, most of them responded that they really liked these little extras, and some came to expect it. However, there were also shoppers, generally young women, who found the gifts made them feel uncomfortable. After asking for more information about a certain type of tomato, one woman told me she felt obliged to buy at least a kilo of them because she had taken up so much of the vendor's time on a busy Saturday. While this gift economy is what makes markets different from supermarkets, this obligation to buy weighed heavily on a number of shoppers.

As the shoppers at the sweet stand in Piazzetta Milano made their purchases, they navigated between anxieties concerning control of their bodies and control of their budgets. The public nature of shopping made each choice open to the possibility of public judgment from vendors and fellow shoppers.

Gleaning at the Market: Food Security and the Elderly

Perhaps the most anxiety-producing element of the Porta Palazzo market is the struggle against food insecurity that can be witnessed each day.[7] When I did research in markets in France, I frequently saw young people gleaning from discarded produce. Some of these could be considered "freegans,"[8] people who could not stand to see all this produce they still deemed edible to go to waste (Black 2008). The people I talked to in France never mentioned being hungry or indicated their gleaning activities were motivated purely by economic necessity. This was not the case in Italy: the people doing the gleaning at Porta Palazzo were elderly, and their search for food was most certainly related to hunger and food insecurity (see Figure 6). An Italian government pension does not ensure subsistence, and if families do not pitch in or directly care for their elders, they will be hungry or cold (Deriu and Sgritta 2005). The informal family social security net is showing signs of collapse.

It was a cold January day, and I was doing my shopping as quickly as I could so I could get home and start making soup. I am not sure why I had never noticed the mounds of garbage that piled up at the fringes of the area with the market stalls in the large resellers' market, but that day I took note. An elderly woman bundled up for the cold weather sifted through the discarded vegetables. I stopped in front of one Italian vendor's stand to watch this activity; I guess I must have stood there too long. The vendor said to me in a cool tone, "Don't stare. It's a disgrace. I can't believe Italy has come to this!" I turned my eyes away and started to discuss the situation with another vendor who had caught my shocked gaze. He told me, "It's the end of the family and the end of the State. We leave our elders to sift through the garbage while we stuff our baskets." The vendor told me that they all knew the old people who came to collect the refuse. They turned a blind eye and made sure there was something edible for these people to pick up. The vendors wanted these hungry people to have some dignity. Another Italian vendor told me, "It makes me want to cry that it comes down to this." The immigrant vendors were far less sympathetic: one Moroccan vendor told me he saw these scavengers as bad for business and criticized Italians for not taking care of their elders. It certainly was a

Figure 6. Gleaning after the market. Photo courtesy of Alice Massano.

heart-wrenching scene to witness each market day, and it spoke volumes about how Italy has changed and how all forms of social security, from both family and State, are failing. This is a problem of epic proportions since Italy has the fastest and largest aging population in all Europe (Testa 2000; Pinelli and Golini 1993).

A few weeks later, I returned to the market toward three in the afternoon to watch as it was dismantled. The stalls had been taken down, and tractors were moving the "garbage" from its various scatterings in the square to two huge mounds. An elderly man and woman were nimbly combing the refuse and shoving slightly damaged carrots, squash, and lettuce into their bags. They worked against the clock and the approaching arm of the crane that picked up the refuse and put it into a truck to be carted off for organic recycling. I did not have the nerve to approach these people. They looked at me and caught my gaze, then quickly looked back down at the ground. I skulked off feeling sick to my stomach.

Food insecurity among the elderly is a huge issue in Italy that goes largely unaddressed by authorities and communities. Although it is socially unacceptable to glean at the market, everyone turns a blind eye. Not everything discarded at the market is inedible, and much of it, particularly produce, is perfectly fit for human consumption after it has been washed and cooked. In some ways, this gleaning can be seen as redistribution, but it still begs the social issue of food insecurity amid abundance and the lack of a stronger sense of moral economy in a society with such abundance, waste, and disparity. Not having enough food to eat is perhaps the most anxiety-producing situation that a human can face.

By the end of my research, I saw around me at Porta Palazzo not only a plentiful world of *cuccagna* (land of plenty) but also an urban landscape filled with complex social relations—many of which abounded with uncertainty, fears of being judged, and an inability to live up to social norms and gender roles. Food was the language in which this anxiety was expressed: food gave a voice to social concerns and change. My own anxieties, fears, and uncertainties were also bound up in my life at the Porta Palazzo market. As I mentioned earlier in this chapter, I initially felt unsure about who I was in the context of the market: I felt the weight of social judgment upon my actions as I found my way around my field. As I became increasingly familiar with the landscape of the market and the people I dealt with on a daily basis, I learned to employ the various scripts that were expected of me. These included playing the role of the immigrant woman, the student, the wife, the shopper, and the worker. As I learned the boundaries of these various performed parts of my social identity at the market, I began to navigate the space adeptly. There were still moments where I overstepped boundaries and pushed the limits of what I could and could not do or say, but every day at Porta Palazzo I learned more about who I was and about how the experience of working and carrying out my daily activities at the market was all about navigating social relations and trusting myself. My experience of being in the markets started out as an anxiety-filled daily chore and ended as a nostalgic stroll in a place I felt as much a part of as the paving stones on the ground. I also learned that some forms of social anxiety are overcome through familiarity, but there are other kinds of uncertainty produced by changes in what I thought I knew intimately. This reflection helped me understand my own initial reactions to the market and those of my fellow shoppers and workers in the face of the major social and economic shifts in their society and daily lives.

Many of the examples in this chapter have combined issues of gender, life stage, consumption, and the anxiety produced by shopping and working in the market. Through what I observed at Porta Palazzo and the conversations I had at the market, I realized that much of the social anxiety that was attributed to economic difficulties, the influx of migrants, and changes in everyday life had a huge impact on social relations and in many ways were a small reflection of the issues facing Italian society on a larger scale. How does increasing economic independence of Italian women affect marriages? Are slim bodies more desirable than plump? How do men bond when there are fewer public social spaces? Why are Italians not more concerned about the elderly and their lack of access to reasonably priced food? As I did my shopping, sold food, and interviewed shoppers, these were some of the questions that stayed with me during my investigation. The market, although public, offers windows into a more intimate private life of citizens. On one hand, it is a place where topics that would otherwise be considered taboo can be broached, whether through a vendor's banter or the purchase of a bag of chocolates. On the other hand, the market is a place where Italians ignore some of the most glaring social issues of the day. As Italian families, diets, and everyday lives change, Italian and migrant food voices express a degree of anxiety amid the usual pleasure associated with food in Italy.

Vitel Tonné (Vitello Tonnato)

The first time I saw this dish,[9] I did not think the combination of veal with tuna sauce was a very good idea. You could say it produced a certain amount of gustatory anxiety on my part—an example of how the unfamiliar can create anxiety. Fortunately, I was brave enough to have a taste and was pleasantly surprised how delicious it is. Along with *bagna caoda*[10] this was the recipe the Saturday crowd at Paolo's stand most discussed and which seemed to be an indicator of authenticity when talking about Piedmontese food. Like *bagna caoda*, *vitel tonné* is a product of the trade between Liguria and Piedmont. It brings together the sea, salted capers, preserved tuna, and the rich pasture lands of Padania, famous for *razza piemontese* cattle. This recipe is a little tricky to prepare at home, but it is one of the most common dishes on restaurant menus throughout Piedmont. Many housewives buy the meat finely cut from the butcher and prepare the sauce themselves.

INGREDIENTS
2–2.5 lb veal roast from leg or loin, boned and tied
1 onion
1 clove garlic
1 carrot
1 stalk celery
10 stalks Italian parsley
1.5 cups dry white wine
kosher salt

FOR THE SAUCE
2 egg yolks
1 cup extra virgin olive oil
juice from 1/2 lemon
25 oz tuna in olive oil
2 tbs capers in salt (rinsed)
salt and white pepper

In a large pot, bring to a boil enough water to cover the meat. Add the wine and the onion, carrot, and celery, all cut into large pieces. Also add the garlic, parsley, and kosher salt. Place the meat in the boiling liquid. Bring to a simmer, cook for an hour, and let cool in the broth. Refrigerate until chilled.

Cut the meat into very thin slices and arrange them on a serving platter. Spread the sauce over the meat just before serving

To make the sauce, put the egg yolks in a bowl with a pinch of salt and a little white pepper. Work the yolks with a wooden spoon until they increase a little in volume. At this point, slowly add the olive oil while stirring the mixture until it is entirely incorporated. The sauce should become soft and creamy. Now, slowly and delicately add the lemon juice.

Finely chop the capers and the tuna together. Stir into the mayonnaise mixture. Chill.

Il Ventre di Torino: Migration and Food

> Walking around the market, I sometimes forget I
> am in Turin. There are people speaking in Arabic,
> English with African accents, Mandarin and
> Romanian. There are numerous *halal* butchers
> whose signage is mainly in Arabic, where Moroccan
> men stand out front talking. I am intrigued by the
> way they cut the meat and how it is displayed—so
> much more vividly red and roughly cut than I am
> used to seeing. It's all just piled in the refrigerator
> cases. I am equally enticed by the Asian grocery
> stores along corso Regina, which are stocked floor
> to ceiling. The smell of fish and rice wafts down via
> delle Orfane and draws me to the door of an African
> restaurant—the menu is written in French. I want to
> taste everything. It's as if all the kitchens of the world
> are filling their larders here at Porta Palazzo.
>
> —Fieldnotes, February 15, 2003

One of the first things that strikes most visitors when they arrive at Porta Palazzo is the multiethnic environment of the market. As mentioned earlier, Porta Palazzo is one of the main receiving areas for migrants in Turin and has been for the last century. The first wave arrived from the Piedmontese countryside at the turn of the twentieth century, followed by migration from the Veneto and the south of Italy after World War II as industry grew in Turin. Over the past two decades, this city has experienced its first modern influx of migrants from outside Italy. Interestingly, this neighborhood has attracted newly arrived migrants in all three waves of migration. Newcomers are drawn to the area by the availability of housing, low rents, and the market. Porta Palazzo has always been a place where people and goods have moved freely in and out of the city.

The market plays a central role in attracting people to the area and serves important social and economic functions for newcomers. In this chapter, I will focus on the most recent wave of migration and the Torinese reactions to their new neighbors. Here I have tried to capture the role of the market and ethnic businesses in the lives of migrants from two different groups: Moroccan vendors and female Nigerian shoppers. My choice of these two groups is somewhat organic: during my fieldwork, these were the people I got to know best as the outcome of a snowball approach to finding participants. It is important to note that these short freeze-frames do not try to give an overall picture of migration in Turin; rather, they zoom in on specific groups and individuals to give a more subjective and personal account of migration and how it relates to life at the market. I have tried to capture these people's view of the migration experience and the role that food plays in their everyday relations.

Migration and Food

The relationship between migration and food has been explored from many perspectives: identity, history, nutrition, and economic prosperity, to name a few (Kershen 2002; Ward and Jenkins 1984; Bates 1997; Ray 2004). Food is something most migrants hold dear; it helps maintain relations in kin groups, strengthens ties to home, and is often deeply linked to memory. Anthropologist David Sutton (2001) argues that food "becomes a point of identification for people displaced by migrations caused by larger global processes" (75). Food brings groups of migrants together each day, whether to eat around the same table, shop together, or buy food from migrant and nonmigrant vendors. Many Italian writers speak of the importance of food in the migration process. Anthropologist Vito Teti claims that southern Italian writers frequently write about a momentary return to their homeland, real or dreamed, that is facilitated by food. The need to find meaning and a sense of place in a new home also happens through the regaining of familiarity with foods that have been lost, through the sacredness that accompanies the act of eating. Eating together, as it occurred in the "lost world," becomes a possible way to recognize oneself and to recognize the Other (Teti 1999: 92–93). The power of memory lies in its ability both to recall and to forget: remembering ties migrants to their homelands, while forgetting makes new situations possible or even bearable. This is how and why new traditions and cuisine are created. This was certainly the case for Italian American immigrants in New York in the twentieth century, who invented traditions that gave them a new identity that maintained their Italianness while confirming their Americanness at the same time (Cinotto 2001). Food plays an important role in giving stability to frequently volatile migrant lives.

Food carries the history and traditions of home for many migrants, providing continuity amid novelty (Delamont 1995: 26). This is perhaps why, when migration occurs, the first ethnic businesses to open are usually food related (grocery stores, butchers, and restaurants) (Cinotto 2001; Marte 2007). Ethnic businesses can also encourage voluntary migration and are important elements in migration networks, which are frequently related to kinship. They offer employment opportunities for newly arrived migrants, who might not have language skills to find jobs in the host country. Although there are cases of exploitation, employment in family-run businesses can offer a sheltered environment (Kershen 2002). Migrants have a high propensity for self-employment, often become middlemen, create ethnic enclaves, and dominate certain occupations (Portes 1995: 25). All these activities depend on social networks, on social capital, and often on informal economies (Peraldi 2001). This entrepreneurship demonstrates the relational embeddedness, the broad network of social relations on which migration networks are often based, and the ability of migrants to mobilize their social capital to find employment or start businesses in the host country (Portes 1995). These businesses often require the transnational activation of social capital and the capacity of individuals to command scarce resources by virtue of their membership in networks across international borders. For example, migrants depend on their contacts in their country of origin for supplies and often labor, while they must use their social capital in the host country to get permits and attract clientele in ethnic communities and the host society. The Gate office at Porta Palazzo has also been working hard to facilitate and encourage migrants to get legal permits for their vending activities in the area. The Gate staff help with the application process and explain some of the basics of doing business in Italy. This is seen as a major step for bringing immigrants into mainstream society and having them contribute to community life. In this manner, two-way connections are built between Turin and the sending countries of the migrants who live and work at Porta Palazzo.

This connection between places is not always as direct as one might think. For instance, the Moroccan and Asian businesses in Turin are connected with established supply routes in France and England. Until recently, there were few direct suppliers of Asian and African foodstuffs in Italy, and these contacts developed much more slowly because large-scale migration is only a recent phenomenon. For this reason, many business owners like Mohammed, who owns and runs a Moroccan butcher shop just off Porta Palazzo, travel to France on a regular basis to stock their stores. France and England have much more long-standing supply routes to ex-colonies (India, Africa, Asia) (Goody 1982; Castellani 2001). If you follow the movement of "ethnic" food from its source, you can trace migration flows. By looking at food, it is also possible to discern to what degree a migrant community has established itself in an area.

The establishment of food-related businesses usually indicates that migrant communities are putting down roots; this development normally occurs when female migrants and families start to join men, usually the first to migrate, who have attained a certain degree of stability in the host country (housing, employment, and sometimes legal immigrant status) (Lee 1992; Phillips 2006). The number of female migrants in Turin has increased greatly in groups that used to be predominantly male (in particular, the Moroccan community), suggesting the firm establishment of these communities. In 2007, 49.7 percent of the immigrant population in Turin were female.[1]

What makes Porta Palazzo particularly interesting is that it has attracted nearly all ethnic groups, from southern Italians to Chinese, as residents, shoppers, and shop owners. Unlike the case in most cities, ethnic enclaves have not formed for individual groups at Porta Palazzo; the area remains ethnically mixed. In and around the market area, ethnic businesses have flourished; there are Asian groceries next to Moroccan music stores and *halal* butchers near African beauty supply shops.

This mixing of ethnic businesses adds to the bazaar atmosphere of the area. As Sharon Zukin (1995: 190) notes, the bazaar generally lacks signage; it exists in contrast to modern commercial spaces and commodity fetishism in which everyday practices and communication are the most important features. Lack of branding and the nearly constant change in the use of retail spaces create commercial forms that elude modern retail forms. At the same time, there are extremely modern examples of trade that reflect global flows of people and goods. Low residential and retail rents, as well as the presence of the market, which attracts a large number of shoppers, are the main explanations for this attraction and proliferation of migrant-owned businesses.

Besides the ethnic shops and restaurants, many market stands are owned or rented by migrants. This is not a new occurrence: the acquisition of market stands by migrants also took place during the 1960s and 1970s when Italian southerners migrated to Turin. It is interesting that, within the market, there is an unofficial division of groups based on the type of goods sold: Moroccans and Tunisians tend to sell fruits and vegetables; Chinese sell imported electronics and trinkets, as well as work at a few stands in the fish market; Africans sell clothing; and Romanians have taken over most meat stands in the two covered markets. Illegal market vendors (those without permits or permanent stands) tend to be migrants and are also divided based on the goods sold: for example, Moroccans sell phone cards, mint, and shopping bags, while Africans sell phone cards (cf. Semi 2004 for more on the informal market at Porta Palazzo). Social networks, supply chains, and cultural values largely explain these divisions of both the informal and formal sectors.

The following ethnographic snapshots focus on some complexities of this multiethnic commerce from the consumer and vendor perspective. They give a glimpse of the stratified relations that are created at the market through commercial transactions and social networks.

Mustafa and Company: Market Integration

I first met Mustafa in April 2003 when I was working with Giovanna in the big produce resellers' market, the largest and most lively section of the open-air market area. The two vendors did not always get along, and there was a lot of banter back and forth between them. As I was standing on the platform next to Giovanna, I could tell that I was cramping her style. In fact, despite wanting to give me a hand with my research, she desperately wanted to pawn me off on someone else. Jokingly, Giovanna suggested that I should work with some of her Moroccan neighbors, and proceeded to introduce me to them. I guess she thought this was a good way of punishing them for giving her a hard time.

Initially, I did not think I would be well received by a group of Moroccan men, and I felt rather nervous. Mustafa's stand faces Giovanna's, and his brother "Giorgio" (his adopted Italian name) and his assistant Abdul have another stand kitty-corner to it. Giorgio told me to give Mustafa a hand, so I jumped up on the vendor's platform alongside Mustafa behind mounds of tired-looking zucchini, cucumbers, and tomatoes. The interrogation began: where was I from, why was I here, was I married, when was my husband going to pick me up, why did I want to work at the market? Mustafa was testing my character, and I knew that honest and reasonable answers to these questions were essential to our successful collaboration. Once the basic questions were answered, Mustafa showed me the ropes: how the scale worked, how to speak to the customers, how to stand my ground, how not to let the customers touch the produce or choose for themselves. Over the next few days, I learned how to have a quick tongue and even faster hands.

Our prices were low, or so it seemed, so we had to meet the real cost by putting a few rotten tomatoes in the bags of customers we did not know, and we insisted that everyone by a kilo and not just one or two zucchini. This was a practice I did not like, but Mustafa was always on my case. Let us just say Mustafa and Giorgio's theory of customer service and sales differed greatly from my own North American experience and expectations. Was it the specific setting of the Porta Palazzo market that accounted for this difference? Was it the great masses pushing through the market aisles and the heavy competition from the other vendors selling exactly the same thing? Or was it just hard economics dictating our business practices?

At times it felt as if it was the two of us against the customers; we really treated most people brusquely (if not rudely), and there were few polite formalities. Mustafa carried this to an extreme: when an old lady complained about the quality and the price of our produce, Mustafa told her to leave and never come back. Mustafa expressed his offense loudly, as if she had insulted his religion, and told her he would never take her money. Of course, this was all part of a performance on the part of both parties: the customer was trying to get a better price, and Mustafa was protecting his economic interests by loudly refuting accusations of low quality and high prices. He had to make himself heard to save himself from public defamation that would be overheard by other customers and vendors. This exchange was very much about saving face. In reality, there are no deals at the market; you always pay the real price depending on the time of day. When customers go home, they may have to throw out half the bad fruit the vendor slyly deals out. This is not always the case, and it is a practice that can be avoided by developing strong relationships with a few vendors—loyalty literally pays in this case. Stuart Plattner (1985) claims that this type of relationship between customer and vendor reduces risk and cost, eventually becoming a factor of value that is created out of abstract social relations, rarely a point of consideration for Western economic theory. This is one of the first lessons I learned about the social aspects of economics, as it is played out in everyday life at the market.

I also learned that economics is a social performance at the market. When necessary, Mustafa put on his "Moroccan hat" to draw the attention of Moroccan clients. He was charming and joked effortlessly with Moroccan women and men. Groups of compatriots gathered around the stall and caught up on news from home and about family. Well-wishers dropped by to congratulate Mustafa on the impending birth of his first child. The market stall also acted as a social focal point for a larger Moroccan community made up of Mustafa's friends, family, and loyal Moroccan clientele. Admittedly, I felt a little left out as these folks asked to be served by Mustafa, but I could understand that they were more comfortable being served in Arabic and by someone they trusted.

Successful market vendors have to have a certain type of personality and keen social skills. For instance, Mustafa has an amazing talent for cross-ing cultural boundaries. Much of it seems well rehearsed and calculated, but there is another level in his exchanges of which he does not seem fully aware. Early in my apprenticeship, Mustafa was teaching me about the importance of vendor calls, and as I watched and learned, I was surprised by his adaptability and business sense. For example, when he saw people pass-ing who looked Romanian, he would yell out "roșie" (tomato) and "castra-vete" (cucumber) in Romanian. This would always get their attention if they were Romanian, and they would stop to ask him how he knew the names of these vegetables in their language. Ethnic stereotyping certainly plays an important part here, and I discovered that migrants have interesting ste-reotypes of the Other as they encounter people from ethnicities they have never had contact with before. Their stereotypes are partly built on experi-ence but they are also influenced by Italian prejudices that fill the media and are part of the everyday discourse of market vendors. The fact that Mustafa is visibly North African made this surprising to the unsuspecting Romanians, but his tactic usually led to a sale. Mustafa's limited acquisition of Romanian, learned at the market from his clients, was a well-calculated business technique.

This strategy did not always work out the way Mustafa planned: there were moments when he did not fully understand what he was mimicking in calls he heard the other vendors chant. In another instance, Mustafa yelled out, "Occhio al finocchio!" (a common vendor call with a double mean-ing) to passing Italian shoppers to draw attention to the fennel at his stand. This is an Italian play on words that literally means "Look at the fennel" or figuratively speaking, "Watch out for the fag." All the Italian vendors around Mustafa would be sniggering at hearing a devout Muslim yell out an essen-tially homophobic remark. I found it hard to explain the double meaning to Mustafa; when I did, he was not amused. Even though he was quick to apply his linguistic skills to make sales, he did not have the linguistic or cultural knowledge to avoid such little pitfalls. As for my own attempts at vendor calls, I was extremely shy and self-conscious at first. Mustafa's insistent bad-gering motivated me, and I started to get the hang of it after a week or two. Initially, I was overly aware of my own status as a foreigner as I yelled out in Italian. My performance was very much about mimicry at the beginning.

I started to get creative near the end of my apprenticeship, making up my own rhymes and enjoying the raw musical and poetic side of the market. That said, who knows what kind of cultural meanings I was missing or misappropriating in my creative attempts at novel sales pitches? Mustafa was surely much more savvy than I in that department.

When I arrived in the morning, Mustafa poured me a cup of sweet mint tea and shared some sweet cakes his wife Fatima had prepared for him. He took great pride in his wife's culinary skills and wanted to share bits and pieces from his homeland. The fact that he had been able to bring his wife to Italy from Casablanca was a show of his success, which he vaunted in small ways. I tried to reciprocate these culinary gifts in my own way by bringing cakes and sweets that are typical of my country (banana bread, oatmeal cookies, Nanaimo bars). These seemed to be appreciated by Mustafa, and, as small as the gesture was, I felt that this helped create some common ground between us. The act of sharing food is often a form of trust and intimacy, and the fact that we were both foreigners in a foreign land brought us closer together as we peered out from behind the big market stall at the sea of Italians and other foreigners who streamed by.[2]

After a few weeks Mustafa confided in me more and more, and his family started to take me under their wing: I was associated with Mustafa and Giorgio wherever I went in the market. Giorgio has been working at the market for seventeen years; he came from Casablanca and started working at the Porta Palazzo market when he arrived in Turin. He never made it clear how he ended up in Turin, but he did underline that he had worked hard and had a good deal of success selling produce. After a few years, he sent for his brother Mustafa, who came and gave him a hand with the stand he had bought. Things went well, and they were able to buy another stand (the one Mustafa runs). Giorgio does all the buying at the big wholesale market (CAAT), and Mustafa returns to the market in the evenings to put up the stalls along with other Moroccans and Tunisians who are charged with this laborious task. Mustafa told me he has a "Bac" (high-school leaving exam) in sciences, but there is no employment in Morocco. He said he had to get out of the country to have some opportunities, but he does not want his other brothers to join him in Italy. Mustafa and the other Moroccans I got to know often idealized Morocco as a place where a better life is lived, despite the economic hardships that have led many families to send their sons to Italy, France, Germany, England, and other European countries.

Although the produce business had been good to Mustafa and Giorgio, they complained of the high risk factor; they put out capital to buy perishable stock and suffered losses when they did not sell it all. The prices of produce also fluctuated greatly, increasing and decreasing the profit margin, because of weather, the war in Iraq (or so they told me), and inflation. A sense of instability was prevalent when Mustafa and Giorgio talked about their business. In fact, Mustafa has no desire to stay on in Italy; it is a means to an end. He calls himself a *meridionale*, an odd Italian reference for a Moroccan to apply to himself; he originally comes from the countryside near Casablanca, although he has moved all his family into the city. He would like to work for ten more years in Italy and then retire to Casablanca, where he has a flat and where the rest of his family is waiting for his return.

I thought it was interesting how someone could spend half of his life in a place and feel so little attachment. This is where our experience as immigrants differed. I was in Italy because I loved the culture, was fascinated by the place, and had married an Italian. I was integrating to some degree. Mustafa saw Italy as a means to an end—a place where he could earn money to send home remittance. For Mustafa, living in Italy was a type of exile, and he worked each day with the hope of returning to a better life in his country. Mustafa and Giorgio had imagined a better life in Italy, and this sense of imagination has been a powerful life-changing force. Arjun Appadurai has focused on the role of imagination in new forms of globalization: "The imagination is now central to all forms of agency, is itself a social fact, and is the key component of the new global order" (1996: 31). Mustafa and Giorgio imagined the economic opportunities that Italy held, and they now imagine a better life that they will have once they are back in Morocco. Standing next to Mustafa each day, I tried to understand the complex relationships between place, social life, and imagination being played out in this immigrant's experience (Appadurai 1996: 55). Returning home and being seen as successful businessmen were always on Mustafa and Giorgio's minds as they lugged vegetables through the market and worked into the wee hours setting up their stalls.

Not all migrants are in it for the long haul: members of Mustafa and

Giorgio's family came for shorter stints and sold produce at rented stands in the market. I discovered the widespread network of their relations one day when I decided to try my hand at cooking some Moroccan cuisine. I announced to Mustafa that I wanted to make couscous; the first thing I had to do was assure him I knew how to cook this dish by explaining the procedure to him while we worked. Once he was satisfied with my technique, he asked Abdul to watch our stand while he took me around to do the shopping. He took me to the *halal* butcher on the square, introduced me, and told the butcher to remember me because I was a good friend. I was using Mustafa's loyalty and our relationship to bypass the longer process of developing my own personal relationship with the butcher (which would have taken some time since I am female and not Moroccan). Mustafa helped me select the meat and made sure I got a good price. Next, we went around to other Moroccan produce vendors to pick up ingredients that we did not have at our own stand: pumpkin, coriander, onions. Following Mustafa around like this, I started to realize how tight-knit the Moroccans are at the market. In general, Moroccans and Tunisians watch each other's backs and give each other a helping hand. Solidarity between ethnic groups tends to form in this way within the market.

The next day when I came to work, Mustafa asked me how my couscous had turned out. I reported that it had been a great success. Judging from his grin, I could tell Mustafa was pleased that he had shared a bit of his culture with me and that I had taken it upon myself to explore Moroccan cuisine. Mustafa took great pride in always eating Moroccan food and not letting his diet become influenced by Italian cuisine. This was largely thanks to his wife who had little or no contact with Italian culture and who only shopped in Moroccan stores around Porta Palazzo and at the market. Food played an important part in Mustafa's nostalgia for Morocco and was an integral part of maintaining "Moroccanness" when under the constant influence of Italian culture. Working around Italian culture even seemed to be part of Mustafa and Giorgio's everyday agenda.

I started to observe the ways in which Mustafa and Giorgio avoided participating in Italian social and political life. This lack of involvement in Italian society was apparent during a strike that took place at the market on April 14, 2003. Like most vendors, Mustafa and Giorgio participated in the strike by not setting up their stands (mainly because they were afraid of being lynched, I suspect), but they told me that they did not feel like part of the protest. They would have preferred to set up their stands, and they saw the strike as something that was making them lose money. They did not attend any of the meetings the town council held at the Sermig, a semipublic space that was created by a religious missionary organization from an old munitions factory, concerning the restoration and reordering of the market. I noticed that, at the meeting called by the city on April 10, 2003, there were few representatives from ethnic minority groups. I asked Mustafa why he did not get involved, and he told me the market politics was none of his business. I was not sure whether he felt no interest in the long-term plans for the market, or he felt threatened by the presence of an angry Italian majority that was perhaps in search of a scapegoat, or it was just too overwhelming to participate in such an event because of limited language skills. Perhaps it was a combination of all these factors. On my return to the market in 2009, I noted that the number of foreigners with stands had increased, and I asked the staff at the Gate whether foreigners were now participating more in the administration of the market. The Gate staff told me that the Moroccans in particular were getting more involved but that the decision processes concerned with the commercial activities of the market remained mired in factional disagreements. Despite all the challenges, I was pleased to see that migrants were including their voices in the discussion.

Perhaps there is truly safety in numbers now, but this was not the case in 2003. I came to understand that the Italian majority were not open to having minorities participate and were very defensive toward outsiders at the market. This attitude came in the form of snide remarks, as well as actual physical threats that occurred inside and outside market hours. During my time working at the market, I witnessed numerous shoving matches between Italians and Moroccans. On one occasion, I was walking by the area where the vendors keep their trucks loaded with stock and saw two men having a heated discussion about whose truck belonged in the disputed spot. The Italian man yelled in the face of the Moroccan, "You foreigners think you can just come here and do as you please. We have rules here!" The Moroccan man responded without raising his voice: "I was here first this morning. The police told me I could park my truck here." The Italian responded, "The police are idiots! I am the one who has been selling in this market longer than you. I will tell you how things work around here!" Shoppers and vendors began to gather, and another Italian man intervened to try to calm down the screaming Italian vendor, who concluded the exchange with several profanities and "Why don't you go back to where you came from!" With that, he stormed off to his market stand, and the Moroccan was left shaking his head. These sorts of incidents happened each day while I was in the field. Rarely did they end in more than pushing and shoving, but they certainly indicated the tension that was ever present between Italians and foreigners working at the market.

When it came to planning the future of the market, the Italian vendors wanted to protect their position, and the foreigners were seen as the number one threat, not as allies in a fight against the city. The Italian vendors wanted to maintain the status quo in every sense. Even if migrants were becoming an important element of the market, in 2003 they had little voice in the bureaucratic processes that shaped the everyday running of the market and were hesitant to speak out. This treatment of newcomers was not much different from the way southern Italian migrants were treated when they arrived en masse during the 1950s and 1960s.

One particularly tense moment came in early 2003, when a march on March 27 passed through the market (not an unusual event since the market has traditionally been a place for protest and political discussion) protesting the impending U.S. invasion of Iraq. *La Stampa*, a national newspaper based in Turin, reported that two hundred foreigners had grouped together and marched through the market on their way to city hall just up nearby via Milano. Police escorted them.[3] I watched from Roberta and Lorenzo's stand where I was working. A thick crowd of market-goers and vendors gathered to watch the protesters as they marched past. A group from the nearby mosque caused quite a stir. They were led by the controversial imam Bouriqi Bouchta, who was quoted in the paper as saying, "It is an unjust war. It is right to resist. We don't want Iraq to become another Anglo-American colony." The political voices in the protest were extremely contradictory. There were other Muslims and foreigners who expressed a strong anti-war view, but the majority were protesting against the anti-Islamic sentiments that had been running high since September 11, 2001. There were banners that denounced Italian racism and discrimination against Muslims and immigrants more generally. This protest, clearly an angry shout-out against the way Italians and their government had been treating immigrants in the years leading up to this event, made tensions run even higher. The flag waving, banner holding, and yelling of the protesters (some Italians but mainly immigrants) only seemed to confirm the negative feelings of the onlookers toward foreigners: "Look at those unruly foreigners. They are about to start a riot." "This is all we need: more civil chaos. We should deport them all!"

I took notes quickly as the people around me made comments about the passing parade of angry protesters. The Iraq War that started in 2003 certainly solidified many of the tensions that already existed between Italians and Muslim immigrants—the media regularly couched the Iraqi conflict in terms of the civilized Western world against Islamic terrorists. The people of Turin and Italian officials viewed the Borgo Dora neighborhood near Porta Palazzo as a potential hotbed of Islamic dissidence. Surveillance of the mosques was increased, and many suspicious eyes were turned toward anyone who looked Arab in the least. A terrorist could be lurking anywhere, even at the market. Perhaps he had just sold you some tomatoes. When the anti-Iraq war protest charged through Porta Palazzo, I was struck by the contrast of ordinary and extraordinary events at the market. My analysis of everyday xenophobia that came from underhanded racial remarks and whispered comments was confirmed by the outpouring of detest expressed by the crowd watching the protest. In just a few minutes of observation, the dynamic between foreigners and Italians in the market was laid bare. After the protest passed through the market, the vendors went back to selling, and the shoppers went back to buying. The Moroccans went back to standing at their stalls next to the Italians standing at their stalls—it was as if nothing had been said: it was business as usual at Porta Palazzo. The protest was like a pressure valve that temporarily exploded and let off steam. In some ways, I saw it as one of the mechanisms that kept the market running smoothly without more serious eruptions. However, the other mitigating factors were economic: everyone was here at the market to make a living or to find sustenance—these higher objectives averted an all-out riot.

Next to politics, religion is an equally inflammatory and touchy issue when it comes to migrants in Italy. In particular, Islam is seen as a threat to the Catholic cohesion of the Italian social fabric (Galesne 2008). Religious practices, places of worship, and fear of an unknown and potentially dangerous foreign group are at the heart of much debate in Turin and at Porta Palazzo. Religion, like food, is an essential element of the identity and culture that migrants bring with them to the host country, and this is no exception for Muslims in Turin. One of the city's most important mosques is located just off the market square (Moschea della Pace in corso Giulio Cesare). This particular mosque has been the focal point for Italian xenophobia toward Muslims; the imam was arrested a number of times, and antiterrorist investigations centered on activities at the mosque. There is a mosque in the Borgo Dora neighborhood because there are many Muslims who reside and work in the area.

One day during a lull in business, Mustafa lamented the fact that he was not able to go and pray during the working day; this is one of the reasons he missed living in Morocco, where religion is an essential part of the day. Religious practice in Morocco marks daily rhythms and time. Many Muslims working in Italy feel out of sync and mention that it takes some time to adjust to another society's rhythms. The city can be seen as a secularizing force that negates the temporal rhythms of religious life (Yom 2005: 35–36). In Turin, there are no calls to prayer; moreover, the ringing of the church bells are largely drowned out by traffic, and their significance is lost on younger generations of Italians, for whom religion is not a central part of their daily lives. Many times I offered to watch the stand while Mustafa went to pray at the mosque that was not more than five minutes away, but he never took me up on it. Perhaps Mustafa was also falling into the increasingly secular ways of Italian culture.

The city still seems unable to erase all religious time and culture; all around Porta Palazzo, the links between Islamic culture and food are apparent, and many of them have an important temporal significance. During Ramadan, this is evident at the moment when the daily fast is broken—an important social moment. Men who are away from their families gather in restaurants and cafés around Porta Palazzo to break bread together. Large pots of *harira* (a hearty Moroccan soup usually eaten during the holy month of Ramadan) bubble all afternoon, and the scent of coriander and ginger wafts out into the streets.[4] I walk by windows filled with shiny, honey-dipped sweets like *zlabia*, *m'hanncha*, and *mescouta* that will restore strength after a hard day of work on an empty stomach. During this important religious season, food connects Moroccan immigrants in Turin to their faith, community, and home (Ismail 2006; D'Alisera 2004).

Mustafa and Giorgio gave me a glimpse of the insular Moroccan world at Porta Palazzo. They trusted me with their business and welcomed me into their homes, something I certainly did not expect the first day I stood next to them behind a pile of cucumbers. Once again, I was surprised by how a strong work ethic and an openness to listening can bring people from diverse cultural backgrounds together. I was worried that I would have a hard time fitting in because I am a woman, but I was pleasantly surprised that I was treated with the utmost respect and not relegated to certain tasks considered suitable for women. Many times during my field experience I had to rethink my own gender and subconscious cultural stereotypes (Golde 1986).

Mustafa and Giorgio are shrewd businessmen who are proud of their accomplishments: they own two stands at the market, and they have brought their wives and families to Italy while sending remittance back to Morocco. Their personal stories demonstrate the way in which long-term migrants create their own communities and networks within the larger structure of the market and market square. Nonetheless, these two Moroccan men had little desire—or felt they had little access—to participate in Italian society on many levels and had no plans for permanent settlement. When I returned to Porta Palazzo in 2007, I was happy to find Mustafa, Giorgio, and Abdul thriving. Mustafa's family had grown, with one young toddler and another child on the way. When I chatted with Mustafa at his market stall, he told me that he still has a dream of taking his family back to Morocco for good. The last time I went to the market in the fall of 2009, I went to see Mustafa and Giorgio. Despite dreams of returning home, they were more ensconced in the market than ever. We talked about the increasing number of Moroccans and foreigners at the market and the general state of business. I could see that Mustafa and Giorgio were now enjoying a degree of seniority and success after years of struggling against discrimination and many hard knocks. The tides seemed to be turning.

At the end of our conversation, Mustafa invited me for dinner. He wanted me to see his new apartment and meet his two daughters. That evening I broke the Ramadan fast with Mustafa and Fatima and their two little girls. The table was heaped with Moroccan delicacies, and Fatima served up a hearty soup. It made me happy to see Mustafa and his family doing so well, and I wondered if they would ever return to Casablanca for more than just summer holidays.

Formal and Informal Economy at the Market

Not all migrants are as above board with their commercial activities as Giorgio and Mustafa. There are a large number of migrants (nearly impossible to enumerate precisely) who are engaged in informal commercial activities at Porta Palazzo—informal in the sense that these vendors do not have permits, do not pay taxes, and operate outside the structures that govern economic exchanges in the formal economy (Feige 1990; Portes and Haller 2005).[5] In general, any place where there is a formal economy, there will also be informal economic activities (Peraldi, Foughali, and Spinouza 1995; Peraldi 2001, 2002).

At Porta Palazzo, I met a number of young Moroccan men who were engaged in a variety of informal commercial activities. For example, the mint vendor that I met on my first day in the field was engaging in underground commerce. The vendors with stands do not like the informal vendors, but they are part of the market landscape. I admired their resourcefulness and their ability to find a way to survive despite not having access to the legal job market—nearly all of them lacked work visas or immigration papers. These young men can be found on the street corners in the market, at the bus stops, and in all the in-between spaces of the legal commercial activities. They are selling phone cards, mint, black tea, bread, coriander, *cabas* (a plastic shopping bag that is popular in Morocco), and occasionally counterfeit handbags (Figure 7).

When I interviewed the market police, I asked them about these illegal vendors and was told that it was more hassle to catch and arrest them than it was to just chase them away. Almost every day I witnessed the cat-and-mouse game between the police and other market officials and these vendors. As soon as they saw the authorities coming, the vendors would pick up their makeshift stands or the merchandise they had spread out on the ground and run away at high speed. During market hours and in the

Figure 7. Moroccan man selling mint in the resellers' area of the Porta Palazzo market, 2009. Photo by Rachel Black.

marketplace, it is rare to see stolen goods offered for sale. However, toward Borgo Dora and after market hours, it is not unusual to be solicited with the offer of stolen car radios, bicycles, and hashish. This trade in drugs and stolen goods falls into the category of illegal economy: "the production and distribution of legally prohibited goods and services" (Portes and Haller 2005: 405). Informal vending is generally accepted, but the authorities are constantly battling illegal economic activities.

Many immigrants turn to the informal and illegal economy as a survival tactic, but when given the opportunity, there are many who gladly participate in the regulated economic activities in the market. Market licenses are a precious commodity at Porta Palazzo: they are seen as a big opportunity to start one's own business, be autonomous, and make a very good living. When I asked the Moroccan and Tunisian vendors I knew how they had gotten started, many of them told me that they rented market permits before actually purchasing a permit from a previous license holder. When I inquired with the market authorities about these practices, I was told it was forbidden to rent or sell a market license. Only the City of Turin has the right to grant a market permit. Not many people, especially not Italians, wanted to talk about the renting, buying, and selling of licenses. As Italians take to the Internet, ads for the sale of businesses at Porta Palazzo are starting to appear. The prices range from 150,000€ for a stall in the covered market to 30,000€ for an ambulant vendor's license in the resellers' market area. It seems that the illegal selling of mint is not the only informal economic activity going on at the market. Selling and renting of market licenses is much more lucrative and potentially exploitative.

Municipal regulations of market licenses abound, but rarely are these fully respected by vendors. Officially, a person or legal entity can only have one authorization to sell goods on public property. The only case where more than one authorization can be held is if an individual inherits a license.[6] Many families have numerous stalls at the market, but the licenses are held under different names of the family members. That is one way around the limit of one license per vendor. Like many dealings in Italy, while these are the official rules, the everyday workings of business in the market are quite different (Herzfeld 1992, 2009).

Licenses are bought, sold, and rented with great frequency. A simple Internet search brings up a number of listings of people selling their vendors' licenses at Porta Palazzo. Often this is the easiest way for migrants to get in on formal market activity and bypass the drawn-out bureaucratic process that is part of getting a license. What is ironic is that migrants generally pass through this informal market of licenses before they can gain access to the formal market. These transactions require passable linguistic skills and a great deal of social capital. If people want to buy a license, they need to have connections, someone who can locate a "legitimate" license for them and who can vouch for their ability to pay and character. Migrants must understand the unspoken rules of these illicit Italian business transactions, perhaps the most difficult knowledge to obtain and skill to master. In addition, market licenses at Porta Palazzo are a limited commodity, and if a person applies, it is not a given that the authorization will be granted. Many of the foreigners I talked to told me how they had started off with rented licenses and later were able to buy licenses from retiring vendors; only the occasional person I met had actually obtained a permit from city hall.

The black market trade in market licenses shows yet another side of the economic activities of the market where legal and illegal activities intermingle. These exchanges reveal the vulnerability and the resourcefulness of migrants attempting to negotiate the complex formal and informal Italian economic system (Ram and Jones 1998). These were difficult topics to broach straight on with the people that I worked with at Porta Palazzo. However, there was constant chatter and whispering about the price of licenses and how it was possible for newcomers to set up a business—at a certain price.

A Chicken in Every Pot? Nigerian Women at the Market

The commercial success of Moroccan produce vendors and the resourcefulness of others are only two aspects of immigrant life at Porta Palazzo. Some groups specialize in selling other goods such as clothing and beauty products, and there are those who come to the market to shop and socialize. The diversity of the people working, shopping, and strolling along at the market makes it an attractive place for newcomers to Turin. It is hard to feel entirely out of place at Porta Palazzo because it is a place where cultures meet and mix. The social side of shopping at the market is just as important for immigrant communities as the commercial side.

One visible minority group at the Porta Palazzo market is African women. They come to do their shopping, buy supplies at the nearby beauty shops, and socialize in front of stores and between the market stalls. I did not work with any sub-Saharan Africans at the Porta Palazzo market. There are not many who have food-related stalls; I chalked this fact up to the Moroccan and Tunisian stronghold that was growing in that sector during my early fieldwork. However, while spending time with Elena, I had the opportunity to get to know a few Nigerian women.

Elena sells live chickens at the farmers' market. At first, I was both fascinated and appalled by this. Elena and Roberto, her husband, come in every day from just outside Cuneo to the south of Turin with their chickens and eggs, as well as other small animals such as rabbits and guinea pigs. Elena explained to me that the chickens she sells no longer produce eggs, and this is a good way to make a bit of money and get rid of them at the same time. Roberto sells eggs on the other side of the market next to Pier with his produce stand. Elena told me that not many Italians buy these chickens because they do not have much meat on them and what there is can be tough and stringy; most of her clients are African women. However, there were a few other ethnic groups that depended on Elena's wares, and I quickly learned about all sorts of culturally diverse food taboos and beliefs. For example, Chinese clients only wanted white rabbits because they are considered lucky in their culture. Elena recounted that Peruvians came to buy guinea pigs to barbecue—a Peruvian specialty. Italians bought them as pets or to feed to their pet snakes. These microfood chains demonstrate that categories of edible and inedible are culturally constructed and learned (Douglas 2002; Leach 1964; Rozin 1982). Animals considered pets for one group are tasty snacks for another.

As I watched a Nigerian woman expertly thrust her hand into a cage and pull out a squawking hen for inspection, my first guess was that African women buy these chickens because they are cheap. They cost €3.50 each, compared to about €5.00 for the cheapest slaughtered chicken sold in supermarkets or in the covered market pavilions at Porta Palazzo. However, I learned that this was not necessarily the only motivation for buying live chickens. Elena told me they wanted to make sacrifices of live animals as part of their religious practices. Some Italians even told me they thought it must be for witchcraft. These are the types of misconceptions that get created when there is no real understanding or communication between different cultural groups, so I decided to go to the source and ask.

One day there was a large group of Nigerian women standing around chatting in pidgin English and waiting for Elena to serve them. At the farmers' market, no one ever really talks to these women because Italians generally put them in the socially stigmatized category of prostitute. Black women can frequently be seen prostituting themselves in the red light districts of Turin, but nearly all these women came to Italy with a hope for a different life. The largest group of women who are sold into prostitution and trafficked in Italy are Nigerian (Aghatise 2004). Luca Trappolin (2005) notes that the women who are not smuggled into the country often obtain work visas under the category of *badanti* (domestic workers). This is another category of migrant work that includes women who are frequently exploited by unethical work practices, informal work arrangements, and the inefficiency of the Italian government to regulate this sector. Whether the women I met in Italy worked as prostitutes or domestic workers, it was likely that they were being exploited in some way. From my own experience, young, foreign, and unwed women are often placed in the category of prostitute or sexually dangerous. This is largely the result of the huge prostitution problems that plague Italy and fuel a steady flow of migrants (particularly from Eastern Europe and Central Africa) who are often forced into the sex trade (Orsini-Jones and Gattullo 2000: 128); due to their low social status, physical "otherness," and rough knowledge of the Italian language, these women are rarely included in everyday social exchanges with the locals. When I approached them, I was happy we were all speaking English. It somehow created a small, instant bond: the "Italians" could not understand what we were saying, and we could talk freely.

After introducing myself, I took the opportunity to ask them what they intended to do with their chickens. They looked at me as if I were completely daft: "We're going to cook them up for dinner!" I wanted to know how they were going to get them from the market to the plate because it did not seem like such an easy task to me. First, Elena put the chickens in cardboard boxes, taped up the tops, and punched air holes; often the customers would participate or do these steps themselves. The chickens then set off with their new mistresses on the bus or tram. Several times I witnessed this transportation of livestock and noticed that most Italian passengers were looking on in horror as the occasional feather and squawk escaped the box in the busy bus. This is one case in which culinary practices create public stigma because of behavior in public places considered outside social norms: people in Italy no longer transport live animals using public transit, but, of course, this practice is the norm in many countries in Africa, India, and South America. During the avian influenza scare in the winter of 2002, Italians were nearly hostile when they witnessed live poultry on public transit.

Once the women got their chickens home, the butchering would take place. This is the part that initially mystified me the most: how did these women manage to kill and pluck a bird in a one-room apartment? It seemed like a very messy business to me. One kind Nigerian woman explained to me that it is done in the bathtub with a pair of scissors: the chicken's throat is punctured, and then the blood is drained out into the tub. Boiling water is used to help remove the feathers. Then the chicken is gutted and ready for the pot. Although no one offered me any specific recipes, I was told that chickens were generally boiled.

So why go to all this trouble when you can buy a chicken at the super-market, which is a lot less hassle? One woman told me that this is just the way that Nigerian women did things. If a woman did not prepare a chicken in this way, she was considered a lazy cook and frowned on by other women. The authenticity of food lies not only in the quality of the ingredients but also in the preparation of the raw materials, as well as the dish. Preparing a dish properly is part of maintaining respectability as a woman in their community.[7] These Nigerian women demonstrate the importance of food in maintaining identity as well as performing gender: real women pluck their own chickens, no matter where they are or what their main occupation may be. Perhaps because they were so socially ostracized, these women felt no need to conform to social norms when it came to provisioning and culinary practices—or it could be such an important element of their daily lives and identity formation that they are uninterested in adapting to the customs of their host society. They did not bat an eye when the Italian on the tram made derogatory remarks: "These Africans are such savages! Who let them into our country?"

Returning to the farmers' market in 2007, my eyes scanned the covered market area—something was missing. Where were Elena and Roberto? I asked my friend Enzo, who raises pigs and sells sausages, what had hap-pened to his fellow vendors and their chickens. Enzo explained that, when the farmers' market underwent renovations in 2006, the administration used this as an excuse to send Elena and Roberto away. They cited concerns about hygiene and the threat of diseases carried by chickens, such as avian flu. Enzo noted that this was a huge loss to the market in terms of authentic-ity: Porta Palazzo had started off as a market where livestock and produce were sold. Not only did the market lose an important part of its traditional composition, but immigrants lost an important source for reasonably priced food that played a key part in their culinary and cultural practices. I left the market wondering about the motives of these hygiene concerns: was the city looking out for public health or trying to break down the cultural practices of certain groups?

A Home Away from Home

Although the situation is different for all migrant groups, Porta Palazzo market offers a taste of home for many, a place to gather and spend time with compatriots. In addition, the market is often one of the first places of contact between Italians and migrants. Commercial exchanges make this contact necessary and at times facilitate a dialogue, although at other times, they can create tension and misunderstanding (Semi 2004). In the end, Porta Palazzo is everyone's market: Chinese farmers, French tourists, Romanian construction workers, Calabrian olive vendors, Nigerian women, Piedmontese *mamme* and Canadian anthropologists. People are free to express and negotiate their public roles and identities in a multitude of ways: through their food choices, how they talk about food, and how they interact with other market-goers.

Food is central to the feeling of unity that the market produces. People find their way to the market because they need to eat. Yet food also works as an identity marker and a point that creates difference; as we saw above, Nigerians buy skinny live chickens out in the open at the farmers' market, whereas Italians buy buttery-looking butchered fowl at the covered markets. What food we eat, how and where we buy, cook, and eat it indicate a great deal about where we are from, our social class, religion, and even personal tastes. While this chapter has offered a glimpse of the Porta Palazzo market as a multicultural place by looking at the migrants who work, shop, and socialize there, the next chapter focuses on the Italian gaze on this new phenomenon of international migration.

Porta Palazzo Couscous

This is a version of the couscous I made after my shopping trip with Mustafa. Couscous is not entirely foreign to Italy: there are many fish-based versions in Sicily. This is a remnant of the Muslim occupation of the island after the Byzantine period. However, couscous is a dish associated with Moroccan culture in the minds of most Italians.

While working at Porta Palazzo, I invested in a *couscousière*, a pot specially designed to steam the couscous over the stew. This cooking method imparts the couscous with the wonderful aroma of the stew below. You can easily replicate this effect by using a large pot topped with a steamer lined in cheesecloth.

Serves 4

INGREDIENTS

1 lb couscous semolina (*not* instant couscous)

1 cup Moroccan olive oil (it has a stronger olive flavor compared to most extra-virgin olive oil)

4 cups water

1 lb lamb (Moroccans cut their meat differently, but I have used neck and a leg of lamb cut up into pieces with the bone in)

1 lb carrots, peeled and cut into large pieces

2 medium turnips, peeled and cut into large pieces

1 lb zucchini, cut into large pieces

1 lb yellow or orange squash or pumpkin, peeled and cut into large pieces

1 can (8 oz.) peeled tomatoes

2 medium white onions, grated

1 can (8 oz.) chickpeas

1 bunch parsley, finely chopped

1 bunch coriander, tied in a bundle

1/2 tsp ground black pepper

1/2 tsp paprika

1/2 tsp *ras el hanout* (a blend of spices commonly used in North African cuisine)

1 cinnamon stick

10 threads saffron soaked in 1/2 cup warm water

salt to taste

In a large bowl, pour a cup of water onto the semolina and work it with your hands so that there are no lumps. Add it to the top of the *couscousière* or steamer lined with cheesecloth. Drizzle the semolina with a little olive oil and place on top of the stew pot half an hour before the end of the cooking time. This will depend on how the meat is cooking. Every so often, use a fork to work the couscous and insure there are no lumps. Add salt to taste.

Meanwhile, place olive oil, onion, parsley, spices, salt, and lamb in a large pot. Cover with water and set at medium-high heat. When the ingredients start to boil, add the prepared carrots, turnips, zucchini, and tomatoes. Simmer for half an hour. Add pumpkin, coriander, and chickpeas. Cook for about fifteen minutes longer until the vegetables are tender.

Once the couscous semolina is cooked, place it in a large serving dish. Make a well in the center of the semolina and place the meat and vegetables there. Ladle the broth over the couscous and meat, making sure it does not get too soupy. You can also serve a bowl of broth on the side. Serve with spicy *harissa* (hot chili sauce).

Traditionally, all diners ate the couscous out of the same plate using their hands. Most Moroccans still eat out of the same platter but using a spoon or piece of bread. This communal dining is how children are taught proper table etiquette and sharing. You may prefer to eat your couscous in separate plates or bowls using a fork or spoon.

CHAPTER 6

Kumalé: Ethnogastronomic Tourism

Constructing Edible Exotica

When I first started frequenting Porta Palazzo, everyone kept telling me I had to talk to Chef Kumalé if I was interested in foreign cuisine. In fact, I kept seeing this name on stickers on the doors of Chinese dry goods shops and Moroccan butchers in and around Porta Palazzo. Who was this mysterious character, the ubiquitous point of reference when it came to foreign cuisine and Porta Palazzo? Was there another anthropologist already in the field I had chosen? Not exactly, but Kumalé seemed to be asking some of the same questions that struck me as I got to know the market: in particular, can food create greater understanding and harmony between Italians and migrants? The chef was organizing tours of the market, its neighboring ethnic food shops, and even abroad in Morocco. He was on television talking about Italy's new immigrants and the exotic cuisine they had brought with them. He was on radio playing world music. He was everywhere I turned. What struck me was that Kumalé was trying to communicate through food: his message was that immigrants were not a huddled mass of unapproachable Others. They could be known through delicious encounters at the table, in the kitchen, and even in the market.

Getting to know Chef Kumalé and following his activities and writings afforded me a number of interesting points of investigation concerning the Porta Palazzo market, ethnogastronomic tourism, and immigration in Italy. Can Chef Kumalé's activities be considered a new form of gastronomic tourism? Can he really help educate Italians about other cultures and the new people they are so reluctant to host?

After hearing all kinds of stories about Kumalé, I made an appointment to meet with the chef. We arranged a meeting before a Japanese cooking class he had organized as part of a cycle of ethnic cooking courses that he ran out of the Circolo de Amicis space in the upscale neighborhood of Borgo Po. Chef Kumalé turned out to be Vittorio Castellani, a middle-aged freelance journalist from Turin. Vittorio talked a mile a minute, with an entertaining aside ready and rehearsed for each topic as he carefully guided the interview I was supposedly conducting.

Castellani revealed that he had given up his day job to follow his passion for culture and food full-time. This is how the character Chef Kumalé was born. The title chef denotes the character's position as someone who prepares food as a profession, and it also gives a sense of status and authority—he is not a cook or a "hash-slinger." The name Kumalé initially sounded Egyptian to me, or like a name from some far-off exotic place, but there was something familiar about it. In reality, for most Torinese, the name is easily identifiable because it is one of the most common expressions in the local dialect of Piedmontese: "cum a l'é," closely related to "come va" in Italian, which means, "how is it going?" Many of Vittorio's activities and programs use similar play on words to engage the curiosity of Italians and to make approaching other cultures a less daunting idea. Castellani's guide to ethnic food in Turin, *Pappamondo: Uomini, migrazioni e pietanze* (2001), uses similar word play. This title turns around the words *pappa* (food, sometimes used for referring to baby food and food more generally) and *mappamondo* (globe of the world), and the play on words comes out as a reference to global food. Popular marketing campaigns for food products underline this point that language can make food more palatable to potential consumers (Schor and Ford 2007). In Italian advertising, through a jingle or friendly cartoon character, from Parmigiano cheese to ready-made pasta, food becomes fun. Is this what the chef was up to, making the Other easier to swallow?

Besides writing guide books and organizing ethnogastronomic tours of the Porta Palazzo market, gastronomic tours abroad, and ethnic cooking classes, Vittorio Castellani also appears and helps orchestrate a variety of events in Italy and abroad that promote ethnic cuisine, writes articles for the Italian press, and hosts a world music show on a local radio station. For some time, Castellani was the "world food" point person for Slow Food. According to the extremely energetic and motivated Castellani, all these activities are aimed at promoting multiculturalism. I was left wondering whether, through his numerous activities, Chef Kumalé was helping commodify culture or promoting cross-cultural understanding. Is it even possible to understand another culture solely through its food? There seems to be something extremely reductive about boiling a culture down to a few dishes or key ingredients.

When Castellani started working with immigrants, he wanted to find a way to create a bridge between Italians and these new arrivals from all over the world. He realized that the press public image of foreigners nearly always focused on the negative aspects of the presence of immigrants (delinquency, unemployment, lack of education), and he wanted to present some of the most enjoyable aspects of cultural diversity: music and food. These are also two aspects of culture that can communicate across barriers, and sharing enhances the experience. This is certainly a beautiful idea.

However, Castellani can send out some mixed messages. Although he expresses a great deal of passion for his subject, he also displays an acute sense of marketing and an ability to transform raw materials, in this case ethnic cuisine, into a clean and easy-to-consume product. On one hand, he knows about an enormous variety of ethnic food, from Moroccan to Japanese. He tries to gain his knowledge directly from the source (women, home cooks, and professional chefs). He spends a great deal of time at the Porta Palazzo market and has developed close personal relationships with many vendors and their families. On the other hand, he has learned that his Italian audiences find it hard to approach these cuisines and see them as potentially threatening unless tamed and presented in a well-packaged and accessible manner. He understands his role as tour guide as well as chef.

Vittorio Castellani's guide to ethnic ingredients is a good example of this well-thought-out presentation of information in an approachable package. The cover (Figure 8) features three smiling ethnic faces of different ages, the font is playful, and the format is easy to leaf through. Inside, ingredients are presented with their names in Italian and in the language of origin and sometimes other languages, followed by an informative but colorful

Figure 8. Chef Kumalé's guide to ethnic cuisine, *Pappamondo*. Photo by Michele d'Ottavio

description of each product. There is also an effort to make the reader aware of the foodways and human processes involved in importing this food to Italy. In the introduction, the voyage that Than, whose family owns an Asian grocery store at Porta Palazzo, makes to France two or three times a month to supply his store serves as a concrete example of the complex chain of provisioning that is behind the ethnic food that can be found in small grocery stores in Turin.

In theory, the *Pappamondo* guide to ethnic ingredients is an excellent initiative to introduce people to ethnic food; it takes the fear and unknown nature out of food products that are a complete novelty in a country where the monoculture of regional Italian cuisine—granted, diverse in itself—has reigned supreme until very recently (Helstosky 2004). As Martin F. Manalansan, IV (2006: 50) suggests, the "cultured foodie" has accumulated enough cultural capital, in this case thanks to the *Pappamondo* culinary guide, to be able to explore the exotic from a position of the culinary consumer. I wanted to know if these guidebooks had really made Porta Palazzo palatable to the Torinese. How widely had they had been distributed (locally they were sold along with *La Stampa* newspaper); was the information useful to people who had no knowledge of how to prepare these products; and did people actually go out and buy the products after reading the guide? Did *Pappamondo* bring new Italian consumers to Porta Palazzo? In the field, I did not encounter anyone with a guidebook or map in hand and I was unable to interview readers of the guide, but I did interview four vendors at the market, in the ethnic grocery stores surrounding the market, and in the San Salvario neighborhood, another ethnically diverse area. One vendor at an Asian market on corso Regina told me: "I haven't seen the guide [as I showed it to him], and I haven't noticed any increase in Italian clients or questions from clients." Two weeks after *Pappamondo* was released, staff members of only one store, which was explicitly mentioned in the guide, told me they had noticed an increase in the number of Italians who entered their store. This led me to believe that the idea was very good but the actual commercial and social impact was limited.

Cooking Up Culture

Chef Kumalé was already carrying through with the missing step in the process of getting people to know the Other through food: he was conducting ethnic cooking classes. In fact, the chef was kind enough to invite me to sit in on a cycle of Moroccan cooking classes. What impressed me most was that the person teaching the class was a middle-aged Moroccan woman who spoke broken Italian but admirably explained and smiled her way through some of the classic dishes of her national cuisine (couscous, tajine, and rice pudding, among other delicacies). Castellani served as a mediator and filled in the gaps, explaining the names and uses of spices, sprinkling the silent moments with anecdotes, and generally keeping things on track. Although the students, mainly middle-aged Italian professionals and housewives, sat in front of a makeshift demonstration kitchen, they were encouraged to help in a hands-on way, kneading dough and stirring stews, while spices and ingredients were passed around to be smelled and touched.

During the course, I met and befriended Marco, a middle-aged professional with a penchant for cooking and eating. I asked Marco why he had decided to take the course, and he told me that he had traveled a lot and always liked to explore new food and cultures. Chef Kumalè's course seemed like a good introduction to Moroccan cuisine. He also mentioned that it was nice to be able to find the ingredients for the dishes in Turin and Rome. Marco was commuting to Rome for work, and he did not know many people in Turin; he explained that the cooking course was a good way to meet people with common interests in this new city where he was spending more and more time. Chef Kumalè's cooking class was a form of entertainment and leisure for many of the participants.

Food preparation and culinary knowledge are oral traditions in many cultures; culinary knowledge is reproduced through a social exchange that relies on the repetition of manual actions and a careful apprenticeship that necessitates communication between cooks (Sutton 2006). The messages contained in cuisine and even just ingredients are not always self-evident. Further information is required to penetrate the superficial image created by many ethnic restaurants, cooking shows, and food journalism—an element that is frequently absent. At times, customers lack the curiosity to look for further meanings behind the simple pleasure of taste, or cuisine is packaged in such a way that it portrays a superficial or homogenized representation of a culture (Classen and Howes 1996: 186).[1] The students in this cooking class were certainly looking to go deeper—they were in search of an authentic experience.

As the Moroccan woman used her hands to work dough in a traditional ceramic platter, I could see the students squirming in their seats. They could not understand the operation and how they could reproduce it. In an effort to help, the woman passed around a lump of dough so everyone could get an idea of the perfect consistency. One of the most interesting aspects from my observations of these classes was the students' unease with the oral tradition and hands-on apprenticeship of Moroccan cooking, with culinary knowledge passed on through doing, rather than written precisely into cookbooks. Luce Giard (de Certeau, Giard, and Mayol 1994: 310) reminds us that the precise written form of modern recipes is only a recent invention in Europe; however, for the students of this class it was something they demanded and found necessary to duplicate the recipes they were witnessing. I was left wondering whether this penchant for exactitudes was driven by the students' desire to create a perfect replica that could be deemed authentic or whether they were just unsure of their newly acquired culinary knowledge and needed precise recipes as a kitchen crutch. Castellani had an assistant who carefully took notes, recording the recipes and translating them into a Western form of culinary knowledge with precise measurements and a list of cooking procedures. This often caused frustration between the Italians and the Moroccan teacher, who when asked for measurements of ingredients, would reply, "a pinch, a handful, you'll just know when the consistency is right." Different methods of knowledge acquisition and communication were negotiated each lesson, and food was certainly the driving force that aided understanding. This was evident when everyone sat down to taste the evening's recipes at the end of class, and the sounds of enjoyment and smiles of satisfaction were universal. The students needed to get their hands dirty, not just sit in their chairs as a passive audience. They were ready and willing to roll up their sleeves when asked.

Mapping Out Diversity in the Foodscape

Where does the Porta Palazzo market stand in this culinary multicultural love-in? In fact, the market was a constant: referred to as a place to locate ingredients, as a center of Moroccan culture and social life and in the presence of numerous Moroccan businesspeople from the market and surrounding area, who were invited to come by and take part. This is how a number of the participants and I came to meet Hasan, who has a store and restaurant just off the market square. Although the market was a reference during the course, it seemed that it was still a faraway place. Were the students actually going to the market to buy supplies? During the third course, I asked a number of the participants if they had been to the market to buy spices and other ingredients. Many of them had visited Hasan's store and told me that, if they had not met him before, they might not have been so comfortable entering such a "foreign place." They also told me they felt more confident knowing what they were looking for and not needing to ask for help. Participants informed me that they had also visited the market itself to buy vegetables for couscous and mint for their tea. In fact, it would seem that Chef Kumalé's plan was working. With a bit of knowledge and a great deal of curiosity, the participants of the course were engaging in an exchange (commercial and social) with Moroccan merchants at Porta Palazzo.

The story does not end here. Perhaps Chef Kumalé did not feel he had quite conquered quite wide enough an audience for spreading the good word about multiculturalism through food. He must have heard me thinking, because he launched another ingenious program centered on the Porta Palazzo market in conjunction with *Pappamondo*. "Turisti per Casa" consists of three itineraries of the multiethnic Porta Palazzo market: 100 percent Arabica, a guide to the Moroccan and Tunisian restaurants and grocery stores; Turin Dakar, a guide to African cuisine at Porta Palazzo; and Ogni Ben di Buddah, an Asian guide to the market area. These guides are neatly folded sheets of glossy paper that have a map of Porta Palazzo on one side indicating the businesses of interest and a description of a number of the venues accompanied by artistic photos that help the imagination travel to exotic places.

The actual mapping of the territory makes Porta Palazzo become solid, knowable, and controllable for the user or potential consumer (La Cecla 1988: 60). In fact, "Turisti per Casa" can be seen as a social political initiative to remap Porta Palazzo and create a new "mental map" that uses food and the friendly face of multiculturalism to draw the Torinese back to the piazza.[2] An itinerary can be planned beforehand using the information provided on the other side of the map. The photos of smiling Moroccans, Chinese, and Africans and some of the products they sell prepare the potential ethnogastronomic tourist for the people he or she might encounter. In recent years, the Porta Palazzo area has been given a very bad reputation largely by the media (Semi 2004; CICSENE 2002). Potential visitors, who may feel nervous or frightened, like the reinforcement of positive images to make them feel safe as they head out for a morning of shopping.

"Turisti per Casa," which means "Tourists at Home," plays on the name of a popular Italian television program, *Turisti per Caso* (Tourists by Chance), in which the two hosts travel to the far reaches of the world by sailboat, train, and other forms of transportation. "Turisti per Casa" suggests that Italians, the Torinese, can travel to exotic places without leaving their city and that, unlike the television program, they can participate through shopping and eating. It must be noted here that most Italians have a particular passion for food: endless television programs report on regional Italian culinary specialties and restaurants, while markets are an essential part of stock footage when talking about climbing food prices and inflation. The number of ethnic restaurants in most major Italian cities is on the rise.

Backyard Tourists Despite Themselves

Although there were previous waves of migration from southern Italy that took many years for locals to adjust to, the Porta Palazzo market has been deeply affected by recent migration, which has brought many exotic, foreign cultures to the backyard of the Torinese. As Rojek and Urry (1997: 4) suggest, this has created an opportunity to experience the Other at home, blurring the lines between the categories of home and away. In many ways, Porta Palazzo has become what Arjun Appadurai (1996: 33) calls an ethnoscape: "the landscape of persons who constitute the shifting world in which we live: tourists, immigrants, refugees, exiles, guest workers." Porta Palazzo is constantly changing, deteriorating, being rebuilt and reimagined by the groups of people who populate this area and by the public administration that manages and controls the physical market space. This idea of tourism, often denoting a Disney-like controlled environment where other cultures can be consumed and put on display for tourists' viewing pleasure, tames the wildness and danger of Porta Palazzo (Black 2007b; Crang 1998: 143). In the case of cuisine, the tourist need not even leave home; the exoticism of the Other is easily transported into kitchen, dining room, or living room through a variety of media and gustatory experiences. Chef Kumalé's activities, from guidebooks to self-guided market tours, fit well into this conception of culinary tourism, "providing us with groundedness from which we can embark on adventures into otherness" (Long 2004: 15).

The ethnogastronomic tourism promoted by Chef Kumalé also creates a sort of spectacle out of the market. Much in the same way the nineteenth-century Parisian boulevard created a place to express social anxieties and a social space where people of all classes could come together, the market square offers a rare space where all people, Torinese or foreigners, can watch and be observed. Much like the nineteenth-century *flâneur*, the ethnograstronomic tourist strolls through the market in search of the exotic but also takes time to display his or her knowledge of the world. The market can be consumed with the eyes and there is no real need to purchase anything, although the environment is decidedly consumption-oriented. Experiencing the market and being present in the space is what is most important. Once more, the pretext of shopping and that of economic exchanges facilitates a moment of contact and a unique cultural exchange around food.

Consuming Otherness

Although Porta Palazzo remains something of a dystopia and subverts most plans to tame or gentrify it, Chef Kumalé's programs make it quite appetizing. These are ideas Turin and the Gate have found very appealing as they attempt to improve the image of this area, which has experienced a great deal of degradation over the past fifty years. As the blurb from the Gate in the "Turisti per Casa" guide puts it, "We are starting with what most succeeds in putting races and different people around the same table: food" (Castellani 2001).[3] This is a tall order for any cook, but particularly appealing for public institutions and political agendas: Chef Kumalé found sponsorship from the city, the Gate, the local chamber of commerce, the Piedmont region, and even the EU for many of his projects that focus on Porta Palazzo.

In this multicultural feeding frenzy, it is important to remember that, initially, the food and products promoted by "Turisti per Casa" were not brought to Porta Palazzo for an Italian market. These goods arrive via a complex supply chain that often passes through France or other European countries due to the lack of direct import networks, and connects Turin to a large part of the world. Demand for foreign food products has grown with the increasing numbers of immigrants living in Turin, in particular, in the areas of Porta Palazzo and San Salvario. Usually, food-related businesses and especially ethnic grocery stores do not begin to appear until migrant communities become well established and women start to arrive after their husbands, brothers, and fathers have found work. Women are still most often the people who shop and prepare meals. Food plays an important role in the lives of these immigrants in Italy: it helps them maintain cultural identity and pass it on to future generations, it is part of nostalgia and the memory of "home," and it plays an important function in community building (Cinotto

2002; Sutton 2001; Counihan 2004). Often imported specialty food items are a large expenditure for migrant shoppers, but they are willing to spend more for products that are necessary for reproducing familiar dishes, often certain spices or vegetables, and sometimes they splurge on an item that may not be necessary but reminds them of home. One Nigerian customer told me, "No, I don't need to buy this Vita Malt, but it reminds me of home and once in a while I treat myself."

The food products in most ethnic shops have not been packaged to appeal specifically to Italian shoppers, and most of the stands run by immigrants at the open-air market are nearly identical to one another. The clientele is very mixed. Although local and foreign tourists frequent Porta Palazzo, it has not become a tourist-oriented market: not many stalls sell prepared or packaged foods, there are plenty of produce vendors, and people can still buy the necessities for everyday cooking and household chores. Even though tourism is an important potential source of clientele for market vendors, their business is largely directed to people who live in the city and shop at the market for their daily needs.

If the products at ethnic shops are not essentially for Italian consumption, how are they received and interpreted by Italian consumers? As we have seen, the food purchased or eaten at the businesses around Porta Palazzo is an important identity marker for the migrants who constitute the majority of shoppers, and the same often holds for a number of the Italian shoppers who venture out on Chef Kumalé's itineraries. By going to ethnic stores and restaurants, much like attending a Moroccan cooking class, these Italians display open-mindedness and curiosity. They may even be overcoming some of their fears. The act of consuming these ethnic goods or the well-packaged culture of migrants can even be seen as a political statement. It is political in that it goes against the overriding sentiment of the right-wing government (in particular, Silvio Berlusconi and the Lega Nord), which seeks to ostracize and marginalize foreigners through its immigration and campaign policies. If the media are any indicator, xenophobia and intolerance are on the rise in Italy. The participants in Chef Kumalé's cooking class were largely middle-aged, liberal professionals, but there are also new culinary tourists who appear at the Porta Palazzo market: young (18–30) Italians who publicly display a cultural

and political outlook that rallies against Silvio Berlusconi's right-wing re-
gime. Eating ethnic food, wearing ethnic clothing, piercing their noses,
socializing at Porta Palazzo, and displaying tattoos are all part of their
counterculture performances. For this group of young Italians, visiting
Porta Palazzo and eating ethnic foods are a loud statement of resistance
to capitalism and xenophobia. This group make their older counterpart of
cooking-class-attending liberals look timid. However, both groups can be
considered tourists to a large degree because they rarely engage in the culture of these culinary Others beyond the plate. They never fully engage the
Moroccan or Chinese communities at Porta Palazzo to try to understand
what that food means to these immigrants in their cultures and what it is
like to be a foreigner living in Italy.

A bunch of coriander is not the same ingredient to every chef. Ethnic
food has different meaning and significance depending on the consumer
(Howes 1996: 5). Igor Kopytoff outlines this process of the transformation of goods in his essay "The Cultural Biography of Things: Commoditization as a Process" (1986). He states that, when taking the biographical
approach to the meaning of objects, one must consider "What are the
recognized 'ages' or periods in the thing's 'life,' and what are the cultural
markers for them? How does the thing's use change with its age, and what
happens to it when it reaches the end of its usefulness?" (67). For example,
harira, a hardy chick pea soup, may be everyday food for Moroccans, but
it is most likely exotic and out of the ordinary for Italian diners at a Moroccan restaurant at Porta Palazzo; a ceramic platter might be a decoration
for the wall for one person and a useful serving dish that denotes social
standing and status for another. Not only the significance but also the use
of the ingredients and objects purchased can vary greatly. Migrants may
use ingredients in dishes from their homeland, or the ingredients may
be incorporated into Italian cuisine to form a new hybrid cuisine, what
Jean-Pierre Poulain refers to as culinary "métissage" (2002b: 31; cf. Howes
1996). This process goes in both directions; for example, it is quite common to see Moroccans buying pasta and using it in the place of couscous
(Aime 2004: 135–36). I even met Italians at the market who were buying
coriander from illegal Moroccan vendors to add to their tomato sauce.
Returning to Kopytoff's idea, it is likely that the social cultural meaning

of these "exotic" foods will change in time—they will become everyday as they are incorporated into culinary practices and become a regular part of the market landscape.

This process is both unconscious and conscious. As Giovanni Semi notes in his study of multiculturalism at Porta Palazzo, there is also a growing trend of Italians who go to ethnic shops to consume culture: "An 'ethnic' product is not only a good but a combination of this with the idea of a culture that is sold along with it" (Semi 2004: 242).[4] In fact, the market has been cornered for ethnic products packaged in a way that makes them easy for Italians to swallow. The Hafa Café (a Moroccan café) and Otium e Sibiriaki (a Siberian restaurant) are both trendy restaurants/cafés in the Quadrilatero Romano area of Porta Palazzo, run by Italians selling ethnic food and culture, with not a single Moroccan or Siberian in sight. The performance is polished and convincing: you can sip your mint tea at a low table while sitting on an embroidered cushion and imagine you are in Marrakech, but really you are only a few steps from Porta Palazzo.

While "Turisti per Casa" and ethnic restaurants encourage contact between Italians and new migrants, the type of contact created is questionable. Can we know people from other cultures simply through their cuisine or by consuming "ethnic" goods? What happens when Italians take over the commoditization of ethnic goods, often subordinating migrants at the same time?[5] For example, no Moroccans work in the front of the house at the Hafa Café; the food served at lunch is prepared at a Moroccan restaurant down the road by Moroccan women working in a small, hot kitchen. Food is perhaps a good introduction to other cultures and is something of particular interest to Italians; however, food and cuisine are languages unto themselves, and the symbolic importance or meaning of certain foods and their usage cannot be gleaned simply by grocery shopping. As Mary Douglas suggests, "A code affords a general set of possibilities for sending particular messages. If food is treated as a code, the messages it encodes will be found in the pattern of social relations being expressed" (1972: 61). Douglas emphasizes the need to put food in a social context; ingredients can be bought and consumed, but if the cultural background and social context are not included, they can be misinterpreted or reinterpreted. In many ways,

Chef Kumalé's cooking courses are helping the Torinese crack some of these cultural codes when it comes to navigating the market or choosing dishes in a Japanese restaurant.

Fear of Small Numbers

Food has an incredible power to evoke and stimulate the senses and, in turn, memory and imagination (Seremetakis 1994; Sutton 2001). Smelling and tasting food are not the only parts of the sensory act of eating; the framing of the gustatory experience is also important. Porta Palazzo is a place where food and the colorful surroundings are key in evoking memory as well as imagination. Immigrants come to the market in search of ingredients from home, foreign tourists come looking for a glimpse of the "real" Turin, and Italians often come in search of the "exotic," which can take the form of ground cumin or eavesdropping on a conversation in Cantonese. Porta Palazzo unites and gathers together the local and the global, creating a rich tapestry of sensory experiences.

As illustrated previously, Italians have been the hesitant hosts of recent waves of immigrants from Europe and beyond. Xenophobic incidents are regularly featured on the *telegiornale* (television news), and racial stereotypes have become largely accepted as part of everyday language. A climate of suspicion, verging on fear, toward foreigners plagues Italian society. Although there is a great deal of diversity from one region of Italy to the next, the image of the Other has been solidified into a dichotomy of "us and them." As I watched the news each evening, I asked myself whether Italy would ever become a multicultural country. Migrants are only a small minority of the population, but they are often framed in a discourse of fear that is actively produced by the media and politicians.[6]

This "fear of small numbers" is particularly grave in moments of economic hardship; and this is when immigrants become the scapegoats for the nation's woes (Appadurai 2006). As Italian anthropologist Marco Aime (2004) has suggested, one of the best ways to overcome the potential cultural tensions of immigration is through one-on-one encounters between Italians and immigrants. It is much harder to loathe or fear someone you know as an individual in comparison to the faceless mass. So where can these two parties meet? In this sense, Porta Palazzo offers an important space for interactions between Italians, immigrants, and all sorts of people from elsewhere who come to visit the area as tourists; transactions that take place at the market are often among the first encounters between these groups. Not only the economic but the social space of the market makes it a fascinating multicultural place. The cross-cultural interactions that take place there occur on many levels: economic, social, psychological, sensorial, and emotional, for instance.

In the popular imagination of immigrants and the Torinese alike, the Porta Palazzo market and neighborhood have become associated with cultural diversity. Sharon Zukin notes that "markets and place are tightly interwoven. At its origins, a market was both a literal place and a symbolic threshold, a 'socially constructed space' and 'a culturally inscribed limit' that nonetheless involved a crossing of boundaries by long-distance trade and socially marginal traders. But markets were also inextricably bound up with the local community" (1991: 9). Traditionally, markets are places where outsiders, be they vendors or shoppers, enter the city and mingle with the townspeople; markets are crossroads where the lines between inside and outside are crossed. On one hand, immigrants come to the area because they know this is a place where they can fit in and often find people who speak their language, cook similar food, and practice the same religion. In addition, the market is often a place where new arrivals can find work, whether casual labor, black market jobs, or entrepreneurial opportunities. On the other hand, the Torinese have come to think of Porta Palazzo as a place where they can find the exotic. We usually think of tourists as people from other places or countries who come to enjoy and discover the local culture of the place they are visiting, but in the case of Porta Palazzo there is a new local form of tourism. Markets have always been popular tourist attractions, and Porta Palazzo is no exception. However, Porta Palazzo has become a unique site for a type of culinary tourism: not the usual tourism that attempts to attract visiting foreigners but a form of tourism where the locals come to indulge their curiosity for the culture of exotic new neighbors.

The Dynamics of Culinary Tourism

Folklorist Lucy Long is largely responsible for coining and exploring the term "culinary tourism." Long explains that "Culinary tourism is more than trying new and exotic foods. The basis of tourism is a perception of otherness of something being different from the usual" (2004: 1). Italians, in particular, often come to Porta Palazzo for just this—they seek to escape the everydayness of life in the city. They come to be transported to a place very different from the usual, and food is what draws them there. Jennie Molz Germann states, "Culinary tourism is not necessarily about knowing or experiencing another culture but about performing a sense of adventure, adaptability, and openness to any other culture. Food and eating are mobilized as material symbols of the global in travelers' performances of cosmopolitanism through which travelers simultaneously transgress and reinforce their own culture's norms" (2007: 77). As I investigated the various forms of culinary tourism at Porta Palazzo, I came to realize that many of these culinary forays into the world of the exotic Other on the part of Italians at the market were not about understanding or getting closer to other cultures; this form of tourism and the market itself offered a space for public performance of liberalmindedness, which could later be reproduced in the kitchen at home for friends or family. Who knew that the cultural capital of a world traveler could be acquired this close to home and was only a tram ride away?

Although the focus here is on ethnic food in general and the ethnic food businesses surrounding the market, many of the ideas about tourism and "ethnoscapes" hold true for the market square as well. As mentioned earlier, markets, spaces for local and foreign trade, have always been places where products brought from areas outside the city and country have been bought and sold. Exotic products are not new to the market, and often novelty items make their first appearance at markets before other stores and places of business. For many Torinese, Porta Palazzo has been a place of culinary discovery for many years, a place of novelty and surprise. Vittorio Castellani is also aware of Porta Palazzo's history and the importance of this market to newly arrived migrants in Turin now and in the past. In effect, Chef Kumalé masterfully brings into play both nostalgia for a place that has an important position in the memory of most Torinese and the excitement of globalization:

The Porta Palazzo market, eternally a meeting place and a place of consumption for "new Torinese," has experienced in the last few years a growth and multiplication of new commercial and cultural activities managed by people of different nationalities and ethnicities. The richness and the variety of humans, culture, and goods that are available today in our city's largest market truly comprise a heritage that is still to be explored, which allows us to travel between the cultures that are there at our doorsteps, a new way through the uses, products and traditions of faraway places and people, which have never been so close before.[7]

This introductory blurb penned by Castellani is full of terms and clichés that are recurrent in the marketing of ethnic products and tourism the world over. The idea that a multiethnic neighborhood offers an opportunity to learn and discover about difference is something novel for Italy since external migration is a relatively new phenomenon. "Turisti per Casa" represents difference as a valuable asset, and something to be explored, rather than feared. The idea of tourism and commerce makes difference seem tame and accessible; it falls into constructed categories, which are familiar and easy to consume. The multiethnic nature of Porta Palazzo has the power to condense distances and space: there is no more need to go further than one's own door step to experience the cultures of the world. This all seems a bit disorienting, and in reality the hum and buzz of the piazza can have this effect on visitors. It can be hard to focus with so much sensory bombardment.

The Limits of Culinary Tourism

Castellani's tours and cooking classes have been effective in creating real understanding and contact certainly between a limited number of Italians and immigrants; however, these activities have a limited scope. Although "Turisti per Casa" is an initiative with very good intentions, it does not seem to be enough to give people printed information and a map and expect them to discover the world. As Daniel Miller notes in *The Dialectics of Shopping* (2001), cuisine is often used as "a symbol of the 'multicultural' or 'cosmopolitan'." This has caused an academic debate between two groups, one who feels this use of food is just a "feel good" experience that does not allow for actual contact with Otherness and another who feels that food has a positive mediating effect in broadening people's attitudes to other cultures (114).

"Turisti per Casa" and Chef Kumalé's promotion of multiculturalism are interesting cases that show alternative possibilities for dealing with tensions caused by the recent increase of immigration in Italian cities. Castellani has presented difference through food, a safe and interesting topic for Italians, and marketed it as tourism. However, the depth of real understanding and the scope of the transmission of knowledge about other cultures have yet to be seen. Are we really eating at the same table together, to use Castellani's words, or do we want takeaway culture that can be consumed in the privacy of our own homes or the controlled environment of a restaurant without giving it further thought? Projects like "Turisti per Casa" encourage Italians to go out and explore other worlds in their own backyard, rather than sitting in front of the television watching terrifying news reports about the situation of migration in Italy or cooking and travel shows. Spending time at the market, engaging in sociability, has potential for undoing destructive and ignorant stereotypes and the growing racist sentiment toward migrants in Italy. There is an urgent need to create opportunities for contact between individuals that helps to humanize the migration experience through first-hand experience and relationships. After spending time with Castellani and learning more about his activities, I was eager to investigate the other forms of tourism I had witnessed while working at the market. I wanted to see how ethnogastronomic tourism at home differed from or compared with the culinary tourism of foreigners just in town for just a short visit.

One type of foreign tourism I regularly observed and investigated were the busloads of French-Italian day-tourists who came to Porta Palazzo on the weekends. Buses came frequently from Grenoble and Lyon, only a few hours away over the Alps. The people I spoke to usually preferred to converse in French, but many explained that their parents or grandparents had been born in Italy and moved to France to find work. One woman, Cécile, told me that, "I came over for the day on an organized tour to buy products I cannot get in France. We really just come for the market. I buy cheese, bread, pasta, and coffee. Sure, we have many of these things in France, but the products that are exported, even the Italian brands, aren't as good. We like our pasta al dente, and the French pasta just overcooks. It also all costs a lot less here at Porta Palazzo." According to Lorenzo and Roberta, who have over fifty years of experience at the market, this French-Italian day-tourism has been going on as long as they could remember. They like the French tourists with their heavily accented Italian: they buy lots of candy to take home.

I found it ironic that these French people came to Porta Palazzo to consume Italianness as much as Italians tour the market in search of the exotic Other. Once again, the market showed me how it has a potential to turn the gaze of the observer and make you aware that you are being observed. Heightened by the frame of tourism, the role of consumption in human relations and the power dynamics seemed all too clear to me when looking at the various merchants and shoppers moving through and around Porta Palazzo.

Throwing Off a Bad Image

Porta Palazzo has struggled to overcome its negative image and attract much of the tourist trade. It is a big working market where petty crime such as pickpocketing is frequent, and the press has heightened the sense of public insecurity by continually reporting immigrant activities in the surrounding areas as potentially dangerous and criminal. During the protests against the Iraq War, local officials and the press saw the market as a site of urban unrest and even a potential target for terrorist attack. All this negative publicity and the lack of offerings geared toward tourists make it difficult for city officials to promote Porta Palazzo as a tourist attraction. The Gate initiated a number of programs to try to enhance the offer at the market. For example, a 1999 program called "Frutti della qualità" was aimed at creating a new management structure for the farmers' market, and a study was carried out to find the strengths and weaknesses of the existing market. The overall appearance of the farmers' market was improved with matching tables, and new vendors were brought in, including a Chinese produce vendor and a few organic offerings. The renovation of the main market area completed just before the 2006 Winter Olympics helped improve the area's image and was the biggest push for attracting tourist traffic during this important international event. Porta Palazzo, with its new paving stones and bright new lights, certainly did put its best foot forward and has continued to improve while remaining a working market that mainly serves the city's needs.

Unlike the Boqueria market in Barcelona or the Borough market in London, Porta Palazzo and the other markets in Turin have not been gentrified to serve tourism or a local elite. The types of merchants and products have not changed to serve this lucrative trade. Although tourism has been an effective way of preserving many waning covered and open-air markets throughout the world, it can be almost impossible in these tourist-oriented markets to buy the ingredients to cook an ordinary meal. For one thing, the prices are so exorbitant that average citizens could not afford to do their daily shopping at these markets. This is not the case with Torinese markets for a number of reasons. Until the 2006 Olympics, Turin was not a major stop on the northern Italian tourism map. There were few services for tourists and even fewer hotels. In the wake of 2006, tourism is growing in Turin, but the offerings still remain limited, and in many ways it is one of the few major Italian cities that has remained unchanged from a tourism perspective and has developed other industries besides tourism. When visitors go to the city's markets, they are getting a glimpse of how the locals really live, shop, and eat. This may not be as sanitized, accessible, or quaint as shopping at the Ferry Plaza market in San Francisco, but it certainly has a degree of authenticity. Porta Palazzo remains a market that serves all the citizens of Turin.

There are many kinds of tourism that take place at the Porta Palazzo market. Most are focused on food, but their motivations, focus, and experience can be incredibly different. This is largely because there are so many different cultures that come together in the market square; curiosity about the Other and the subjectification of foreign culinary practices are nearly unavoidable. Many of the foreigners at Porta Palazzo are anything but tourists, and many of the Torinese who come to the market looking for the exotic are far from regular market shoppers. In all forms of tourism, there is a desire to explore another world and lose oneself in the unfamiliar or even a desire to engage in nostalgia for a lost cultural link.

Carrot Salad Scented with Orange Blossom Water

This is another Moroccan recipe, one I learned while attending Chef Kumalé's cooking class. It is very easy to prepare and makes an excellent opener for the couscous in the previous chapter.

INGREDIENTS
10 large carrots
1 juicy orange
1 tbsp sugar
1/2 tsp ground cinnamon
1 tbsp orange blossom water

FOR GARNISH
a handful of walnuts or fried almonds
a few mint leaves

Peel and grate the carrots and put them in the juice from the orange. Flavor with cinnamon and orange blossom water. Mix well and place in a serving dish. Garnish with nuts and mint.

Nostrano: The Farmers' Market, Local Food, and Place

As I turn the corner and head behind the Mercato dell'Orologio (Alimentare IV) at Porta Palazzo, I feel as if I have entered into the heart of Piedmont. The light, sounds, and smells are different here. The sun filters through the cast-iron roof of the *tettoia dei contadini* (farmers' market area) and warms the chilly fall air. Chickens squawk, and shoppers yell greetings in Piedmontese: "Bun di!" A man walks by with a steaming cup of espresso and stops in front of a cheese stand: the smell of goat cheese overwhelms the rich scent of the coffee.

The farmers' market engages all the senses and transports shoppers to another time and place when Turin had stronger ties with the surrounding countryside. The shopper vividly experiences the seasons in this part of the market: in summer, the stands are piled high with local fruits and vegetables, while in winter, the shivering vendors huddle around nearly barren tables displaying a few potatoes and maybe some winter squash. Although the Porta Palazzo farmers' market seems timeless, this age-old market has undergone a number of changes over the past decades, many of which I witnessed during my research there. While conducting my fieldwork at the *mercato dei contadini*, I began to think about the importance of local food and how it connects cities to their hinterlands in a very social way. I also began to look at how local food is constructed and challenged each day by the people who shop and sell their wares at the market.

Situated under a nineteenth-century cast-iron structure behind the Mercato dell'Orologio pavilion, the farmers' market is different from the rest of the Porta Palazzo (Figure 9). This was something I realized the moment I

Figure 9. Under the *tettoia* of the Porta Palazzo farmers' market, 2009. Photo by Rachel Black.

turned the corner and my gaze scanned across this relatively peaceful little market. The space is smaller and more sheltered than the rest of the piazza; in many ways, it is more intimate because one can see from one end to the other: it is not a maze like the big resellers' market. The fact that each stand does not have its own structure and awning makes this market seem more like a community, a coherent whole. When the *mercato dei contadini* is at its busiest, the shoppers have to press through the crowds and are sometimes jostled by other customers as they wait their turn in front of the low, flat tables loaded with seasonal produce. Unlike the resellers' market, customers are face to face with the farmer—a shopper does not have to look up at the vendor. The spatial relations have a huge impact on the way people interact and socialize in this part of the market.

What makes this part of Porta Palazzo unique is that this is where the city and the countryside meet and have met for over a century. It is one of the few places where urban consumers come in contact with the people who produce their food, an experience that is becoming increasingly rare (Robinson and Hartenfeld 2007). The old woman behind the table hands me a beautiful bouquet of radishes with the dirt still clinging to them and tells me about how dry this growing season has been. Going to the Porta Palazzo farmers' market puts people in touch with the areas surrounding the city and gives city dwellers a sense of another reality, that of country life. The farmers' market may seem like a remnant of the past in a cityscape that has done away with many of its rural contacts; but most important, this market puts people in touch with their food and the people who produce it.

The *mercato dei contadini* may seem as if it is from another time, and it can also seem like another place. When I go to the farmers' market, I feel as if I have left Turin because vendors and clients often speak in the local dialect (Torinese or Piedmontese);[1] conversely, for most Torinese, there is nothing more local than this market. There are few places in Turin where people still converse in the local dialects; this is one of the reasons young people are not learning the local dialects, which are falling out of use. Torinese is the dialect spoken in the city of Turin, and Piedmontese is spoken in the countryside.[2] They are similar in many ways, but the pronunciation is quite different; even the pronunciation of Piedmontese can vary wildly from town to town. Dialects have now fallen out of fashion in Turin, but once they were a status symbol and a social form of elitism: the managers at the Fiat car factories would speak to each other in Piedmontese and Torinese so that the workers from the south could not understand them. Now the only people speaking dialect in the city are the elderly. Coincidentally, they make up the majority of the regular farmers' market shoppers. The farmers at the market also speak Piedmontese, which is still quite frequently spoken in most villages. I noticed that these linguistic exchanges created a special bond between farmer and client—two dying breeds?

As in the city, children in the countryside do not want to speak in dialect. One of the farmers I worked with, Pietro, explained that he usually speaks to his children in Piedmontese; they understand, but they always reply in Italian: "They are embarrassed. Speaking Piedmontese sounds silly [*buffo*]. It's backward." He felt it was a shame that his children would not speak his dialect, but he chalked it up to one of the changes of the world that he could not fight against. The farmers' market is one of the last places where one can hear these two dialects being spoken. It is possible that the sound of the *mercato dei contadino* will be very different in a decade from now. One thing that will not change is the seasons.

Shoppers in this special part of the piazza become very aware of the passage of time: the Porta Palazzo farmers' market is one of the few places left in the city where seasonal changes can be felt and observed. Stands are sparse in winter and abundant in summer; "special" holiday foods appear at specific times of the year and only at those times (Delamont 1995). There is a frenzy around the harvest of tomatoes at the end of the summer, as people purchase cases to make preserves. Certain fruits are related to a specific time of the year: strawberries in May, apricots in June, watermelons in August. The various harvests mark out time, and often there is a festive atmosphere around the appearance of certain produce at the market (du Boulay and Williams 1987), not to mention the abundance and commotion of the market at Christmas. Religious festivities are quietly celebrated under the gaze of the Madonnina, who watches over the market from her privileged position high above the swarming shoppers; she reminds market-goers of the deep-seated religious beliefs of rural life (Figure 10).

There are other corners of religious symbolism at Porta Palazzo: all the covered markets have small shrines where shoppers and vendors can stop to light a candle or say a prayer. I noticed people crossing themselves as they passed the Virgin, but rarely did I see anyone stop for much longer than a few seconds. Less obvious symbols of Catholic culture also appear at the market: foods for preparing special dishes, usually symbolic themselves, appear on tables and make their way home to tables for holiday feasts. For

Figure 10. The farmers' market *Madonnina*. Photo by Rachel Black.

example, eggs are in abundance at Easter for special baked goods such as the ubiquitous *colomba* (a dove-shaped panettone). In this case, food plays an important part in marking time through religious festivities, as well as the passing of seasons (Delamont 1995).

Mercato dei Contadini: Constructing Local Food

Pietro, Roberto, Elena, and Enzo are a few of the many farmers and artisans who let me into their world that oscillates between this corner of the city and the lush farmlands that spread out around Turin from Cuneo to the Susa Valley. I have tried to capture a bit of this world that is very intimate, demanding, and, despite its timeless appearance, ever-changing. During the time I spent at the farmers' market, I came to realize that the social interactions that take place there are just as important as the food and the goods sold. Food sold in the *mercato dei contadini* is instilled with value that has to do with place, local knowledge, and social relations. The market connects people to place—in the city and the surrounding regions. My observations led me to think more about how this sense of place and local food is not just bought and sold but created.

What is local food to the Torinese, and does the term *terroir* mean something to Italians as they shop at the farmers' market? Do Italians shop for the taste of a specific place? Amy Trubek's *The Taste of Place: A Cultural Journey into Terroir* (2008) explores the ways the concept of *terroir* can be applied to food; it looks at how place can invest food with meaning, even taste. I was intrigued by how Trubek compares the concept of *terroir* in the French and North American contexts. I wondered if I could contribute something to the discussion by looking at the Italian interpretations of this term through local food at the *mercato dei contadini*.

The *Collins English Dictionary* defines *terroir* as "the complete natural environment in which a particular wine is produced, including factors such as the soil, topography, and climate." *Terroir* with reference to food is now used frequently when talking about local and traditional food production (Leynse 2006). It is also often used in opposition to industrial or fast food (Abramson 2007). Trubek has tried to flesh out this slippery term and looked at specific cultural contexts, including Italy.

Toward the end of *Taste of Place*, Trubek considers the role of the Slow Food movement and the organization's leader Carlo Petrini in preserving the sense of place in Italian food. Trubek believes that, as in France, Italian farmers have a privileged place in the popular Italian imagination. However, Italy has had a very different agricultural history from its French neighbors, and farmers do not have the same position in Italian society as in France. In fact, Slow Food has actually been working on raising the social profile of farmers. Unlike in France, farmers do not have a privileged place in the social imagination of most Italians. Most of agricultural Italy labored under *mezzadria*, an oppressive form of sharecropping, or the *latifundia* system (in which all farmers worked as day laborers for large landowners—often the Catholic Church—up until the 1960s). In fact, Italian law did not officially ban *mezzadria* until 1982.[3] Although this system was prevalent in central Italy, agriculture in northern Italy had its share of hardships, including massive outmigration from the countryside to the factories of major cities from the 1950s to the 1970s. There were few people left to work the land, and those who returned did so only to help during the harvest.

Italian peasants lived in relative poverty and had very low levels of education. Italian authors helped solidify the image of the Italian peasant as a brutish, ignorant being who constantly suffered the injustices of the Church, the State, the privileged, and nature. Beppe Fenoglio's *La Malora* (1954) and Cesare Pavese's *La Luna e i falò* (1950) epitomized the hardship of peasants in Piedmont, while Ignazio Silone's *Fontamara* (1931) illustrated the ignorance of peasants in the region of Abruzzo, revealing their long suffering as they struggled to work the land and survive. Italy's agrarian past is recent history, and the popular image of the farmer is tied to times of hardship. In an attempt to move beyond the stereotypes cemented by literature, Slow Food has run campaigns to improve the image of farmers, underlining the importance of agricultural labor and its social contribution. Slow Food has tried to communicate to Italians that growing food and working the land are respectable occupations that should be recognized and that the hard work of farming should be rewarded appropriately. Wendell Berry's "eating is an agricultural act" has become a Slow Food mantra. This attempt to change the social standing of farmers is a slow process that is made more difficult by the expansion of industrial agriculture and the continuing exploitation of migrant workers in Italy (Gatti 2006; Lagnà 2006).

For these historical reasons, there has been little or no back-to-the-land movement in Italy. Why would anyone want to farm? It is hard work! The Italian countryside has been emptying out steadily since the 1950s, and there has been no reversal. Older generations may still have nostalgia for farming, but they are generally appeased by small, urban garden plots. This connection to the land certainly has not been passed on to younger generations. While Italians seem reluctant to get their hands dirty, foreigners are taking up the hoe and starting small-scale, organic farms in some parts of Italy. Rather than a sea change, this small movement seems to be more of a romantic fantasy about the Italian countryside à la Frances Mayes (1997).

After spending several months at the *mercato dei contadini*, I found the concept of *terroir* just as romantic as starting an organic farm. *Terroir* really does not seem to be a notion consciously associated with farming in Italy (perhaps except for grape growing for wine production) at a grassroots level. There is no equivalent term in the Italian language. *Terroir* is a borrowed term applied by Italian marketing campaigns or by famous chefs in television interviews. In general, the act of farming is still swept under the rug in Italy. It is dirty. It represents the opposite of the modern ideal of a rich consumer society, which is something that only started to become a reality in Italy in the 1960s and 1970s. The Italian shoppers I spoke with at the market seemed to value the idea of local food but had little concept that a specific *terroir* could create a unique product. Although they value diversity and unique products from specific places, *terroir* is not part of the vocabulary of the average Torinese shopper or of the Piedmontese farmers. Perhaps it exists, but not in a concrete or well-articulated way.

At the same time, Italian industrial food producers are trying to co-opt the concept of *terroir*; place lends authenticity to their products. Many marketing campaigns for regional products in Italian supermarkets have been successful (for example, Terre d'Italia has been an important success story for promoting regional products throughout Italy[4]), but local produce makes rare appearances at supermarkets and can even be hard to find at local markets. The logistics of supermarket distribution privilege central-ization and economics over fresh local food. The ideas of "food miles" and the "100-mile diet" are just starting to reach the more enlightened Italian consumers, but there is still not a general demand for local, sustainable food in Italy (Rubino 2011; Smith and Mackinnon 2007). At Porta Palazzo, price tends to be the bottom line, and industrial produce is generally the cheapest option.

Local food is produced at the market itself, rather than just in the field on the farm. Trubek (2008) places emphasis on the role origins have on sen-sory experience and authenticity when it comes to cuisine; this is what she calls "the locational philosophy of taste" (a term borrowed from the world of wine). Does it taste better if it has dirt on it? Is it a more authentic carrot if the farmer hands it to me? The farmers' market builds that link to place and typicity in many ways, and perhaps the transparency of origins even makes this food taste better to some consumers. Aurier, Fort, and Sirieix (2005) found that consumers place enhanced value on local food and are willing to pay more for it. In North America, popular figures like Michael Pollan and Alice Waters are strong advocates for local food and have had an impact on the way many Americans think about food and its production. In Italy, Carlo Petrini is becoming more of a household name and plays a similar role in underlining the value of local agriculture.

The *mercato dei contadini* is certainly involved in the "production of locality" that ties the food sold there to nearby farms (Appadurai 1996). From my discussions with Torinese shoppers, I gathered that ideas of *ter-roir* and local food were really just givens to most Italians—there was no other choice than to eat local and seasonal food because that was all the markets had to offer until recently. Not until refrigerated trucks began to transport produce all over Europe did this situation started to change. Even after international food hit markets in Italy, Italians (other than farmers) did not think much about this: most food sold in local markets and supermarkets had no indication of its origins until a national labeling law was introduced in 2002.[5] People just assumed the fruits and vegetables were produced in Italy.

Only recently have Italians begun to think about where and how their food is produced. Groups such as Slow Food and the media have begun to raise awareness but the local and organic food movements are still nascent.[6] At the same time, Italians express a fierce pride in foodstuffs produced in Italy. With the introduction of DOP (*denominazione di origine protetta*; protected designation of origin) and DOC (*denominazione di origine controllata*; controlled designation of origin) certifications, the Italian government is beginning to get serious about authenticating, protecting, and promoting local and culturally unique food and drink. Increasing international competition and cases of fraud make this, on one hand, an important economic move and, on the other hand, a strategy that encourages cultural reproduction of local cuisine. However, these certification systems are not without their politics and complications.[7] Beyond labels, I was curious to know how the shoppers at the *mercato dei contadini* created connections between food and place, or not, and if this played a role in their choice to shop here at the farmers' market.

I asked a number of shoppers and clients at Pietro's stand why they preferred to shop at the farmers' market. One client responded, "The vegetables just taste better when they are local." Another told me, "I feel better knowing where my food comes from. There are so many food scares these days." Most shoppers made comments about quality (mainly with reference to taste) and food safety, but ultimately quality seemed to mean produced in Italy. I would argue that these perceptions were deeply influenced by the relation created when food is bought from a farmer. Living in a city can be an alienating experience, particularly when it comes to food and nature, and feeling connected to the land adds value and reassurance to the food people purchase at the market. It is also reassuring to be able to ask the producer questions about the produce, how it was grown and what the season had been like (Bérard and Marchenay 2004). Shoppers are becoming more aware of food safety and the ecological impact of food miles; this is one of the reasons consumers have begun to have a renewed appreciation for farmers' markets.

Perceived value (economic, salutary, and gustatory) is certainly a factor in the appreciation of local food. At the same time, the clientele at the farmers' market is mixed. I conducted a small survey from which I got a better idea of the client base. The majority of shoppers are elderly

Torinese who shop at Porta Palazzo out of habit and often because they do not like the "poor quality" of the produce they find elsewhere. Many people from this group also told me they thought they got more for their money at Porta Palazzo. There are young Italians who are attracted by the quality of the produce and enjoy meeting farmers, but this group also sees these outings as a leisure activity that includes shopping, socializing, and drinking. Then there is a minority group of immigrants from a wide variety of backgrounds who frequent very specific stands (mainly stands with eggs, Chinese produce, and live animals). For many shoppers, the motivation may not be to seek out the taste of *terroir*, but in the end, value is added to the purchases that they make at the farmers' market by having contact with producers and engaging in discussions about food. From my research, I concluded that authenticity was not determined by place and taste alone; the social connections to the people producing the food were essential to most shoppers' perceptions of quality at the farmers' market. In many ways, how Italians talked about food and place comes from not being so far removed historically from agricultural production.

Local food is surely a cultural construction, but on the other hand, it must also be something one can certify and put a label on. Local food is potentially tangible. After all the questions I had asked about people's perception of local food, I still did not have a concrete idea of how to determine the provenance of much of the food that was laid out each day in the *mercato dei contadini*. Most of the produce signs read "nostrano." What does this term mean?

Nostrano: Defining the Location of Local

Walking around the farmers' market one morning, I noticed the municipal police, *vigili urbani*, hassling a vendor. After they left, I went to see what the trouble was all about. Giuseppe, a market gardener, explained that the authorities are now enforcing a law that says all produce at the market must be labeled with its price, grade, and origin. The Gate office had handed out specially made signs as part of a larger marketing campaign, but Giuseppe told me he had forgotten to put out his signs. The *vigili* were giving him a reminder. I looked down at Giuseppe's signs and I noticed that, on the box that was labeled "origine," it read "nostrano."

The term *nostrano*, which literally means "ours," is often used in Italian markets and shops to denote fruits and vegetables that have been grown in Italy (technically, Giuseppe's sign should have read "Italia" to conform to Italian law; *nostrano* is not a legal term). At the Porta Palazzo farmers' market, the term means grown on the farm (usually by the person making the claim); it suggests something that is genuine and that has tradition and comes from local soil. This possessive pronoun takes back some of its function even when used as an adjective: the farmer is possessive of the produce and proud of what he or she is selling. There is a nationalistic connotation in the term *nostrano*: anything grown in Italy must be better than produce grown elsewhere. Melissa Caldwell talks about a similar use of the Russian term *nash* ("our own" in Russian) in her work on changing foodways in postsocialist Russia: "the 'nash' system is both a segmentary system of inclusionary and exclusionary identity and a marker of sentimental solidarity and imagined uniformity" (2002: 309). Although *nash* has specific ties to socialism and the construction of fellowship and social responsibility that are unique to the Russian context, this term works in many similar ways to the Italian *nostrano* denomination for food. *Nostrano* is also seen as a way of guarding against all that is foreign and threatening and is often tied to a belief that *nostrano* products are healthier and of better quality.

The health aspects of food have come to the fore of public discourse since recent food scares (contamination, including Listeria, E. coli, and salmonella and use of toxic herbicides and pesticides) have been highly publicized in the Italian media, raising consumer awareness of the risks that their food can pose. In addition, Italy's rejection of GMO (genetically modified organism) crops, despite EU approval, has given yet another meaning to *nostrano*—Italian produce is not genetically modified. Although many food scares have been directly associated with Italian agriculture and food production (for example, the recent dioxin contamination of *mozzarella di bufala* from Campania in spring 2008), buying food from the person who produced it somehow assures safety and quality for many consumers (the traceability is perhaps the most reassuring aspect of these exchanges, although there is little scientific evidence such food is any safer). The concept of *nostrano* evokes ideas of produce that is "home grown," which has a connection to local places and culinary culture—this is positive and desirable. However, this is not always the case.

Nostrano is not only about economic exclusion; there is even a hint of xenophobia in this unofficial geographic indication. Lemons that are labeled *nostrano* might have been grown in Sicily or Calabria, hardly that close to Turin but still Italian. Are those lemons still considered "local" food? Long beans grown and sold by Chinese immigrants in fields near Chivasso, a town not far from Turin, are never labeled *nostrano*. When I asked one Piedmontese customer if he felt the produce sold and produced by local Chinese farmers at the market could be considered *nostrano*, he replied: "Absolutely not! Those vegetables have nothing to do with Italian food." This is when I realized that the idea of *nostrano* is deeply tied to concepts of what is Italian culture and what is not. This unofficial declaration of Italian origin is not without its nationalistic side, and the exclusion of local products that are deemed Other is the norm. From what I observed at the *mercato dei contadini*, *nostrano* really does mean food that is "ours" in terms of both national production and culinary culture.

The Farm and the City

Food that is produced too close to home can also be problematic. In cities, it is difficult to think of food as being produced locally. For many Italians, there is a strong feeling that food should not be produced in cities or too close to urban areas; it would not be safe, clean, or orderly. The farm is best kept at a distance (along with the agricultural past). The farmers' market is one of the last links. In Western Europe, this connection has been weakened over the last century; with modern transportation, refrigeration, and increasingly centralized food distribution and production, local farms are often marginalized from urban food distribution networks.[8] As regulations tighten and profits shrink, small-scale farming is struggling to stay in the market.[9] In many cases, people living in Italian cities are losing the choice and possibility of buying local food. Although the press and foodies laud the local, large-scale food distribution trends are moving away from local and even Italian food.

Only recently have municipal governments began to encourage or promote farmers' markets as essential elements of urban foodscapes. Despite an increasing demand for organic produce and an interest in locally produced food on the part of consumers, the farmers I worked with did not echo these positive trends in the evaluation of their state of affairs.[10] Why is local food so scarce, and what are the repercussions of this dwindling local food supply? It does not seem that local food in Italy is undesirable or unappreciated. There is a disconnection from agricultural production.

Some Italian municipalities are starting to see the potential and benefits for developing markets to help improve food security and access. Farmers' markets offer much needed encouragement to local producers and, in turn, assure that the city has access to food. Local food production has recently been in the media spotlight due to the rising cost of petroleum and transportation. Many cities are taking into consideration the possibility that local farms may someday be the only viable and economical source of food.

There is more to food than food security alone. David Sutton (2001) and Carole Counihan (1984) note that the decline in the significance of seasonal food patterns leads to the breakdown of social bonds; food no longer needs to be shared in order to survive. The rise of "global food," food that is transported from all over the world and sold at all times of the year without consideration for the seasons, is contributing to a loss of place and cultural disorientation away from local practices. Food becomes less crucial to social relations. Seremetakis (1994) also argues that standardization of regulations around food has led to a decline in regional diversity, which leads to an identity crisis because of the disappearance of acts of social reproduction as well as biodiversity. This can be seen in regulations imposed on farmers' markets by the EU and, as a result, by local administrations (Black 2004; Leitch 2000): dairy products without refrigeration can no longer be sold in the market, prepared foods are limited due to rigid hygiene standards, and meat products are strictly controlled. It is true that globalization does not necessarily lead to homogenization and that it often creates new hybrids (Miller 1995b; Wilk 2006); however, without places like the Porta Palazzo market, there would be few outlets for selling local varieties of vegetables; farmers' markets are important because they help maintain biodiversity. Fruits and vegetables that are specific to a certain region are usually ingredients in local recipes. For instance, the *cardo gobbo* (cardoon, a plant in the artichoke family that was deemed in danger and culturally important enough to make it one of Slow Food's first *presidia* products[11]), the Martin Sec pear, and certain seasonal field greens are examples some of the local produce that one can find only at the *mercato dei contadini* and only when they are in season. Dishes such as *bagna caoda*, *pere cotte* (cooked pears), and *omelette alle erbe* (herb omelet) would drop out of the Piedmontese culinary repertoire without these ingredients.

"Global food" is only one kind of globalization of food systems: the way we shop is another. Shopping at the farmers' market for some is a form of resistance to globalization and the speed of modern life—it takes time to shop at the market. Wendy Parkins and Geoffrey Craig argue that slowness can be seen as a resistance to the ever-increasing speed of modern life (2006: 1–2). They note that "whether making bread or growing heirloom vegetables, there is a dual impulse towards time and history in such 'slow' practices which connects a mindfulness in the present with a heightened awareness of historicity" (2006: 41). The same holds true for the act of going to market, where shoppers reconnect with their senses as well as the past. A number of the young shoppers I interviewed told me that shopping at the farmers' market fit in with their political views: "I'm a little bit of a Marxist, and I think that it is important to cut out middlemen. I want to support famers directly and capitalists as little as possible. I refuse to shop at Auchan." One woman told me, "It's a pleasure to shop at the Porta Palazzo. For me everything about food from shopping to eating should be a pleasure. Supermarkets make me feel nauseous." Going to the market in Italy is no longer the only alternative for everyday provisioning; therefore, it is increasingly becoming a conscious choice, and in many ways, it can be seen as an act of resistance to faster, more efficient alternatives for procuring food (Honoré 2005).

A Sense of Place

Can food evoke a sense of place? Typical dishes and local wines have a strong identification with place, but it is the ingredients that really connect food with a specific geography, history, and culture. The names of fruits and vegetables are often accompanied by place names (capon from Morozzo, gray rabbit from Carmagnola, strawberries from Tortona), or they take their names from places (Castelmagno, Macagn, and Montébore cheeses). Not only is this an indication of incredible biodiversity in Italy, but it reflects the diversity of the culinary culture of this country. At the same time, this biodiversity and culinary richness are under attack. The Piedmontese varieties of pears, cherries, and apples are being replaced by popular "global" varieties whose names have become agricultural trademarks: William pears, Granny Smith apples, and Concord grapes, to name a few. What has happened to agricultural diversity and culinary culture when we are all growing the same plants and using the same ingredients? Even at the market it is not uncommon for consumers to shop for name brands when it comes to fruit: for example, Melinda apples and Del Monte pineapples. The farmers' market is one of the few places where local varieties are still sold; production is small, and these are often aesthetically imperfect fruits that appeal only to a small clientele.

For many, diversity is not the main appeal of the market. To some shoppers, a tomato is just a tomato. If tomatoes cost two euros a kilo in the farmers' market and a euro fifty in the resellers' market, guess where shoppers will buy their tomato? Price is the bottom line for many people, is particularly in these difficult economic times. The farmers I worked with frequently expressed the challenges of being a market farmer: long hours, labor costs, and small profit margins. The farmers at Porta Palazzo and most neighborhood markets have to compete with the resellers, who at times are right next to them selling similar produce at much lower prices. This makes it challenging for them to command higher prices. The *mercato dei contadini* is a niche market in many ways: the prices are higher, but the value that is added is the knowledge of the producers; a wide variety of produce (many local and heritage varieties); and the freshness of the food. Not all shoppers appreciate these qualities, and many cannot be bothered to walk across the street to see what is on sale in this part of the market.

Pietro, a farmer I worked with for several months, explained that there was a lack of local knowledge about what fruits are from the area and what time of year they are harvested. I overheard Pietro explain several times why the pears he was selling were so small. With the Martin Sec pears, a famed variety that can be difficult to find, Pietro explained to one client that they were hard because they had to be cooked. He proceeded to give the customer a recipe for Martin Sec pears cooked in Nebbiolo, a local red wine from the Langhe region. This is just one example of the disappearance of local knowledge that would have been common knowledge even twenty years ago.

In part, this loss of connection with production (and use) is due to the impersonal commercialization of agriculture and waning culinary apprenticeship. What makes the farmers' market experience different from that in the rest of the market is the passing along of rural knowledge, history, and culinary information. Pietro often had to explain what type of beet greens he was selling and how to cook them, in addition to giving detailed descriptions of agricultural practices and the personal sacrifices involved in raising a crop. He would spend time explaining to me which apples could be stored for the winter (if you had the space or the right conditions, unlikely for most city dwellers). These explanations helped Pietro's customers and his Canadian apprentice understand what life was like in the Piedmontese countryside. It is a place where nothing is wasted, where everything has its season, and where practical knowledge of farming, food preservation, and preparation are essential to survival. Much of this knowledge is being lost, but in its own small way, the *mercato dei contadini* is helping preserve some of it through the oral traditions passed along from countryside to city in the small conversations of the market. The social life and verbal exchanges of the market can be seen as the glue that connects these two worlds.

Dammi la ricetta! Talking About Food, Reproducing Culture

The farmers' market is an important place for people to learn about food and cooking. The social life of the market offers many examples of how culture is reproduced through discussion about food. Although social reproduction has been widely studied through eating and cooking (Sutton 2001; Douglas 1972), there is little research on food shopping, which seems ripe for this type of analysis due to its everyday, repetitive nature. Daniel Miller's (2001) study of shopping in England posits the idea that shopping in general is a normative activity in which people often mediate between complex contradictions in their public and private lives. For provisioning in particular, the complexity of the shopper's selection of food and the relationships in the family are mediated in each choice. In addition, the social performance of the act of shopping in a place, the market, requires multiple social interactions and exchanges. Buying food at the market is one of the most public forms of food provisioning: there are many necessary exchanges, and there are many opportunities to be observed. At the farmers' market, many clients appear to display their food choices proudly; by shopping at the *mercato dei contadini*, customers are confirming their social values, their desire for local food and culinary knowledge. A young woman cradles her market basket brimming with kale, lettuce, and onions. Others are just following the mundane routine of everyday grocery shopping—this is how they have always gotten their food. An old man is dragging a dusty cart on wheels. He quickly deposits his purchases in its belly as if feeding a hungry dog who is following him. There are innumerable types of shoppers and ways to do the shopping. Everyone has his or her own approach, relationships with vendors, and ways of speaking to fellow shoppers. Some are chatty, others are silent, but most everyone is listening. The discussions that take place at and between market stalls are part of affirming these choices, which, in turn, create an understanding and consensus about what is local food. Food discourses at the farmers' market not only help define personal and group identities but also determine the value of food from a gustatory and cultural perspective.

Food is certainly bought and sold at the farmers' market, but what is perhaps just as important is that food is talked about. This culinary discourse is not always merely informational; it is often "phatic." Language is used "to maintain and build social relations rather than communicate new information" (Sutton 2001: 111). I heard a vendor and a client (both men) comparing recipes for *bagna caoda* (see the recipe below); rather than just a recipe exchange, it seemed to be a way of learning more about the other person, where they were from, how they were raised, and if they shared similar tastes. Both men knew how to make the dish, but the subtle differences interested them both. How much garlic should be used, and how finely should it be chopped? The critical question is whether cream is added (not using cream is the sure sign of a purist). Often a discussion about food or a request for information about products being sold is the beginning of more personal conversations or eventually friendships.

In other cases, talking about food can really be a way to talk about lived experiences, emotions, the past, and so on. For example, in her research Meredith Abarca (2004) uses *charlas culinarias* (culinary chats) that center on the life experiences of working-class Mexican women. Similarly, Carole Counihan (2004) uses life-centered food histories to look at changes in gender relations in contemporary Florence. In Italy, discussions about food are an important means to communicate things that are often difficult to say without the guise of a culinary discourse. How does a woman talk about her battle with diabetes with total strangers? How does a man discuss the lack of love in his life with other men? He shares recipes that are intertwined with heartfelt lamentations of nights at the table alone and a desire to share a plate of pasta. Food can be love, but it can also be sadness or consolation when there is no one there to share it with.

During my time at the Porta Palazzo market, people used food as a medium for talking about health, politics, masculinity, families, and the past, to name just a few topics. These types of discussions easily come to life in the informal atmosphere of the market. This is particularly true in the *mercato dei contadini*, which is much smaller and more intimate than most shopping places. After only a few weeks, I was a regular, and my conversations with vendors and other habitual customers started where they last left off and were usually on rather personal topics. My experience at the market led me to believe that all this chitchat has the effect of giving meaning to place. The farmers' market at Porta Palazzo is not an empty space devoid of significance—it is invested with personal experience and relationships that are built around commercial exchange and work.

After circling the *mercato dei contadini* for months, I was starting to have a good rapport with a few of the farmers there. In particular, I found myself becoming part of a social group that often gathered around one of the cheese stands. My main contact at the farmers' market was a man named Paolo, the cheese vendor at the center of this circle. Paolo introduced me to many of the other people I worked with and brought me into the inner circle of his acquaintances at the market. Focusing on the conversations and exchanges around Paolo's market stall, I began to understand what types of social relations develop at the market. Of course, there were people who just wanted to talk about the weather, but there were others who had formed more meaningful relationships after years of shopping at the *mercato dei contadini*. At Paolo's stand, friendships grew between people from very different backgrounds: there were woodworkers, an opera singer, a semiprofessional guitar player, students, the unemployed, and many more. Conversations over a slice of cheese and glass of wine often turned into a discussion of a seasonal recipe that then turned into a dinner invitation. My web of acquaintances grew quickly as I became part of this social scene. I constantly marveled that this type of "social integration" could happen in no other place than a market. Perhaps it was just Paolo's cheese stand. Was there something particularly special about the social life that thrived around this one vendor? Although it became the social hub of the market for me, there are other hubs like this; some of them focus on a specific stand, while others are just meeting points in the market focused more on the habitual attendees.

Paolo's family makes cheese in Val di Susa, and he travels near and far buying cheese from other cheese makers, which he sells four days of the week at the Porta Palazzo farmers' market. He was thirty-five when I met him in 2002 and had been selling cheese on and off at farmers' markets and other regional markets for the past eight years. Paolo presented his wares in a slightly more careful manner than most of the other vendors, with more attention to aesthetic appeal. Large baskets held delicious *tuma* from Val di Susa, a runny gorgonzola was left with its wood wrapping to hold it together, and little goat cheeses prepared and packaged with pepper and herbs were just a few of the finer touches that set this stand apart. There were other cheese sellers, but most pull their cheeses out of plastic tubs or do not make any effort to present their wares in an appealing manner. The combination of presentation and Paolo's charm made this stand one of the farmers' market's great successes (at least from a social perspective).

When I first started to frequent the farmers' market, it was not easy to approach the farmers and ask if I could spend some time at their stands or actually work with them. The Piedmontese farmers with their leathery skin and dialect-flecked Italian seemed out of my reach. Fortunately, the burly fellow selling cheese, Paolo, noticed a shy young woman lurking nearby. He asked me what I was up to. I introduced myself and proceeded to explain that I was studying the Porta Palazzo market and that I wanted to find out more about its daily running by spending time there. I mentioned I was looking to work with people and if possible sell food. He said that he did not think he could use my help (he already had a number of helpers), but promised to give me a hand. I met nearly all my initial contacts through Paolo, who was friends with most of the younger farmers. After several mornings with Paolo, what I found most remarkable were the close relations he kept with his customers and the atmosphere he created around his stand. As I got to know Paolo's customers, I realized that many made a special trip to Porta Palazzo to spend time at this stand and that others saw a visit with Paolo as a highlight to their market outing.

This was particularly true on Saturday. Around lunch, a small group of regulars would gather to spend time gossiping, exchanging recipes, talking politics, or just shooting the breeze. A few of the younger farmers from neighboring stands would join and sometimes contribute some of their products to creating a *merendina* (a little snack) for everyone. Enzo, a butcher from Cisterna d'Asti, would throw in one of his sausages, Pietro would bring some tomatoes, and I would buy bread from a stand at the covered pavilion. Paolo made us all sandwiches thick with gorgonzola cheese, and Enzo would pour wine made by his cousin down the road in Cisterna into plastic cups he kept hidden under his stand. A few of Paolo's regular customers and friends would join in: there was Eric, a young Moroccan who was one of Paolo's helpers; Gianni, a Brazilian musician; Filippo, an opera singer; and "Pantani" (nicknamed for his likeness to the famous Italian cyclist) a bit of a lost soul with a penchant for culinary experimentation. Often there was a group of six to eight people drinking, eating, and talking; all the while, Paolo would serve a steady stream of customers as they approached. The atmosphere was very festive, and the topics of conversation ranged from how to make *tajarin* (a local egg pasta) to what sexual positions were most satisfying for women. Politics were generally avoided, and pleasure was generally the main focus of most discussions. This seemed appropriate, given that the market is a place that bombards the senses and piques the imagination about the pleasures of food and meals to come. There were few barriers, taboos, or limits to what could be discussed at Paolo's stand on a Saturday afternoon.

During the time I spent at the farmers' market, Paolo's cheese stand served as a base for my research, and Paolo was an important point of reference. After several months, I felt very much part of this little group of regulars, and when I did not show up, particularly on a Saturday, people would ask me where I had been. There was truly a sense of group cohesion. At times, things would get a bit too personal for me when people would inquire into my private life and criticize my choices. I did not hesitate to push back, and I was often told I was a cold northerner or a backward American. I tried to take it all with a grain of salt.

When I tried to leave the field in 2003 because I found it difficult to gain the perspective I felt I needed to start writing, I stopped attending the Saturday market altogether. I found it was Paolo's stand that I missed most. I wondered if other people felt the same attachment to certain stands and the social life of the market. During informal interviews with the other groupies of the cheese stand, I discovered that this was indeed the case. Gianni told me he would come down to the market to hang out even if he did not have any shopping to do. He saw the market as a square that had a recreational and social value, not just a place to buy food. When I talked to the others, I was not surprised to find they had similar responses and feelings about Porta Palazzo. I also interviewed other shoppers and found that this social aspect of the market was just as important to them. Gianni, an elderly widower who has lived in Borgo Dora for fifteen years, told me that the time he spent talking to his friends (vendors and other shoppers) at the market made up the bulk of his social life. Other than going for a coffee in the bar downstairs from his apartment, he did not have much opportunity to socialize. For many elderly folks, the Saturday market, in particular, is the height of their social week. You can often find groups of elderly people chitchatting at the fringes of the farmers' market. I also asked Eric if the market was part of his social life. I had rarely seen him talking to other Moroccans in the farmers' market. He told me that the farmers' market was his job, but that he would usually go before or after work to the other side of the square to one of the bars under the porticoes to have coffee with friends, exchange a few words, and get news from Moroccan acquaintances. They would talk about soccer, Morocco, and troubles with work and getting a visa to stay in Italy. The more I asked about people's social lives in the market, the more I understood the importance of the market as a public space.

Social life at Porta Palazzo is constant, but it is also constantly changing. I was quite surprised that, after I had left the field for about four months and came back to pay a visit, Paolo was no longer selling cheese at the Porta Palazzo farmers' market. Enzo explained that Paolo had been fighting with the market administration about the size and position of his stand. He had frequently complained that this was just a pretext for trying to get rid of him; others were envious of his success and wanted to see him gone. Apparently, the conflict reached a point at which Paolo actually left. Enzo was shocked by Paolo's departure and told me that Paolo had run up debts with his friends and left without paying. I decided to give Paolo a call to find out what really happened. When I spoke to him about his reasons for leaving, he told me it also had to do with quarreling in his family. He had left the cheese business altogether and was working in a factory doing manual labor the last time I talked to him.

This was the end of an era at the *mercato dei contadini*. When I went back to the market in November 2007, I saw Paolo's brother-in-law selling cheese, with Pantani as his helper, at the very same stand. There was not the same social atmosphere around the cheese stand, but my friend Enzo, the young butcher who sells *salame* and cured pork, had taken over as the social hub for young farmers and clients. I headed over to join in. It was as if I had not skipped a beat. However, I did notice that much of the tone of the discussions had changed: they were more focused on food, its production, and the politics of artisanal food. Unlike Paolo, Enzo is responsible for the production of his goods, from fattening the hog to butchering it and curing the meat. He is an authority on *salumeria* and is outspoken about the way things should be done. It is not unheard of to hear him rail against industrial production and the sad state of Italian traditions. The people gathered around Enzo praised his work, asking him how he long he aged the *salame* and breed he preferred for pigs. All this attention did not stop Enzo from opening a bottle of Barbera and cutting samples of cured ham and *salame* for everyone. Once the wine began to flow, he told me about his children, who were now nearly adults. He also shyly pulled me aside (I was expecting him to ask me something very personal as he used to) and told me his long-time girlfriend was expecting another child; they might even get married after all these years. It seemed as if Enzo was also growing up. I missed Paolo, but I could see that the farmers' market had not lost its social and festive atmosphere. Sociability, food, and drink were elements that did not go away when one key actor left. That life went on despite Paolo's absence led me to believe that sociability is intrinsic to this place and is fostered through personal connections that are built on everyday experience.

Tradition Confronts Modernity: An Important Place for Farmers' Markets in the Future

Farmers' markets in the United States are making a strong comeback as consumers demand greater choice and transparency in their food supply. The publication of books such as *The 100-Mile Diet* (Smith and Mackinnon 2007) has also raised North Americans' interest in local food, particularly in the face of rising food and fuel prices. Municipalities are increasingly using farmers' markets as a way to animate neighborhoods and create spaces for sociability. The situation in Europe is slightly different: this may be largely due to the difficulties of small-scale farmers and their inability to compete with the large agribusinesses that dominate the market. In addition, the presence of farmers at markets is often taken for granted. In Italy, low prices, above all else, tend to be the priority for most shoppers. However, there are signs that this is changing; for example, Turin started to organize farmers' markets (*mercati dei produttori*) in the historic Piazza delle Erbe on weekends and even on Sundays as a way of promoting local produce and gastronomic specialties. Unfortunately, prices tend to be higher than at regular markets, and the focus is not as much on produce. A lot of the goods on offer are finished products such as jams, sausages, and breads. These markets are not really meant to provide basic foodstuffs at accessible prices; they are symbolic showcases rather than working, everyday markets for all the city's inhabitants. For this reason, it is important that there are markets in Italy that are alive, not merely museums to an imagined agricultural past and nonexistent culinary cultures.

The popularity of the Slow Food movement is also a positive sign that Italians are becoming more concerned with preserving their culinary heritage as a living heritage from the field to the table. However, many journalists, writers, and academics have criticized these food movements as elitist and lacking in popular appeal (Chrzan 2004). Why shouldn't everyone have access to food that is good, clean, and fair? (Petrini 2007). Slow Food has even begun an initiative in Italy called *mercati della terra*, as an attempt to revive local, producer-only markets.[12] Groups such as Coldiretti, originally founded after World War II by the Democratic Christian party, also try to support small-scale farming by creating a loan structure, lobbying for government subsidies, and promoting Italian produce.

Despite these positive developments, the farmers I got to know at Porta Palazzo told me that it was hard to make a living, and that most of them no longer wanted to work the land. Pietro told me that he was working hard to give his children a better education than he had, and that he wanted them to have more choices for their futures. Pietro finished middle school (*scuola media*), went to help his father full time in the fields, and later started selling at the market as well. In fact, Pietro still had some of his father's faithful clients. Like most small-scale farmers at the *mercato dei contadini*, Pietro does not employ any farm labor; he and his family do all the work, a difficult situation. Pietro has taken on most of the burden in order to give his children time to study and have lives outside the farm. This scenario is not unfamiliar, and the family farm in Italy seems increasingly unsustainable.

If this is a trend—small-scale farmers leaving the land or their children not wanting to carry on farming—who will provide the produce at farmers' markets in the future if this is a livelihood that is no longer being passed along from generation to generation? Perhaps immigrants will become a stronger presence at farmers' markets since they often come from places that are more connected to the land and food production. There is one Chinese family who have an allotment garden on the outskirts of Turin and come and sell their Chinese produce (cabbage, tubers, and other greens) at the farmers' market. They are an anomaly, and Piedmontese farmers still predominate, but maybe they are representative of a trend that will take off in the future as immigrants gain access to land for cultivating food. Another possibility might be growers' collectives like the group of fruit producers from the Cuneo area who come to sell apples at the market—greater strength in numbers.

The future of the farmers' market will certainly depend on the desire of farmers to come to the city to sell their wares, but it will also depend on the policies of promotion and management pursued by the municipality and the market management. Recent renovations to the market and an advertising campaign have tried to bring the farmers' market up to speed with modern marketing by giving it a commercial image. However, this has risked compromising the "authenticity" and local specificity of the place; the removal of paving stones for hygiene and safety reasons was just one of the changes that took away from the farmers' market atmosphere. The farmers heavily criticized this renovation project. In addition, Agriteco, the former management company of the *mercato dei contadini*, tried to homogenize the presentation of the farmers' stands: nearly all the stands consist of standard aluminum tables rented from Agriteco; they have a color-coordinated green skirting that creates a homogeneous, "clean" look; farmers have been encouraged to purchase aprons with the Agriteco logo on them, and they sell plastic shopping bags with the same logo. These last two initiatives are part of a marketing program that mimics supermarket tactics through branding and creating a visible, recognizable name. This effort has both positive and negative effects. On one hand, the market has more visibility, and hygiene standards were brought up to European norms. On the other hand, homogenization takes away from the original nature of the place and tries to convert it into the likeness of a supermarket. Is this what people who shop at the farmers' market want? I spoke to a number of long-time regular customers who told me that they had been put out by the renovation and missed the chaotic, festive atmosphere the market had before. A few mentioned that they liked the new surface because they no longer fell in big holes as they did their shopping, and no one mentioned concerns about hygiene. The people most resistant to change were the farmers, who did not see any reason for it. Like the vendors in the resellers' market, the farmers resisted change because they wanted to protect their position (literally), they lacked faith in the administration, and they wanted to continue as they always had.

The farmers' market can potentially play an important part in revitalizing public places in cities. It is a place that offers contact between city dwellers and farm folk—one of the last connections. From a social and linguistic perspective, the *mercato dei contadini* is essential for the exchange of local knowledge concerning language, food, and rural customs. At the farmers' market, sociability and food are intertwined in all exchange activities, giving meaning to daily life. All the actors at the farmers' market play a part in turning urban space into a public place.

I know I am not the only person who turns the corner behind the Mercato dell'Orologio and feels as if she has left the city and entered into a Piedmont of the past. This is a place where history remains in the recipes that are exchanged and in the way that people relate to each other, which is often slow, at times diffident and always based on day-in, day-out reputations that are built over time.

Bagna Caoda

The name of this dish can be translated literally as "warm bath." It is one of the most typical dishes of Piedmont. It is best eaten with a big group of friends when the weather is cold in the fall and winter. The sauce can also be used on grilled vegetables or to top off a flan.

Developed along the salt route that runs through the Langhe, this dish features salted anchovies and olive oil from Liguria that were integral to this trade. It is a perfect blend of local produce and products that were the fruit of commercial connections. The first written record of this dish dates to the eighteenth century when it was cited in the *Cuoco Piemontese* (Serventi 1995), and it is a pillar of *cucina povera* in Piedmont. Barbera and Dolcetto, two simple wines from the Langhe, usually accompany this dish. Be warned that you will likely be enveloped in a beautiful perfume of garlic the following day after eating *bagna caoda*.

This is a recipe that I developed by talking to people at the market and tasting different versions of this dish. Rosa Cerrato's recipe in the Slow Food *Ricette di osterie di Langa* (1992) also served as a point of reference. The vegetables used might vary depending on availability.

INGREDIENTS

3 heads garlic

4 cups milk

3 cups extra virgin olive oil

9.5 oz. salted anchovies, rinsed and deboned

2 cardoons, with the fibers removed

2 yellow peppers

6 Jerusalem artichokes

2 roasted beets

6 boiled potatoes

6 carrots

1 Savoy cabbage

1 cauliflower

Carefully peel the cloves of garlic, and remove the green center piece, if you are using garlic that is not very fresh. Put the garlic in a saucepan, and add the milk. Cook on low heat for an hour. Drain off the milk, and crush the garlic with a fork. Place the garlic in an earthenware pot; then add the anchovies and olive oil. Heat and stir until the ingredients become a homogeneous cream. The sauce is now ready to be served. In Piedmont, most families have little earthenware dishes that have candles underneath. What is important is to keep the sauce warm at the table.

Cut the vegetables into pieces, and place on serving platters. You can use any raw or cooked vegetables that you like. Traditionally, cardoons and peppers were the only vegetables used in this dish. Place the warm sauce, and vegetables on table. People should serve themselves and dip the vegetables into the *bagna caoda*.

La Piazza—City, Public Space, and Sociability

I walked out into the square—*la piazza*. I was standing in the middle of an empty space framed by high- and low-rise buildings. I could feel the void in the cityscape around me. Are there really any empty spaces in the city? I began to notice movement and the sound of metal wheels grinding against paving stones reached my ears from the carts being hauled out from the surrounding streets. The clatter of metal rang out in the square as the silent workers began to construct the market stalls. Bundled up in their winter coats, these burly men barely noticed me watching. The piazza was changing shape before my eyes, the market taking form—barren gray tracts of stone were now a maze full of life.

When I first started my fieldwork at Porta Palazzo, I thought the future was anything but bright for traditional forms of retailing such as open-air markets. I saw historic institutions failing to keep up with the times and respond to changes in urban life—the slowness of the market seemed to be overwhelmed by a new everyday speediness. Increased competition from supermarkets and hard discount stores as well as changing consumer perceptions and hygiene standards toward food markets are some of the main reasons for this decline. The changing nature of work and leisure time in Italy and the lack of renewal of infrastructure on the part of cities were also taking their toll. Decisions made about the development and the future of markets in Turin were largely dependent on the municipal administration. With so many parties involved and so many vested interests, the decision-making process for making changes to markets was not going to be easy. I personally witnessed the conflicts and negotiations that preceded the renovations at Porta Palazzo, which showed me the difficulties of civic processes when it came to provisioning the city and deciding on the use of public space. The story of Porta Palazzo is remarkable considering that markets are not generally profit-making institutions for cities. Looking beyond practical economics, the City of Turin decided to make an investment in markets because of their social, cultural, and historical importance.

As I finish writing this book, I have a new optimism that Turin is setting an example for other Italian and European cities of how to revitalize urban marketplaces. Statistics for Italy indicate that markets still capture an important portion of food provisioning, despite the strong presence of supermarkets. According to researchers at Bocconi University, ambulant markets on public land represent 17 percent of all Italian retail business. After a decline that lasted until 1999, markets in Italy are now growing at a slow and steady pace (Premazzi and Colaprice 2005). However, there are still few statistical data about open-air markets; researchers studying food distribution have mainly focused on supermarkets. The lack of data made my qualitative research seem more pressing. What was really going on beyond the numbers at markets? After over ten years spent in and around markets, I was convinced that their success was based on something more than what statistical or demographic studies could tell me.

Porta Palazzo may not be the typical neighborhood market, but it represents the major trends that I noticed on my frequent visits to smaller markets in Turin and occasional outings to markets throughout Italy. First of all, it is evident that market shoppers in Italy are ageing. Pensioners shop frequently at markets because of low prices; they also come for the social aspect of the market, because they have an abundance of free time, and out of convenience (if they live in neighboring areas). Second, immigrants are important new clients at the market and have certainly helped maintain the vitality of these institutions. Both socially and economically, the market is central to integrating immigrants into mainstream Italian society. Third, markets in Italy also tend to be frequented more on Saturday (they are not normally held on Sunday). These are big changes that I have seen at markets in Italy in the past ten years. Many of them bode well for the future of markets.

However, if someone asks market vendors about the current state of markets, they will usually tell the person that business has dropped off and that it was much better in the past. Although these comments often reflect immediate economic crises (layoffs at local factories and inflation after the introduction of the euro, to name a few), they do not take into account some of the positive trends (immigrants as new clients, the low price of whole-sale goods due to industrial production). The future may not be that grim, with the recent expansion of this form of retailing and new investment in infrastructure by some cities. In addition, new niche markets for local and organic food bode well for markets. Early in the twenty-first century in Europe, markets are more pertinent than ever, as Europeans realize the risk of losing touch with local food production and culture. They also understand that markets are important public institutions that offer a unique space for social life.

In the years I spent at the Porta Palazzo market, I observed that the market is a series of intimate daily interactions between humans and built spaces that facilitate social relations. These interactions bring meaning to places and daily life. The empty square is just a shadow of itself without the market. It is impossible to imagine Porta Palazzo and the vast spaces of Piazza della Repubblica without the market. This is perhaps at the crux of my fascination with markets: what is a city without human activity and interaction? What happens when there are no public spaces to facilitate exchanges? What is life like without chance meetings between neighbors and strangers? From the moment I first set foot in a European market to the time when I said my goodbyes at Porta Palazzo, I could not stop thinking about the social and cultural importance of markets.

The Markets as a Social Space

The square and the street are urban spaces that can have many functions. They are spaces waiting for city-dwellers to give them meaning through everyday uses and acts of sociability. A market can be the showcase of a neighborhood and even an attraction that draws people from outside the area. It is undeniable that markets promote social interaction and animate neighborhoods.

Studies of markets that focus on ethnographic perspectives are still needed because they illuminate the changing attitudes toward the use of public spaces in urban settings. Where else in the city can people talk to complete strangers and neighbors, discuss their health and political concerns, and exchange a recipe? Many small towns in Italy have an area known as the *passeggiata*, where the town's people walk up and down along a boulevard or park socializing. There are many similarities between the *passeggiata* and the market. Giovanna Del Negro calls this a "ritualized performance" of the town's culture, which is essential for social cohesion (2004: 3). The *passeggiata*, like the market, transforms a public place into a social space. Porta Palazzo, like the promenade in Del Negro's fictitious town of Sasso, is a place where people negotiate their changing society, where gender roles are challenged, the economy is discussed and politics are sometimes marched down the street in a protest. One difference is that the people who socialize during the *passeggiata* generally know each other or have a social connection. This practice of public sociability and display generally only occurs in small towns; the *passeggiata* generally does not happen in larger cities in Italy. Scale remains a problem. Certainly, there are other forms of social life in public places in cities: having a coffee or a drink in a bar with a patio, spending time in a park, or attending a performance in a square. Many of these activities are related to consumption in one form or another, and they do not necessarily require people to socialize with one another. Many cities plan events that encourage social and cultural exchanges; however, it is more difficult to engineer places and activities that invite spontaneous social interactions.

Public space has become highly controlled and contested, and this has not helped social life in cities: loitering in a square or hanging out on street corners or at building entrances is often associated with delinquency and disorder. Public gatherings are frequently monitored. Social gatherings tend to be increasingly associated with private spaces and consumption (private homes, bars, cafés, and malls). In particular, Turin is known as a city where private and social life happens behind closed doors.

Markets are one of the few places in the public sphere that are conducive to sociability. Public parks are perhaps the only other public spaces set aside for social activities, yet their use is usually relegated to leisure time (Low 2000). In many northern Italian cities, markets are the last vestiges of lively public spaces that are now dwindling. The impact of the automobile also needs to be considered here: many public spaces have been turned into parking lots, and shopping malls in peripheral areas often eclipse markets as preferred venues for shopping. This is a trend that Turin has attempted to counter by turning one of the largest squares, Piazza San Carlo, and other important thoroughfares into pedestrian areas. Nonetheless, the automobile has certainly sped up everyday life and changed our conceptions of distance and space. This is important to note in a city like Turin where automobiles have not only been central to the economy but also to the actual development of the city with a major emphasis placed on car-friendly urban planning.

If the automobile is an individualizing and antisocial element in the city, the market is its opposite—people are thrown together in a shared space, rather than compartmentalized. This book has tried to look at the socializing nature of the market. This is particularly important for a city like Turin where the automobile rules and where social life has largely been relegated to private spaces. For many years, the result was a degradation of public spaces and a lack of civic pride. In the past ten years, the people of Turin and the municipality have made giant steps in revitalizing the city. Porta Palazzo is a reflection of these efforts.

The Persistence of Porta Palazzo

The market may seem like an outdated institution that should have been done away with long ago; it can even be considered a form of resistance to modernity. The market persists because many of the people involved are stuck in their ways—the market is an integral part of their lives. At Porta Palazzo, it is evident, especially during the week, that the majority of clients are elderly. For this generation, the market has always been the most obvious way to do the daily shopping and an excellent way to get the most reasonably priced and freshest produce. The market also offers an important social moment for these shoppers. Many elderly people in Italian cities lead very solitary lives if they do not live with their extended family. Elderly people living on their own are increasingly becoming the norm in Italy. It may sound odd, but the elderly are the lifeblood of markets like Porta Palazzo. In return, the market offers reasonably priced food and community to these people who hold fast to their habit of shopping in the market. In the extreme, as illustrated in Chapter 4, gleaning at the market offers a free supply of food that can be critical for food-insecure pensioners living in and around the market area. This is one of the important unofficial functions of the market.

Another group that keeps the market going are the local farmers. Pietro, Paolo, Enzo, and Roberto may face new challenges and a struggle to stay at the market, but they feel it is worth the effort. Pietro continually told me about the autonomy that the market afforded him: he is his own boss and can decide his own price. Sure, if he sold his produce at the wholesale market, he would not have to make the long drive into the city and back to the farm several days a week. He would have more time to work on the farm, but he told me he would also miss the social life. Going to the market is a routine he has been following from when he was a child accompanying his father to the Porta Palazzo market. Porta Palazzo is part of Pietro and his farm—he cannot imagine having it any other way.

There is another group of people who naturally gravitate to the market out of habit: immigrants. This group of newcomers has breathed a second life into Porta Palazzo. The market offers reasonably priced food, work, community, and familiarity. Mustafa and Giorgio were drawn to the market when they arrived in Turin, and it has become their subsistence in every way. Without immigrants from Romania, China, Morocco, and Nigeria, the market would not be as vibrant or vital. For most immigrants, the market is the most familiar and advantageous way to do the shopping. Although they are far from home, immigrants stick with what they know, even if the form might be slightly different. Like the Italians who came from the south before them, Turin's recent immigrants are struggling to make a place for themselves at the market. Slowly, they are making it their home and the center of their communities. It is hard to imagine Porta

Palazzo without immigrants, and it will surely remain a central place for new arrivals to the city.

Emergent Market Culture

Some of the people who keep the market going may be set in their ways, but the market also persists thanks to change. The immigrants have brought new products, new ways, and new problems with them to the market. New foodstuffs and ethnic shops have caught the attention of the locals; Italians are curious to know the Other. Ethnogastronomic tours of the market set Porta Palazzo in an exotic new light while also playing a role in the appropriation of culture. At the same time, these initiatives have helped change the way that the Torinese consider the market: immigrants are not criminals but people with rich cultures that add something to the city. Developing tourism is a fine balancing act because it often risks dominating the character of a market by turning it into a consumable object that becomes just a shell of local culture. This has not been the case with Porta Palazzo, and it may be due simply to scale or the constant influx of outsiders who invest themselves in the market as vendors, shoppers, and visitors. Porta Palazzo persists as a popular market that serves the city and swallows up the tourists without much notice. Fortunately, recent renovations have improved the appearance of the market square without altering its everyday workings.

The area around the market has been transformed by urban renewal projects, and some neighborhoods, like the Quadrilatero Romano, have felt the impact of gentrification. Housing prices have risen, and quaint cafés have popped up in quiet squares and along pedestrian-only streets. The market is a meeting point for the different areas around Piazza della Repubblica, both gentrified and downtrodden, but it is also a point of conflict. Low-income residents are thankful that the market offers food at reasonable prices. Artists, students, and hipsters love the market, its colors, liveliness, and fresh food. The new middle-class residents, however, often complain that the market is dirty and disorderly. They see it as a haven for petty crime. The day-to-day life around the market is a negotiation between diverse residents, market-goers, and vendors. Encounters in the market square vary from hostile and criminal to amicable and social. Porta Palazzo market represents all walks of life, and the commercial activities of the square mediate some of the social tension that is born out of cultural differences. The market has changed a great deal, but there is something essentially the same about the social and commercial activities that have always taken place there.

Porta Palazzo Market and Urban Renewal

The last time I visited the Gate office, in 2009, I was surprised to find a rather discouraged group and negative energy in the air. It did not seem that the people currently working there could see their success; they just seemed frustrated by the constant resistance they encountered when they tried to implement programs. Luca Cianfriglia, the director, told me it was frustrating and difficult trying to listen to all the people who work, shop, and manage the market because each group is fractured and has its own agenda—there is no unified voice. The people involved in the daily activities of the market have little desire to collaborate and cooperate. They do not have much vision beyond the immediate future—an almost insurmountable roadblock when it comes to implementing changes and trying to renovate a market.

Despite all the difficulties they encountered, the Gate and the City of Turin carried out some very important physical improvements to the market that make shopping and working a better experience. As the ethnographic snapshots in this book attest, these changes were not made without meeting great resistance and persevering despite a lack of consensus. Everyone complained before the renovations started and moaned even more once they started; however, now nearly everyone seems very happy with the results. The people of Turin are proud of Porta Palazzo, which certainly was not the case in 2001 when I started my research and the area was run down and in need of repair. The recent renovations have raised the morale and the status of the market. The City of Turin has shown a major commitment to Porta Palazzo and has dedicated funds to turning the area around from an urban slum to a vibrant part of the downtown core. With all the different interests that kept colliding during the planning process, at times it seemed as if the project would never get off the ground—consensus building largely failed. I think this is the reason the employees of the Gate felt frustrated and were unable to realize that their work had paid off in many visible ways.

I visited the market infrequently during the renovation, but when I returned in 2009 after the work had been completed, I was astounded by the transformation that had taken place. It was three years after Turin had hosted the Olympics, and the feeling of prosperity and renewal could still be felt at the market.

Room for Change

The case of the Porta Palazzo and its transformation is an important example for European cities that want to improve their markets and invest in their social and cultural vibrancy. It is a good sign that many municipalities are starting to see the positive aspect of urban market places and the benefits that they bring to city life. From when I started my research in 2001, I have noticed that there is a new openness to supporting markets. Certainly, most administrators see markets as beneficial to the local economy because they draw in potential customers and create an atmosphere that encourages commercial exchanges in fixed and ambulant businesses. For this reason, markets should be kept at the heart of neighborhoods rather than marginalized or relocated to periphery areas (shopping center parking lots, vacant lots, and city blocks). In some communities, markets have been pushed out of the center of the city because of the cost and effort of closing off streets and cleaning up after the market closes. Some cities have cited traffic issues and lack of parking as reasons for moving markets to peripheral areas. These communities are missing out on the positive benefits of open-air markets, while severely limiting food access in the city center. Porta Palazzo is a case in point that shows how a market can be used to revitalize a neighborhood.

There are some other practical aspects that market organizers should consider, such as the fact that people's use of time has changed, especially for women who have traditionally been in charge of family provisioning. Most people who work outside the home can no longer do their shopping, or socializing, during market hours (normally from 8 a.m. to 1 p.m.), and this is the biggest cause for the decline in business at markets. For this reason, municipalities need to reconsider the logic behind present market hours and perhaps extend or change market hours to coincide with most people's use of time. This is something that has not been done in Turin. On one hand, many of the vendors at Porta Palazzo who resell produce they buy at the wholesale market have complained about this type of proposal—they like their hours just as they are. On the other hand, the farmers at the *mercato dei contadini* whom I talked to about the idea of an evening market thought it was great. They could work in their fields all day and then come to market; in that way, they would not lose a day of work on the farm. Many people would prefer to shop at markets, but their daily work schedule does not permit them to do so. Resistance to change will always be part of urban planning and renovation, but markets are flexible places that have adapted through the centuries to meet the provisioning needs of the city.

The risk remains that markets will become purely destinations for weekend leisure. What directions can markets take to survive and flourish while staying true to their regional character? One of the reasons tourists like markets is that they represent diversity and local character. However, as more tourists flood markets, local vendors and products are usually harder and harder to find. Do markets risk Disneyfication as they become leisure sites? If this occurs, they may lose their true function and meaning as sites of everyday sociability and provisioning. Here we are talking about a type of sociability that is associated with the mundane daily activity of grocery shopping and less with spectacle. Will governments and local interest groups think to protect something as seemingly pedestrian as grocery shopping? What kind of protection can be given to such complex sites? This is a double-edged question because, like all living things, markets must change and adapt in time. Preservation must not mean the halting of organic processes of change. Markets that are purely associated with free time and leisure risk becoming outdoor malls that play on nostalgia for a lost and imagined past (Bressière 1998; Stewart 1988). These types of markets are generally accessible only to affluent individuals, rather than being popular places where everyone can afford to shop and people from all walks of life will come to socialize. Market administrators can play an important role in helping markets maintain their integrity and social usefulness.

Municipalities, the custodians of markets, must play an active role in encouraging markets, and administrators must learn to see them as essential places for sociability in the urban fabric, not only as points of food distribution (as was often the case in the past) or tourist attractions. Perhaps the best way to see markets is as integral, living heritage sites. Unlike museums and monuments, markets are in constant change and are central to the livelihoods of thousands of people in a city and the surrounding countryside. Many attempts to modernize markets have resulted in irreparable damage that takes away from the uniqueness that characterizes each market; site-sensitive interventions need to be carried out to bring markets up to European Union standards for hygiene and safety (Black 2004). Like good building restoration, the best of the original is brought forward, while modern improvements are in keeping with the site or are undetectable.

The people of Turin are beginning to return to Porta Palazzo and their neighborhood markets and are rediscovering the pleasures of this kind of shopping, from the social experience to the delicious food that they can find. This revival is largely due to the Torinese realizing that they want a place to shop besides the supermarket. The revitalization of the city as whole is reflected in the state of its markets. From the turnaround of the failing local industrial economy in the 1980s and 1990s to the reinvention of Turin as the host city for the 2006 Winter Olympics, the Porta Palazzo market has mirrored this urban decline and renewal. Work still needs to be done, and every day poses new challenges for the markets of Turin, but Porta Palazzo offers a fascinating case study that demonstrates the importance and resilience of open-air markets in Europe.

Although it is easier to focus on the big picture of the market as an institution, the complexity, personalities, and passions of the people who participate make markets truly extraordinary places. Through the people and their daily interactions, the marketplace takes on life and meaning. The time I spent in markets taught me that these are not waning sites of tradition and history; they are dynamic places of lively sociability that resist homogenization and remain open to the general public. Markets have always embraced globalization as a force that creates diversity and encourages social, economic, and cultural exchanges across borders and barriers, making them extremely timely institutions that have the potential to bring people together and help create community.

NOTES

Introduction: Going to Market

1. Food and Agriculture Organization (FAO) statistics show that the average Italian has increased his or her caloric intake by 30 percent in the past fifty years. http://www.fao.org/newsroom/en/news/2008/1000871/index.html, accessed May 6, 2011.

2. I use the term "foodscape" to talk about the outlook where people can buy or produce food. In this sense, the idea of foodscape is tied to food access.

3. It should be noted that recently there have been a number of studies by anthropologists on farmers' markets in the United States. Cf. Markowitz 2010; Robinson and Hartenfeld 2007. There is still little published work on markets in Western Europe.

4. "Chilometro zero" (zero kilometers) is ironically adopted from the Italian car industry. New cars sold at a special discounted price once they are licensed are called "chilometro zero" cars.

Chapter 1. The Market as a Field

1. All names are pseudonyms except for those of public figures.

2. Due to the setting of the market, I asked for verbal consent from participants. I felt that presenting people with written consent forms would have immediately alienated me and put me on the side of public officials and authorities. There was a great deal of diffidence toward these figures, and I was eager to build rapport while applying ethical research practices. Studying at an Italian university allowed me this choice.

3. In particular, professional photographer Michele D'Ottavio did a series of photos of the Porta Palazzo market, and a group of filmmakers associated with the production group Kinoetika produced a number of documentary films focused on the market, including *Quattro canti del mercato* (2006) and *Ricette e ritratti* (2005).

Chapter 2. The Evolution of a Market

1. Moving slaughterhouses out of cities was quite common in nineteenth-century Europe. Concerns for hygiene and the desire to have a clean, modern city center were the main motivations (cf. Lee 2008).

2. Filippo Juvarra (1678–1736) played an important role in transforming Turin into one of the Baroque capitals of Europe. He is famous for other important structures in and around Turin: Palazzina Stupinigi, Basilica di Superga, and the façade and ceremonial staircase of Palazzo Madama in the heart of Turin.

3. Plan général d'embellissement pour la Ville de Turin, March 30, 1852, Archivio Storico della Citta di Torino (Tipi e disegni, role 13B).

4. In 2008, during the world food crisis, there were food riots in Haiti, India, Senegal, and Uzbekistan, among other countries.

5. One of the main reasons for the renovation of the monumental Halles de Paris in the mid-nineteenth century and its final destruction in 1969 was that the market bred pestilence and was considered a threat to public health (Thompson 1997)

6. It is important to remember that until the second half of the nineteenth century Italian cuisine was still very regional and extremely heterogeneous (cf. Helstosky 2004).

7. *Meridionali* is a pejorative term used by northern Italians about southern Italians. It makes direct reference to geographic origin and has historically been used in northern Italy as a term of discrimination and exclusion.

8. Official statistics showed that 9.4 percent of the population of Turin were foreign migrants in 2006. For Circonscrizione 7, the census area in which Porta Palazzo is located, 15.2 percent of the population were foreigners (Rava 2007).

Chapter 3. A Neighborhood, a Square, and a Market

1. Comune di Torino 2007.

2. Massimiliano Fuksas did not like the idea of putting his name on a shopping mall, and this is why the structure is now officially called the Centro Palatino. It would seem that the worlds of art and commerce collided in that end on this project. Fuksas was not present at the official inauguration on March 25, 2011. See "Porta Palazzo, dopo 13 anni di lavoro Centro Palatino è realtà," *Torino Today*, http://www.torinotoday.it/cronaca/centro-palatino-nuovo-mercato-coperto-fuksas-porta-palazzo.html, accessed May 26, 2011.

3. See http://www.centropalatino.it/, accessed May 26, 2011, for more information.

4. Snow was placed in the *ghiacciaie* during the winter until ice blocks were formed. These cool, underground cellars would help keep produce through the hot spring and summer months. There are still some of these wonderful storage spaces left (although snow is no longer used), but one has to know where to look around the streets adjacent to the market to find them. These underground areas are also part of Porta Palazzo's complexity. They form a secret geography that only reveals itself to those who have an intimate knowledge of the area.

5. The Gate offices were moved in May 2011 to a nearby location on the Piazza della Repubblica.

6. Auchan is a large French supermarket chain that can be found throughout Italy.

7. Art. 10 Reg. CE 2081/92 FESR.

8. TAR Piemonte, Tribunale Amministrativo Regionale, is the court responsible for hearing complaints against administrative bodies and projects in the region of Piemonte.

9. Renovations to the square were required to conform with EU regulations for food vending. The historic paving stones no longer met the hygiene code because health authorities found they were too difficult to clean and the uneven, slippery surface posed safety issues for those using the square.

10. Many people in Italy believe that the evil eye is a look that can be cast by an envious neighbor or onlooker that will bring about injury or bad luck. Anthropologists have given a great deal of attention to the study of the evil eye in Mediterranean cultures. Many, in particular Michael Herzfeld, have questioned whether the evil eye is a pan-Mediterranean phenomenon. Herzfeld 1984 argues the need to consider the unique linguistic and culture context of the evil eye.

11. The Központi Vásárcsarnok (Budapest), Borough Market (London), and La Boqueria (Barcelona) were also among the founding members of the European Association of Markets.

Chapter 4. *Fare la spesa*: Shopping, Morality, and Anxiety at the Market

1. In Turin, most people eat lunch between 1 and 3 p.m. It was common to return home for lunch, but this is now changing as Italians work farther from home and working hours in general are changing.

2. This quote is not verbatim but from notes written shortly after this conversation, Fieldnotes March 27, 2003.

3. There are a number of unions and associations that most vendors belong to. These include FIVA (Federazione italiana venditori aree pubbliche), ANVA

(Associazione nazionale venditori ambulanti), and Coldiretti (Federazione colti-vatori diretti). Rigid mentalities refers to the desire to maintain a status quo and the feeling that, if something has always been a certain way, there is no need for it to change. A lack of imagination and of a positive outlook that change can help improve the current situation was common among my informants at Porta Pala-zzo. While living in Lyon, France, I saw that a very successful night market had been established in front of one of the main commuter train stations. Nothing of this sort had ever been tried in Turin.

4. Catholic holidays and observances still rule daily life in Italy. More and more shops are beginning to have hours on Sundays in Turin, but many Torinese are firmly against this trend. Sunday is not considered a market day.

5. According to the ISTAT data analyzed by Saraceno, "in 1995, 56 percent of 25-to-29-year-olds lived in their parents' home, compared to the 31 percent EU average" (49).

6. *Vitel tonné* is a Piedmontese dish made from thin slices of roast veal smoth-ered in a creamy tuna sauce.

7. Food security was defined by WHO and the World Food Summit in 1996 as that "when all people at all times have access to sufficient, safe, nutritious food to maintain a healthy and active life," http://www.who.int/trade/glossary/story028/en, accessed July 16, 2011.

8. Freegans are a group of people attempting to boycott the capitalist eco-nomic system through a number of strategies such as waste reclamation; cf. Fla-nagan 2003.

9. This recipe comes from Maria Dotta, in Gambera (1992).

10. *Bagna caoda* is a bath of anchovies, garlic, and oil that is usually served in a communal dish and kept warm over a flame. Diners dip raw vegetables into the warm bath. See recipe in Chapter 7.

Chapter 5. Il Ventre di Torino: Migration and Food

1. Osservatorio Interistituzionale sugli stranieri in provincia di Torino, 2007, http://www.comune.torino.it/statistica/osservatorio/stranieri/2007/, accessed Au-gust 14, 2010.

2. Other anthropologists have experienced similar feelings of affinity with their participants as outsiders. Two of the most famous examples include Victor Turner and Muchona (Turner 1967) and Marcel Griaule and Ogotemmeli (Griaule 1948).

3. "La città e la crisi del Golfo," *La Stampa*, March 27, 2003, 49, http://archivio.

lastampa.it/LaStampaArchivio/main/History/tmpl_viewObj.jsp?objid=4026557, accessed July 10, 2010.

4. *Harira* usually includes chicken, chickpeas, and tomato, but each cook creates her own recipe by adding ingredients such as egg, cumin, rice, saffron, ginger, and coriander. The variations are endless. The idea of measuring out the soup from a communal pot has a great deal of social importance and plays a part in creating community through the sharing of food.

5. Based on Edgar Feige's earlier work (1990), Portes and Haller define informal economy was actions that "bypass the costs, and are excluded from the protection of, laws and administrative rules" (2005: 405). The mint and other ambulant vendors who occupy the in-between spaces at Porta Palazzo fall into this category.

6. The City of Turin clearly defines the process and regulations that govern the granting of licenses to sell at markets and in other public venues in art. 5, comma 2, del D.L. vol. 114/98, which makes reference to the Parliamentary act D.G.R. 2 aprile 2001, n. 32–2642.

7. This same concept of female identity and pride through food is expressed through the preparation of tamales in Mexico. Cf. Pilcher 1998.

Chapter 6. Kumalé: Ethnogastronomic Tourism

1. This leads us to the highly charged debate about authenticity, unfortunately not within the scope of this chapter. For more on authenticity, see Abarca 2004. For more on Chinese restaurants and cultural authenticity, see Lee and Fin 2005.

2. Here I have drawn on Franco La Cecla's idea of "mappa mentale": "E il gioco del 'punto di vista' spaziale il cui organo è tutto il corpo in movimento, il corpo individuale e sociale. La mappa mentale di un insediamento è una esperienza intersoggettiva" (1993: 34). It would be interesting to superimpose Dominic Hislop's mental maps created by migrants with the mental maps of Turin created by Torinese who had participated in Castellani's "Turisti per Casa."

3. "Partiamo da ciò che più riesce a mettere allo stesso tavolo razze e persone diverse: il cibo."

4. "Un prodotto 'etnico' non è solo una merce ma la combinazione di questa con un'idea di cultura che viene venduta assieme."

5. For more on the ethnic division of labor in restaurants, see Zukin 1995.

6. Based on 2008 ISTAT statistics, the number of foreigners in Italy has more than tripled since 1991. Although many remain uncounted, there are 3,891,295 foreigners living in Italy, making up 6.5 percent of the population,

http://www.repubblica.it/2009/02/sezioni/cronaca/istat-popolazione/istat-popo-lazione/istat-popolazione.html, accessed July 14, 2010.

7. "Il mercato di Porta Palazzo, da sempre luogo d=incontro e consumo dei 'nuovi torinesi', ha registrato negli ultimi anni la nascita ed il moltiplicarsi di molte nuove attività commerciali e culturali gestite in prima persona di nazionalità ed etnie diverse. La ricchezza e la varietà di uomini, culture e merci oggi presenti nel più grande mercato della nostra città, costituisce un autentico patrimonio ancora tutto da esplorare che ci permette de viaggiare tra le culture che abbiamo sotto casa, in modo nuovo e inedito tra usi, prodotti e tradizioni di quelle terre e genti lontane, che non ci sono mai stati così vicine."

Chapter 7. *Nostrano*: The Farmers' Market, Local Food, and Place

1. Piemontese and Torinese are similar dialects and have strong linguistic connections to both French and Italian. For more information, see http://www.piemont.org/.

2. A 2003 study carried out by Euromarket for the Province of Torino indicated that 40 percent of rural inhabitants could speak Piemontese proficiently and another 36 percent could not speak but claimed to understand the dialect. The majority of respondents in both groups were over age fifty, http://www.gruppi.consiglioregionale.piemonte.it/mistoriformisti/piemontese.htm.

3. Legge 3 maggio 1982, n. 203.

4. Cf. IRES 2001.

5. Federal law D. LGS. N. 306/02 makes it obligatory for all retailers to indicate clearly the type, origin, quality category, and price of the produce being sold.

6. Although Italy is one of the largest producers of organic products in Europe, most of these goods are exported to countries such as Germany, Austria, and Great Britain. Organic food is still considered a niche market product in Italy (Berardini et al. 2004).

7. For more on the cultural politics and economics of food certifications in Italy, see Leitch's excellent article on lardo di Colonnata that demonstrates some of the fierce local battles over "traditional" foods (2000). For a comparative study, see also Bérard and Marchenay (2004) for more on the politics of food certifications in France.

8. Ashley et al. 2004b: 106; Humphrey 1998.

9. According to the Istituto Nazionale di Economia Agraria (INEA) (2003), agricultural business in northwest Italy decreased by 39.5 percent in 2000, while the average area cultivated increased, meaning that small-scale farming gave way to larger production.

10. Coldiretti 2004.

11. Slow Food began a foundation for biodiversity to safeguard culinary traditions and biodiversity throughout the world. Slow Food does this by encouraging the growing and use of "heritage" varieties of plant and animals.

12. http://www.mercatidellaterra.com/, accessed August 11, 2008.

BIBLIOGRAPHY

Abarca, M. (2004). Authentic or not, it's original. *Food and Foodways* 12: 1–25.

———. (2006). *Voices in the kitchen: Views of food and the world from working-class Mexican and Mexican American women*. College Station: Texas A & M University Press.

Abramson, J. (2007). *Food culture in France*. Westport, Conn.: Greenwood Press.

Aghatise, E. (2004). Trafficking for prostitution in Italy: Possible effects of government proposals for legislation of brothels. *Violence Against Women* 10, 10: 1126–55.

Aime, M. (2002). *La casa di nessuno: I mercati in Africa occidentale*. Torino: Bollati Boringhieri.

———. (2004). *Eccessi di culture*. Torino: Giulio Einaudi.

Allasino, E. and L. Bulsei. (1994) *Le Chiavi della città: Politiche per gli immigrati a Torino e Lione*. Turin: IRES.

Amit, V. (1999). *Constructing the field: Ethnographic fieldwork in the contemporary world*. New York: Routledge.

Anderson, B. (1983). *Imagined communities: Reflections on the origin and spread of nationalism*. London: Verso.

Angli, P. (2004). The market and the unity of territory and city. In J. Angli et al., *Mercados del Mediterráneo*. Barcelona: IEMED & Lunwerg.

Appadurai, A., ed. (1986). *The social life of things: Commodities in cultural perspective*. Cambridge: Cambridge University Press.

———. (1988). How to make a national cuisine: Cookbooks in contemporary India. *Comparative Studies in Society and History* 30, 1: 3–24.

———. (1996). *Modernity at large: Cultural dimensions of globalization*. Public Worlds 1. Minneapolis: University of Minnesota Press.

———. (2006). *Fear of small numbers: An essay on the geography of anger*. Durham, N.C.: Duke University Press.

Ashley, B., J. Hollows, S. Jones, and B. Taylor, eds. (2004a). *Food and cultural studies*. Studies in Consumption and Markets. London: Routledge.

———. (2004b). Shopping for food. In Ashley et al., eds., *Food and cultural studies*. London: Routledge. 105–22.

Atlas, M. (2002). Femminielli of Naples: Contemporary prostitutes neither male nor female, between family, the Catholic Church and gay and lesbian politics. Presented at Association for the Study of Modern Italy Annual Conference, London. November.

Augé, M. (1986). *Un ethnologue dans le métro*. Paris: Hachette.

———. (1995). *Non-places: Introduction to an anthropology of supermodernity*. Trans. J. Howe. London: Verso.

Aurier, P., F. Fort, and L. Sirieix. (2005). Exploring terroir product meanings for the consumer. *Anthropology of Food* 4 (May). http://aof.revues.org/document187.html, accessed August 9, 2008.

Avakian, A. V., ed. (2005). *Through the kitchen window: Women explore the meaning of food and cooking*. New York: Berg.

Bacaria, J. (2004). The machinery of markets. In Angli et al., *Mercados del Mediterráneo*. Barcelona: IEMED & Lunwerg. 214–19.

Bacchiddu, G. (2004). Stepping between different worlds: Reflections before, during and after fieldwork. *Matters Journal* 6, 2. http://www.anthropologymatters.com/index.php?journal=anth_mattersandpage=articleandop=viewandpath[]=95, accessed May 28, 2011.

Back, L. (1993). Gender participation: Masculinity and fieldwork in a south London adolescent community. In D. Bell, P. Caplan, and W. J. Karim, eds., *Gendered fields: Women, men and ethnography*. London: Routledge: 215–33.

Bairati, P., P. Melograni, and L. Scaraffia. (1988). *La famiglia italiana dall'ottocento ad oggi*. Storia e società. Roma: Laterza.

Bakhtin, M. M. (1984). *Rabelais and his world*. Trans. H. Iswolsky. Bloomington: Indiana University Press.

Baldwin, P. (1990). *The politics of social solidarity: Class bases of the European welfare state, 1875–1975*. Cambridge: Cambridge University Press.

Barndt, D. (2007). *Tangled routes: Women, work and globalization on the tomato trail*. 2nd ed. Lanham, Md.: Rowman and Littlefield.

Barrett, G. A., T. Jones, and D. McEvoy. (2001). Socio-economic and policy dimensions of the mixed embeddedness of ethnic minority business in Britain. *Journal of Ethnic and Migration Studies* 27, 2: 241–58.

Barthes, R. (1957). *Mythologies*. Paris: Seuil.

Barzini, L. (1964). *The Italians*. New York: Penguin.

Bassett, T. S., C. Blanc-Pamard, and J. Boutrais. (2001). Constructing locality: The terroir in West Africa. *Africa: The Journal of the International African Institute* 77, 1: 104–29.

Bates, T. M. (1997). *Race, self-employment, and upward mobility: An illusive American dream*. Baltimore: Johns Hopkins University Press.

Baudrillard, J. (1981). *For a critique of the political economy of the sign*. St. Louis: Telos.

Bauman, R. and C. L. Briggs. (1990). Poetics and performance as critical perspectives on language and social life. *Annual Review of Anthropology* 19: 59–88.

Beardsworth, A. and T. Keil. (1997). *Sociology on the menu: An invitation to the study of food and society*. London: Routledge.

Belasco, W. J. (1989). *Appetite for change: How the counterculture took on the food industry, 1966–1988*. New York: Pantheon.

Belasco, W. J. and P. Scranton. (2002). *Food nations: Selling taste in consumer societies*. New York: Routledge.

Bell, D. (1993). Introduction: the context. In P. Caplan, W.-J. Karim, and D. Bell, eds., *Gendered field: Women, men and ethnography*. London: Routledge. 1–18.

———. (1997). *Consuming geographies: We are where we eat*. London: Routledge.

Belmonte, T. (1979). *The broken fountain*. New York: Columbia University Press.

Benelli, E. and. R. Bassoli. (1998). Gli stili alimentari oggi. In A. Capatti, A. De Bernardi, and A. Varni, eds., *Storia d'Italia Annali 13. L'alimentazione*. Turin: Einaudi.

Benjamin, W. and R. Tiedemann. (1999). *The arcades project*. Cambridge, Mass.: Belknap Press of Harvard University Press.

Bentley, A. (1998). From culinary other to mainstream American: Meaning and uses of south-western cuisine. *Southern Folklore* 55, 3: 238–52.

Bérard, L. and P. Marchenay. (2004). *Les produits de terroir: Entre cultures et règlements*. Paris: CNRS.

Berardini, L, F. Ciannavei, D. Marino and F. Spagnuolo. (2004). Lo scenario dell'agricoltura biologica in Italia. Ministero Politiche Agricole e Forestali, working paper, http://www.inea.it/public/pdf_articoli/816.pdf, accessed August 26, 2011.

Beriss, D. and D. Sutton, eds. (2007). *The restaurant nook: Ethnographies of where we eat*. New York: Berg.

Bestor, T. C. (1999). Wholesale sushi: Culture and commodity in Tokyo's Tsukiji Market. In S. Low, ed., *Theorizing the city: The new urban anthropology reader*. New Brunswick, N.J.: Rutgers University Press. 201–42.

———. (2004). *Tsukiji: The fish market at the center of the world*. Berkeley: University of California Press.

Bevilacqua, P. (1980). *Le campagne del Mezzogiorno tra fascismo e dopoguerra: Il caso di Calabria*. Turin: Einaudi.

———, ed. (1989). *Storia dell'agricoltura italiana in età contemporanea*. Venezia: Marsilio.

Bianchi, C. (1975). *Porta Palazzo e il Balon: Storia e mito*. Turin: Piemonte in Bancarella.

Billari, F. et al. (2002). Household and union formation in Mediterranean families: Italy and Spain. In E. Klijzing and M. Corijn, eds., *Dynamics of fertility and partnership in Europe: Insight and lessons from comparative research*, vol. 2. New York: United Nations. 17–41.

Black, R. E. (2004). The Porta Palazzo farmers' market: Local food, regulations and changing traditions. *Anthropology of Food* 3. http://aof.revues.org/document157.html, accessed August 10, 2008.

———. (2007a). Eating garbage: Socially marginal provisioning practices." In J. MacClancy, J. Henry, and H. Macbeth, eds., *Consuming the inedible: Neglected dimensions of food choice*. Oxford: Berghahn. 141–50.

———. (2007b). Porta Palazzo: The market as a tourist attraction. In J. Tresserras and F. X. Medina, eds., *Patrimonio gastrónomico y turismo cultural en el Mediterráneo*. Barcelona: Ibertur, Universitat de Barcelona i Institut Europeu de la Mediterrània. 327–44.

Bogart, B. A. and W. L. Montell. (1981). *From memory to history: Using oral sources in local historical research*. Nashville, Tenn.: American Association for State and Local History.

Boneschi, M. (2002). *Voci di casa*. Milan: Frassinelli.

Bourdieu, P. (1972). *Esquisse d'une théorie de la pratique précédé de trois études d'ethnologie kabyle*. Geneva: Droz.

———. (1984). *Distinction: A social critique of the judgment of taste*. Cambridge, Mass.: Harvard University Press.

———. (1990). *The logic of practice*. Stanford, Calif.: Stanford University Press.

Braudel, F. (1981). *The structures of everyday life: Civilization and capitalism, 15th–18th century*. Vol. 1. New York: Harper and Row.

Bressière, J. (1998). Local development and heritage: Traditional food and cuisine as tourist attractions in rural areas. *Sociologia Ruralis* 38, 1: 21–34.

Bromley, R. D. F. (1998). Market-place trading and the transformation of retail space in the expanding Latin American city. *Urban Studies* 35, 8: 1311–33.

Brooks, D. (2000). *Bobos in paradise: The new upper class and how they got there*. New York: Simon & Schuster.

Brownlie, P., S. Hewer, and S. Home. (2005). Culinary tourism: An exploratory reading of contemporary representations of cooking. *Consumption, Markets and Culture* 8, 1: 7–26.

Burnett, J. (1989). *Plenty and want: A social history of food in England from 1815 to the present day*. London: Routledge.

Butler, J. (1990). *Gender trouble: Feminism and the subversion of identity*. New York: Routledge.

———. (1993). *Bodies that matter: On the discursive limits of "sex."* New York: Routledge.

Calabi, D. (2004). *The market and the city: Square, street and architecture in early modern Europe*. Aldershot: Ashgate.

Caldwell, M. (2002). The taste of nationalism: Food politics in postsocialist Moscow. *Ethnos* 67, 3: 295–319.

Capatti, A. and M. Montanari. (1999). *La cucina italiana: Storia di una cultura*. Rome: Laterza.

Caplan, P. (1997). *Food, health, and identity*. London: Routledge.

Castellanos, E. and S. Bergstresser. (2006). Food fights at the EU table: The gastronomic assertion of Italian distinctiveness. In T. Wilson, ed., *Food, drink and identity in Europe,*. European studies: An Interdisciplinary Series in European Culture, History and Politics 24. Amsterdam, Rodopi. 179–202.

Castellani, V. (2001). *Pappamondo: Uomini, migrazioni e pietanze*. Turin: The Gate.

———. (2004). Markets and the Mediterranean in the third millennium. In Angli et al., *Mercados del Mediterráneo*. Barcelona: IEMED and Lunwerg. 260–63.

Castronovo, V. and A. D'Orsi. (1987). *Torino*. Rome: Laterza.

Cavallaro, V. (2008). Il ruolo economico dei mercati ambulanti e il piano della Città di Torino. In D. Coppo, A. Osello et al., *Il disegno di luoghi e mercati a Torino*. Torino: Celid. 49–59.

Charef, M. (1999). *La circulation migratoire marocaine: Un pont entre deux rives*. Rabat: Sud Contact.

Chiva, I. (1980). Les places marchandes et le monde rural. *Études Rurales* 78–80: 7–14.

Christaller, W. (1968). *Die zentralen Orte in Süddeutschland: Eine ökonomisch-geographische Untersuchung über die Gesetzmässigkeit der Verbreitung und Entwicklung der Siedlungen mit städtischen Funktionen*, 3rd unveränderte Aufl ed. Darmstadt: Wissenschaftliche Buchgesellschaft.

Christaller, W. and C. W. Baskin. (1966). *Central places in southern Germany*. Englewood Cliffs, N.J: Prentice-Hall.

Chrzan, J. (2004). Slow food: What, why, and to where? *Food, Culture and Society* 7, 2: 117–32.

———. (2008). Applied anthropology, politics and small-town life. *Anthropology News* 49, 2: 22–23.

CICSENE (Centro Italiano di Collaborazione per lo sviluppo Edilizio delle Nazione emergenti). (1997). *Un mercato e i suoi rioni: Studio sull'area di Porta Palazzo Torino*. Cuneo: Stampa AGAM.

———. (2002). *Relazione sulle trasformazioni dell'area di Porta Palazzo, 1996–2001*. Cuneo: Stampa AGAM.

Cinotto, S. (2001). *Una famiglia che mangia insieme: Cibo ed etnicità nella comunità italoamericana di New York, 1920–1940*. Torino: Otto Editore.

Classen, C. and D. Howes. (1996). The dynamics and ethics of cross-cultural consumption. In D. Howes, ed., *Cross-cultural consumption: global markets, local realities*. London: Routledge. 178–94

Classen, C., D. Howes, and A. Synnott. (1994). *Aroma: The cultural history of smell*. London: Routledge.

Clément, P. (1999). *Foires et marchés d'Occitanie: De l'antiquité à l'an 2000*. Montpellier: Presses du Languedoc.

Clifford, J. (1997). *Routes: Travel and translation in the late twentieth century*. Cambridge, Mass.: Harvard University Press.

Clywik, H. (2001). Notes from the field: Emotions of place in the production and interpretation of text. *Social Research Methodology* 4, 3: 241–50.

Coldiretti. (2004). *Agricoltura, consumi alimentari ed evoluzione dei mercati: I nuovi scenari di riferimento*. VII Rapporto Nomisma. http://www.coldiretti.it/rapporto_nomisma/CAPITOLO%201%20definitivo.doc, accessed August 26, 2011.

Coleman, S., ed. (2009). *Multi-sited ethnography: Problems and possibilities in the translocation of research methods*. Oxford: Taylor and Francis.

Comaroff, J. (1996). The empire's old clothes: Refashioning the colonial subject. In D. Howes, ed., *Commodities and cultural borders*. New York: Routledge.

Comaroff, J. L. and J. Comaroff (1992). *Ethnography and the historical imagination*. Boulder, Colo.: Westview Press.

Contreras, J. (2004). Markets of the Mediterranean. In Angli et al., *Mercados del Mediterráneo*. Barcelona: IEMED & Lunwerg. 211–14.

Cook, I. and P. Crang. (1996). The world on a plate: Culinary culture, displacement and geographical knowledge. *Journal of Material Culture* 1: 131–53.

Coppo, D. et al. (2008). *Il disegno di luoghi e mercati a Torino*. Torino: Celid.

Corbeau, J.-P. and J.-P. Poulain. (2002). *Penser l'alimentation: Entre imaginaire et rationalité*. Toulouse: Privat.

Counihan, C. (1984). Bread as word: Food habits and social relations in modernizing Sardinia. *Anthropological Quarterly* 57, 2: 47–59.

———. (1999). *The anthropology of food and body: Gender, meaning and power*. New York: Routledge.

———. (2004). *Around the Tuscan table: Food, family and gender in twentieth-century Florence*. New York: Routledge.

Counihan, C. and P. Van Esterik, eds. (1997). *Food and culture: A reader*. New York; Routledge.

Crang, M. (1998). *Cultural geography*. New York: Routledge.

Crewe, L. and N. Gregson (1998). Tales of the unexpected: Exploring car boot sales as marginal spaces of contemporary consumption. *Transactions of the Institute of British Geography* 23, 1: 39–53.

Crosby, A. W. (1972). *The Columbian exchange: Biological and cultural consequences of 1492*. Westport, Conn: Greenwood.

Cusack, I. (2000). African cuisines: Recipes for nation building? *Journal of African Cultural Studies* 13, 2: 207–25.

Czakó, A. and E. Sik. (1999). Characteristics and origins of the Comecon open-air markets in Hungary. *International Journal of Urban and Regional Research* 23, 4: 716–37.

D'Alisera, J. (2004). *An imagined geography: Sierra Leonean Muslims in America*. Philadelphia: University of Pennsylvania Press.

Darby, W. J., P. Ghalioungui, and L. Grivetti. (1977). *Food: The gift of Osiris*. New York: Academic Press.

Darnton, R. (1984). *The great cat massacre and other episodes in French cultural history*. New York: Basic Books.

Davies, C. A. (1999). *Reflexive ethnography: A guide to researching selves and others*. New York: Routledge.

de Certeau, M., L. Giard, and P. Mayol. (1980). *L'invention du quotidien*. Paris: Union générale d'Éditions.

———. (1994). *L'invention du quotidien*. Vol. 2, *habiter, cuisiner*. Paris: Gallimard.

de Garine, I. (2001). Views about food prejudice and stereotypes. *Social Science Information* 40, 3: 487–507.

Delamont, S. (1995). *Appetites and identities: An introduction to the social anthropology of Western Europe*. London: Routledge.

de la Pradelle, M. (1995). Market exchange and the social construction of public space. *French Cultural Studies* 6: 359–71.

———. (1996). *Les vendredis de Carpentras: Faire son marché, en Provence ou ailleurs*. Paris: Fayard.

Del Negro, G. (2004). *The Passeggiata and popular culture in an Italian town: Folklore and the performance of modernity*. Montreal: McGill-Queens University Press.

den Hartog, A. P. (2003). Technological innovations and eating out as a mass phenomenon in Europe: A preamble. In M. Jacobs and P. Scholliers, eds., *Eating out in Europe: Picnics, gourmet dining and snacks since the late eighteenth century*. Oxford: Berg. 263–80.

Deriu, F. and G. B. Sgritta. (2005). *L'età dell'incertezza: Insicurezza, sfiducia e paura nella condizione anziana oggi*. Milano: FrancoAngeli.

Deutsch, J. (2005). Please pass the chicken tits: Rethinking men and cooking at an urban firehouse. *Food and Foodways* 13, 1: 91–114.

Donzelot, J. (1984). *L'invention du social: Essai sur le déclin des passions politiques*. Paris: Fayard.

Douglas, M. (1972). Deciphering a meal. *Daedalus* 10 (Winter): 61–81.

———, ed. 1987. *Constructive drinking: Perspectives on drink from anthropology*. New York: Cambridge University Press.

———. (1990). Foreword: No free gifts. In M. Mauss, *The Gift: The form and reason for exchange in archaic societies*. London: Routledge.

———. (2002/1966). *Purity and danger: An analysis of concepts of pollution and taboo*. New York: Routledge.

Douglas, M. and B. C. Isherwood. (1996/1979). *The world of goods: Towards an anthropology of consumption*. New York: Routledge.

Drobnick, J. (2006). Eating nothing: Cooking aromas in art and culture. In J. Drobnick, ed., *The smell culture reader*. Oxford: Berg. 342–56.

Du Bois, C. (1941). Attitudes towards food and hunger in Alor. In L. Spier, A. I. Hallowell, and S. S. Newman, eds., *Language, culture and personality: Essays in memory of Edward Sapir*. Menasha, Wis.: Sapir Memorial Publication Fund.

du Boulay, J. and R. Williams. (1987). Amoral familism and the image of limited good: A critique from a European perspective. *Anthropology Quarterly* 60: 12–24.

Duggan, C. (1994). *A concise history of Italy*. Cambridge: Cambridge University Press.

Dundes, A., ed. (1982). *The evil eye: A casebook*. Madison: University of Wisconsin Press.

Edgell, S., A. Ward, and R. Hetherington. (1996). *Consumption matters: The product and experience of consumption*. Oxford: Blackwell.

Edwards, L., S. Occhipinti, and S. Ryan. (2000). Food and immigration: The indigestion trope contests the sophistication narrative. *Journal of Intercultural Studies* 21, 3: 297–308.

Elias, N. (1965). *Logiques de l'exclusion*. Paris: Fayard.

Elliot, A. (2001). *Concepts of self*. Cambridge: Blackwell.

Falzon, M., ed. (2009). *Multi-sited ethnography: Theory, praxis and locality in contemporary research*. Burlington, Vt.: Ashgate.

Featherstone, M. (1991). *Consumer culture and postmodernism*. London: Sage.

Feige, E. L. (1990). Defining and estimating underground economies: The new institutional economic approach. *World Development* 18: 989–1002.

Féraud, O. (2003). "Les voix du marché: Le cri marchand et son écoute." Undergraduate dissertation, Université de Paris X Nanterre.

Ferguson, P. P. (2005). Eating orders: Markets, menus and meals. *Journal of Modern History* 77 (September): 275–300.

Ferguson, P. P. and S. Zukin (1995). What is cooking? *Theory and Society* 24: 193–95.

Ferro-Luzzi, A. and S. Sette. (1989). The Mediterranean diet: An attempt to define its present and past composition. *Nutrition* 43: 13–29.

Ferrol, G. (1993). *Intégration et exclusion: Dans la société française contemporaine*. Lille: Presses Universitaires de Lille.

Findlay, A. M., R. Paddison, and J. A. Dawson. (1990). *Retailing environments in developing countries*. London: Routledge.

Fischler, C. (2000). The "McDonaldization" of culture. In J-L. Flandrin and M. Montanari, eds., *Food: A culinary history from antiquity to the present*. New York: Penguin.

Fitzgerald, D. (2004). Ethnographies of migration. UCLA Department of Sociology: Theory and Research in Comparative Social Analysis Paper 19. http://www.sscnet.ucla.edu/soc/soc237/papers/dfitzgerald.pdf, accessed August 10, 2008.

Flanagan, B. (2003,) The sell-by foragers. *The Observer*. http://observer.guardian.co.uk/cash/story/0,,1091014,00.html, accessed June 2, 2006.

Fofi, G. (1975). *L'immigrazione meridionale a Torino*. Milan: Feltrinellie.

Foucault, M. (1995). *Discipline and punish: The birth of the prison*. New York: Vintage.

Frayn. J. M. (1993). *Markets and fairs in Roman Italy*. Oxford: Clarendon.

Freeman, J. (2004). *The making of the modern kitchen: A cultural history*. Oxford: Berg.

Freidlander, W. A. (1962). *Individualism and social welfare: An analysis of the system of social security and social welfare in France*. New York: Free Press.

French, M. and J. Phillips. (2000). *Cheated not poisoned? Food regulation in the United Kingdom, 1875–1938*. Manchester: Manchester University Press.

Friedman, J. (1990). Being in the world: Globalization and localization. In M. Featherstone, ed., *Global culture: Nationalism, globalization and modernity*. London: Sage.

Galesne, N. (2008). Islam en Italie: Cris de guerre médiatiques et roulements de tambours politiques. *Pensée Midi* 26, 4: 67–80.

Galt, A. H. (1982). The evil eye as synthetic image and its meaning on the island of Pantelleria, Italy. *American Ethnologist* 9, 4: 664–81.

Gambera, Armando, ed. (1992). *Ricette di osterie di Langa: I sapori di un territorio*. Bra: Slow Food Editore.

Gans, H. J. (1962). *The urban villagers: Group and class in the life of Italian-Americans*. New York: Free Press.

Gatti, F. (2006). I was a slave in Puglia. *L'Espresso*. http://espresso.repubblica.it/dettaglio/I-%20was-a-slave-in-Puglia/1373950//5, accessed May 28, 2011.

Geertz, C. (1978). The bazaar economy: Information and search in peasant marketing. *American Economic Review* 68, 2: 28–32.

———. (1988). *Works and lives: The anthropologist as author*. Stanford, Calif.: Stanford University Press.

Germann, J. M. (2007). Eating difference: The cosmopolitan mobilities of culinary tourism. *Space and culture* 10, 1: 77–93.

Giddens, A. (1991). *Modernity and self-identity: Self and society in the late modern age.* Stanford, Calif.: Stanford University Press.

Ginsborg, P. (1990). *A history of contemporary Italy: Society and politics, 1943–1988.* New York: Penguin.

Glass, R. L. (1964). *London: Aspects of change.* London: MacGibbon and Kee.

Goffman, I. (1959). *The presentation of self in everyday life.* New York: Doubleday.

Golde, P., ed. (1986). *Women in the field: Anthropological experiences.* Berkeley: University of California Press.

Goody, J. (1982). *Cooking, cuisine and class: A study in comparative sociology.* Cambridge: Cambridge University Press.

Grafmeyer, Y. (1994). *Sociologie urbaine.* Paris: Nathan Université.

Granovetter, M. (1991). Economic action and social structure: The problem of embeddedness. *American Journal of Sociology* 91: 481–510.

Gregory, J. (1984). The myth of the male ethnographer and the women's world. *American Anthropologist* 86, 2: 316–27.

Griaule, M. (1948). *Dieu d'eau: Conversations avec Ogotemmeli.* Paris: Éditions du Chêne.

Grillo, R. and J. Pratt. (2002). *The politics of recognizing difference: Multiculturalism Italian style.* Aldershot: Ashgate.

Grivetti, L. E. (1996). Wine: The food with two faces. In P. E. McGovern, ed., *The origins and ancient history of wine.* Amsterdam: Gordon and Breach.

———. (2004). *Cultural aspects of nutrition: The integration of art and science.* Oxford: Oxford University Press.

Gupta, A. and J. Ferguson. (1997). *Culture, power, place: Explorations in critical anthropology.* Durham, N.C.: Duke University Press.

Habermas, J. (1989). *The structural transformation of the public sphere: An inquiry into a category of bourgeois society.* Trans. T. Burger. Cambridge, Mass.: MIT Press.

Hall, S. M. (2009). "Private life" and "work life": Difficulties and dilemmas when making and maintaining friendships with ethnographic participants. *Area* 41, 3: 263–72.

Hannerz, U. (1980). *Exploring the city: Inquiries toward an urban anthropology.* New York: Columbia University Press.

———. (1996). *Transnational connections: Culture, people, places.* London: Routledge.

———. (2003). Being there...and there...and there! Reflections on multi-site ethnography. *Ethnography* 4, 2: 201–16.

Harper, D. and P. Faccioli. (2009). *The Italian way: Food and social life.* Chicago: University of Chicago Press.

Harris, M. (1997). The abominable pig. In C. Counihan and P. Van Estrik, eds., *Food and culture*. New York: Routledge. 67–79.

Hart, K. (1973). Informal income opportunities and urban underemployment in Ghana. *Journal of Modern African Studies* 11, 1: 61–89.

———. (1990). The idea of the economy: Six modern dissenters. In R. Friedland and A. F. Roberston, eds., *Beyond the marketplace: Rethinking economy and society*. New York: de Gruyter.

Heldke, L. (2003). *Exotic appetites: Ruminations of a food adventurer*. New York: Routledge.

———. (2005). But is it authentic? Culinary travel and the search for the genuine artifact. In C. Korsmeyer, ed., *The taste culture reader: Experiencing food and drink*. New York: Berg.

Helstosky, C. (2004). *Garlic and oil: Food and politics in Italy*. Oxford: Berg.

Henochsberg, M. (2001). *La place du marché*. Paris: Denoel.

Herzfeld, M. (1981). Meaning and morality: A semiotic approach to evil eye accusations in a Greek village. *American Ethnologist* 8, 3: 560–74.

———. (1984). The horns of the Mediterraneanist dilemma. *American Ethnologist* 11, 3: 439–54.

———. (1992). *The social production of indifference: Exploring the symbolic roots of western indifference*. Oxford: Berg.

———. (2009). Convictions: Embodied rhetorics of earnest belief. In I. Stecker and S. Tyler, eds., *Culture and Rhetoric*. Oxford: Berghahn. 182–206.

Hess, A. (2007). The social bonds of cooking: Gastronomic society in the Basque Country. *Cultural Sociology* 1, 3 (November): 383–407.

Highmore, B. (2002). *Everyday life and cultural theory: An introduction*. London: Routledge.

Hislop, Dominic. (2002). Reroute: A remapping of the city of Torino, based on the view of recent migrants. Torino Biennale of Young Art. http://www.bighope.hu/dominic/art/index.html accessed August 26, 2011.

Hochschild, A. R. (1989). *The second shift: Working parents and the revolution at home*. New York: Viking Penguin.

———. (1997). *The time bind: When work becomes home and home becomes work*. New York: Viking Penguin.

Honoré, C. (2005). *In praise of slowness*. New York: HarperOne.

Howes, D. (1996). *Cross-cultural consumption: Global markets, local realities*. London: Routledge.

Hsu, E. (2007). Participant experience: Learning to be an acupuncturist, and not becoming one. In G. de Neve and M. Unnithan, eds., *Critical journeys: The making of anthropologists*. London: Sage: 149–63.

Huag, S. (2008). Migration networks and migration decision-making. *Journal of Ethnic and Migration Studies* 34, 4: 585–605.

Huggan, G. (2000). Exoticism, ethnicity and the multicultural fallacy. In I. Santaolalla, ed., *New Exoticisms: Changing patterns in the construction of otherness*. Amsterdam: Rodopi.

Humphrey, K. (1998). *Shelf life: Supermarkets and the changing cultures of consumption*. Cambridge: Cambridge University Press.

INEA (Istituto Nazionale di Economia Agraria) (2003). L'agricoltura italiana conta. http://www.inea.it/pdf/itaconta2003ita.pdf, accessed September 9, 2005.

IRES (Istituto Ricerche Economico Sociali). (1991). *Uguali e diversi: Il mondo culturale, le reti di rapporto, i lavori degli immigrati non europei a Torino*. Turin: IRES

———. (1992). *Rumore: Atteggiamenti verso gli immigrati stranieri*. Turin: IRES.

———. (2001). *La cascina nel carrello: Tipico alimentare e grande distribuzione*. Turin: IRES.

———. (2003). *Il consumatore in cascina: Tipico alimentare e vendite dirette*. Turin: IRES.

Ismail, R. (2006). Ramadan and Bussorah Street: The spirit of place. *Geojournal* 66, 3: 243–56.

ISTAT (Istituto nazionale di statistica). (2005). Gli stranieri in Italia: analisi dei dati censuari. December 15. http://www.istat.it/salastampa/comunicati/non_calendario/20051215_01/, accessed August 7, 2008.

Jacobs, M. and P. Scholliers. (2003). *Eating out in Europe: Picnics, gourmet dining, and snacks since the late eighteenth century*. Oxford: Berg.

Jah, C. A. (2004). Markets in the northern and southern Mediterranean: A historical perspective. In J. Angli et al., *Mercados del Mediterráneo*. Barcelona: IEMED & Lunwerg. 219–25.

Johnston, J. and S. Baumann. (2010). *Foodies: Democracy and distinction in the gourmet foodscape*. New York: Routledge.

Joseph, M. (1999). Introduction: New hybridity and performance. In M. Joseph and J. N. Fink, eds., *Performing hybridity*. Minneapolis: University of Minnesota Press.

Katrk, K. (2005). Food and belonging: At "home" in "alien kitchens." In A. V. Avakian, ed., *Through the kitchen window: Women explore the intimate meanings of food and cooking*. New York: Berg. 263–75.

Kaplan, J. (1980). *A woman's conflict: The special relationship between women and food*. Englewood Cliffs, N.J.: Prentice-Hall.

Kaplan, S. (1996). *The bakers of Paris and the bread question, 1700–1775*. Durham, N.C.: Duke University Press.

Kelleher, W. (2003). *The troubles in Ballybogoin: Memory and identity in Northern Ireland*. Ann Arbor: University of Michigan Press.

Kershen, A. J. (2002). *Food in the migrant experience*. Aldershot: Ashgate.

King, R., G. Lazaridis, and C. G. Tsardanides. (2000). *Eldorado or fortress? Migration in southern Europe*. New York: St. Martin's.

Klepper, N. (1999). *Taste of Romania: Its cookery and glimpses of its history, folklore, art, literature and poetry*. New York: Hippoerene.

Kopytoff, I. (1986). The cultural biography of things: Commoditization as process. In A. Appadurai, ed., *The social life of things: Commodities in cultural perspective*. New York: Cambridge University Press. 64–91.

La Cecla, F. (1988). *Perdersi: L'uomo senza ambiente*. Rome: Laterza.

———. (1993). *Mente locale: Per un'antropologia dell'abitare*. Milan: Eleuthera.

Lagnà, G. (2006). The EU's "basic values" and irregular migrants: Common principles for integration or exclusion? *Migration online*. http://www.temaasyl. se/Documents/Organisationer/Ovriga/Lagana%20-%20Basic%20values%20 and%20irregular%20migrants.pdf, accessed May 28, 2011.

Langman, L. (1992). Neon cages: Shopping for subjectivity. In R. Shields, ed., *Lifestyle shopping: The subject of consumption*. London: Routledge.

Lapavitsas, C. (2004). Commodities and gifts: Why commodities represent more than market relations. *Science and Society* 68, 1: 33–56.

Latouche, S. (2002). Introduzione: Il mercato, l'agora e l'acropoli. In M. Aime, *La casa di nessuno: I mercati in Africa occidentale*. Torino: Bollati Botinghieri.

Leach, E. (1964). Anthropological categories of verbal abuse. In Eric Lenneberg, ed., *New directions in the study of language*. Cambridge, Mass.: MIT Press.

Lee, D. O. (1992). Commodification of ethnicity: The social spatial reproduction of immigrant entrepreneurs. *Urban Affairs* 28, 2: 258–75.

Lee, N. and R. Munro. (2001). *The consumption of mass*. Oxford: Blackwell/Sociological Review.

Lee, P. Y., ed. (2008). *Meat, modernity and the rise of the slaughterhouse*. Lebanon: University of New Hampshire Press.

Lee, S. and G. A. Fin. (2005). The presentation of ethnic authenticity: Chinese food as social accomplishment. *Sociology Quarterly* 36, 3: 535–53.

Lefebvre, H. (1947). *Critique de la vie quotidienne*. Vol. 1. Paris: L'Arche.

Leitch, A. (2000). The social life of lardo: Slow food in fast times. *Asia Pacific Journal of Anthropology* (formerly *Canberra Anthropology*) 1: 103–18.

Levenstein, H. A. (2003). *Paradox of plenty: A social history of eating in modern America*. Berkeley: University of California Press.

Levi, F. and S. Musso. (2004). *Torino da capitale politica a capitale dell'industria: Il mercato economico (1950–1970)*. Torino: Archivio Storico della Città di Torino.

Lévi-Strauss, C. (1964). *Le cru et le cuit*. Paris: Plon.

Leynse, W. (2006). Journeys through "ingestible topography": Socializing the "situated eater" in France. In T. Wilson, ed., *Food, Drink and Identity in Europe*. European studies: An Interdisciplinary Series in European Culture, History and Politics 24. Amsterdam, Rodopi.

Lindenfeld, J. (1990). *Speech and sociability at French urban marketplaces*. Philadelphia: Benjamins.

List, J. (2009). The economics of open-air markets. NBER working paper, October. http://www.nber.org/papers/w15420, accessed May 6, 2011.

Lockwood, W. G. (1975). *European Moslems: Economy and ethnicity in western Bosnia*. New York: Academic Press.

Long, L. M. (1998). Culinary tourism: A folkloristic perspective on eating otherness. *Southern Folklore* 55, 3.

———, ed. (2004). *Culinary tourism*. Lexington: University Press of Kentucky.

Low, S. M. (1999). *Theorizing the city: The new urban anthropology reader*. New Brunswick, N.J.: Rutgers University Press.

———. (2000). *On the plaza: The politics of public space and culture*. Austin: University of Texas Press.

Low, S. M. and D. Lawrence-Zúñiga. (2003). *The anthropology of space and place: Locating culture*. Malden, Mass.: Blackwell.

Low, S. M. and N. Smith. (2005). *The politics of public space*. New York: Routledge.

Low, S. M., D. Taplin, and S. Scheld. (2005). *Rethinking urban parks: Public space and cultural diversity*. Austin: University of Texas Press.

Lu, S. and G. A. Fine. (1995). The presentation of ethnic authenticity: Chinese food as a social accomplishment. *Sociology Quarterly* 36, 3: 535–53.

Lunt, P. K. and S. M. Livingstone. (1992). *Mass consumption and personal identity: Everyday economic experience*. Philadelphia: Open University Press.

Maher, V. (1996). Immigration and social identities. In D. Forgacs and R. Lumley, eds., *Italian cultural studies*. Oxford: Oxford University Press. 160–77.

Maho, J. (1980). Les aspects non économiques des foires et marchés. *Études Rurales* 78–79–80: 65–68.

Maida, B. (2004). Nuovi prodotti, nuovi consumi. In F. Levi and S. Musso, eds., *Torino: da capitale politica a capitale industriale: il miracolo economico (1950–1970)*. Turin: Archivio Storico della Città di Torino.

Malerba, C. (1997). *Ambulanti, mercati, fiere, botteghe: Il cammino storico del piccolo commercio nella sua evoluzione socio-economica*. Emilia Romagna: Nuovo Cescot; Trenta: Grafiche Futura.

Manalansan, M. F., IV. (2006). Immigrant lives and the politics of olfaction in the global city. In J. Drobnick, ed., *The smell culture reader*. Oxford: Berg. 41–52.

Mann, B. (1976). The Ethics of fieldwork in an urban bar. In M. Rynkiewich and

J. Spradley, eds., *Ethics and anthropology: Dilemmas in fieldwork*. Malabar, Fla.: Kreiger. 95–109.

Marcus, G. (1995). Ethnography in/of the world system: The emergence of multi-sited ethnography. *Annual Review of Anthropology* 24: 95–117.

Marcus, G. (1998). *Anthropology through thick and thin*. Princeton, NJ: Princeton University Press.

Maritano, L. (2000a). Popular racism, modernity and Europe: An ethnography on Turin (Italy). Paper presented at the European Political-Economy Infrastructure Consortium (EPIC) Ionian Conference, 2000.

———. (2000b). Rappresentazione degli immigrati a Torino: Problemi per l'antirazzismo. *Afriche e Orienti* 3–4: 124–30.

Markowitz, F. and M. Ashkenazi. (1999). *Sex, sexuality, and the anthropologist*. Urbana: University of Illinois Press.

Markowitz, L. (2010). Expanding access and alternatives: Building farmers' markets in low-income communities. *Food and Foodways* 18, 1–2: 66–80.

Marsden, T., A. Flynn, and M. Harrison. (2000). *Consuming interests: The social provision of foods*. London: UCL Press.

Marte, Lidia. (2007). Foodmaps: Tracing boundaries of "home" through food relations. *Food and Foodways* 15, 3–4: 261–89.

Mauss, M. (1950). *Essai sur le don*. New York: Routledge.

Marx, K. (1994). The commodity. In L. H. Simon, ed., *Karl Marx: Selected Writings*. Cambridge: Hackett.

Mayes, Frances. (1997). *Under the Tuscan sun: At home in Italy*. New York: Broadway Books.

Medina, X. (2004). The markets of the future: Some thoughts and the outlook. In J. Angli et al., *Mercados del Mediterráneo*. Barcelona: IEMED and Lunwerg. 264–68.

Meyer, B. and P. Geschiere, eds. (1999). *Globalization and identity: Dialectics of flow and closure*. Oxford: Blackwell.

Micheli, G. A. (1996). New patterns of family formation in Italy: Which tools for which interpretations. *Genus* 52, 1–2: 15–52.

Miller, D. (1987). *Material culture and mass consumption*. New York: Blackwell.

———. (1995a). *Acknowledging consumption: A review of new studies*. New York: Routledge.

———. (1995b). Consumption and commodities. *Annual Review of Anthropology* 24: 141–61.

———. (2001). *The dialectics of shopping*. Lewis Henry Morgan Lectures 1998. Chicago: University of Chicago Press.

Mintz, S. W. (1985). *Sweetness and power: The place of sugar in modern history*. New York: Viking.

———. (1996). *Tasting food, tasting freedom: Excursions into eating, culture, and the past*. Boston: Beacon Press.

Moati, P. (2001). *L'avenir de la grande distribution*. Paris: Jacob.

Mott, L., R. H. Silin, and S. W. Mintz. (1975). *A supplementary bibliography on marketing and marketplaces*. Monticello, Ill.: Council of Planning Librarians.

Mumford, L. (1961). *The city in history: Its origins, its transformations, and its prospects*. New York: Harcourt, Brace.

Nestle, M. (2002). *Food politics: How the food industry influences nutrition and health*. Berkeley: University of California Press.

Ong, A. (1999). *Flexible citizenship: The cultural logics of transnationality*. Durham, N.C.: Duke University Press.

Orsini-Jones, M. and F. Gattullo. (2000). Migrant. In F. Anthias and G. Lazaridis, eds. *Gender and migration in southern Europe: Women on the move*. New York: Berg. 128–49.

Ortner, S. (1974). Is female to male as nature is to culture? In M. Z. Rosaldo and Louise Lamphere, eds., *Women, culture and society*. Stanford, Calif.: Stanford University Press. 67–87.

Osservatorio Interistituzionale sugli stranieri in provincia di Torino. (2004). *Rapporto 2003*. Turin: Osservatorio.

Parkins, W. and G. Craig. (2006). *Slow living*. New York: Berg.

Passerini, L. (1988). *Storia e soggettività: Le fonti orali, le memoria*. Scandicci (Firenze): Nuova Italia.

Paxson, H. (2008). Post-pasteurian cultures: The microbiopolitics of raw-milk cheese in the United States. *Cultural Anthropology* 23, 1: 15–47.

Peraldi, M., ed. (2001). *Cabas et containers: Activités marchandes informelles et réseaux migrants transfrontaliers*. Paris: Maisonneuve and Larose.

———, ed. (2002). *La fin des norias? Réseaux migrants dans les économies marchandes en Méditerranée*. Paris: Maisonneuve and Larose.

Peraldi, M., N. Foughali, and N. Spinouza. (1995). Les marchés des pauvres: Espace commercial et espace public. *Revue Européenne des Migration Internationales* 11: 77–97.

Peterson, R. (2005). In search of authenticity. *Journal of Management Studies* 42, 5: 1083–98.

Petrini, C. (2007). *Slow food nation: Why our food should be good, clean and fair*. Trans. C. Furlan and J. Hunt. New York: Rizzoli.

Phillips, L. (2006). Food and globalization. *Annual Review of Anthropology* 35: 37–57.

Picon, A. (2001). Espaces publics, espaces dangereux. *Geocarrefour* 76, 1: 23–26.

Pilcher, J. (1998). *Que vivan los tamales! Food and the making of Mexican identity.* Albuquerque: University of New Mexico Press.

Pinelli, A. and A. Golini. (1993). *Population aging in Italy.* Malta: INIA/CICRED.

Pink, S. (2001). *Doing visual ethnography: Images, media, and representation in research.* London: Sage.

Plattner, S. (1985). *Markets and marketing.* Lanham, Md.: University Press of America.

———. (1989). *Economic anthropology.* Stanford, Calif.: Stanford University Press.

Polanyi, K. (1944). *The great transformation: The political and economic origins of our time.* Boston: Beacon Press.

———. (1957). *Trade and market in the early empires: Economies in history and theory.* Glencoe, Ill: Free Press.

Portes, A. (1995). *The economic sociology of immigration: Essays on networks, ethnicity, and entrepreneurship.* New York: Russell Sage.

———. (1999). La mondialisation par le bas, l'émergence des communautés transnationales. *Actes de la Recherche en Sciences Sociales* 129: 5–25.

Portes, A. and M. Castells. (1989). *The informal economy: Studies in advanced and less developed countries.* Baltimore: Johns Hopkins University Press.

Portes, A. and W. Haller. (2005). The Informal economy. In N. J. Smelser and R. Swedberg, eds., *The handbook of economic sociology.* Princeton, N.J.: Princeton University Press: 403–28.

Portes, A. and J. Sensenbrenner. (1993). Embeddedness and immigration: Notes on the social determinants of economic action. *American Journal of Sociology* 98: 1320–50.

Poulain, J.-P. (2002a). *Manger aujourd'hui: Attitudes, normes et pratiques.* Toulouse: Privat.

———. (2002b). *Sociologies de l'alimentation: Les mangeurs et l'espace social alimentaire.* Paris: Presses Universitaires de France.

Premazzi, K. and E. Colaprice. (2005). In giro per mercati, mercatini e fiere: Si fa shopping e se ne dice un gran bene. *GDOWEER,* May 11, 2005: 42–44.

Prioton, P. (2000). *Les marchés de Provence.* Geneva: Aubanel.

Probyn, E. (1993). *Sexing the self: Gendered positions in cultural studies.* London: Routledge.

Pugliese, E. (2002). *L'Italia tra migrazioni internazionali e migrazioni interne.* Bologna: Mulino.

Ram, M. and T. Jones. (1998). *Ethnic minorities in business.* Milton Keynes: Small Business Research Trust.

Rava, A. (2007). Dati statistici sull'immigrazione straniera a Torino nel 2006.

Comune di Torino. http://www.comune.torino.it/statistica/osservatorio/stran-ieri/2006/index.htm, accessed July 6, 2008.

Ray, K. (2004). *The migrant's table: Meals and memories in Bengali-American house-holds.* Philadelphia: Temple University Press.

Reed-Danahay, D. (1997). *Auto/ethnography: Rewriting the self and the social.* Oxford: Berg.

Richardson, M. (1982). Being-in-the-market versus being-in-the-plaza: Material culture and the construction of social reality in Spanish America. *American Ethnological Society* 9: 421–36.

Robinson, J. M. and J. A. Hartenfeld. (2007). *The farmers' market book: Growing food, cultivating community.* Bloomington: University of Indiana Press.

Rojek, C. and J. Urry. (1997). *Touring cultures: Transformations of travel and theory.* London: Routledge.

Ross, K. (1995). *Fast cars, clean bodies: Decolonization and the reordering of French culture.* Cambridge, Mass.: MIT Press.

Rossi, A. S. (1993). The future in the making: Recent trends in work-family interface. *American Journal of Orthopsychiatry* 62, 2: 166–76.

Rozin, P. (1982). Human food selection: The interaction between biology, culture, and individual experience. In L. M. Barker, ed., *The psychobiology of human food selection.* Westport, Conn.: AVI. 225–54.

Rozin, P., C. Fischler, S. Imada, A. Sarcubin, and A. Wrzsniewski. (1999). Attitudes to food and the role of food in life in the U.S.A., Japan, Flemish Belgium and France: Possible implications for the diet-health debate. *Appetite* 33, 2: 163–80.

Rubino, M. (2011). Farmer's market in controtendenza cresce la spesa a chilometro zero. *La Repubblica,* May 25. http://www.repubblica.it/economia/2011/05/25/news/farmer_s_market_in_controtendenza_cresce_la_spesa_a_km_zero-16733210/index.html?ref=search, accessed May 28, 2011.

Ruby, J. (2000). *Picturing culture: Explorations of film and anthropology.* Chicago: University of Chicago Press.

Sacchi, P. and P. P. Viazzo (2003). *Più di un sud: Studi antropologici sull'immigrazione a Torino.* Milano: FrancoAngeli.

Salih, R. (2003). *Gender in transnationalism: Home, longing and belonging among Moroccan migrant women.* New York: Routledge.

Saraceno, C. (2004). The Italian family from the 1960s to the present. *Modern Italy* 9, 1: 47–57.

Schlosser, E. (2001). *Fast food nation: The dark side of the all-American meal.* New York: Houghton Mifflin.

Schmiechen, J. and K. Carls. (1999). *The British market hall: A social and architectural history.* New Haven, Conn.: Yale University Press.

Schor, J. and M. Ford. (2007). From tastes great to cool: Children's food marketing and the rise of the symbolic. *Journal of Law, Medicine and Ethics* 35, 1: 10–21.

Sciardet, H. (2003). *Les marchands de l'aube: Ethnographie et théorie du commerce aux Puces de Saint-Ouen.* Paris: Economica.

Seligmann, L. J. (2001). *Women traders in cross-cultural perspective: Mediating identities, marketing wares.* Stanford, Calif.: Stanford University Press.

Semi, G. (2004). Le multiculturalisme quotidien: Porta Palazzo entre commerce et conflit. Doctoral dissertation, Universitá degli Studi di Torino, EHESS, Paris.

Sennett, R. (1977). *The fall of public man.* Cambridge: Cambridge University Press.

Seremetakis, C. N. (1994). The memory of the senses: Pts. 1 and 2. In C. N. Seremetakis, ed., *The senses still: Perception and memory as material culture in modernity.* Boulder, Colo.: Westview. 1–43.

Serventi, S., ed. (1995). *Il cuoco piemontese perfezionato a Parigi 1776* (Torino, 1776). Bra: Slow Food.

Shakow, D. (1981). The municipal farmer's market as an urban service. *Economic Geography* 57, 1: 68–77.

Sik, E. and C. Wallace. (1999). The development of open-air markets in East-Central Europe. *International Journal of Urban and Regional Research* 23, 4: 697–714.

Simmel, G. (1990). *The philosophy of money.* London: Routledge.

——. (1949). The Sociology of sociability. Trans. C. Hughes. *American Journal of Sociology* 55, 3: 254–61.

—— (1997). *Simmel on culture: Selected writings.* Ed. D. Frisby and M. Featherstone. London: Sage.

Skinner, G. W. (1964). Marketing and social structure in rural China. *Journal of Asian Studies* 24: 3–43.

——. (1985). Rural marketing in China: Revival and reappraisal. In S. Plattner, ed., *Markets and marketing.* Lanham, Md.: University Press of America. 7–47.

Smith, A. and J. B. Mackinnon. (2007). *The 100-mile diet: A year of local eating.* Toronto: Random House Canada.

Smith, R. H. T. (1978). *Market-place trade: Periodic markets, hawkers, and traders in Africa, Asia, and Latin America.* Vancouver: Centre for Transportation Studies.

Smith, T. B. (1997). The ideology of charity, the image of the English poor law, and debates over the right to assistance in France, 1830–1905. *Historical Journal* 40, 4: 997–1032.

Sobal, J. (2005). Men, meat and marriage: Models of masculinity. *Food and Foodways* 13, 1: 201–29.

Sorcinelli, P. (1982). *La pellagra e la morte: Medici condotti, malattia e società alla fine del XIX secolo.* Ancona: Lavoro Editoriale.

————. (1992). *Gli italiani e il cibo: Appetiti, digiuni e rinunce dalla realtà contadina alla società del benessere*. Bologna: CLUEB.

Spang, R. (2000). *The invention of the restaurant: Paris and modern gastronomic culture*. Cambridge, Mass.: Harvard University Press.

Sperber, G. (2002). *The art of Romanian cooking*. Gretna, La.: Pelican.

Stallybrass, P. and A. White. (1986). *The politics and poetics of transgression*. London: Methuen.

Stanziani, A. (2005). *Histoire de la qualité alimentaire: XIXe–XXe siècle*. Paris: Seuil.

Stewart, K. (1988). Nostalgi: A polemic. *Cultural Anthropology* 3, 3: 227–41.

Striffler, S. (2002). Inside a poultry processing plant: An ethnographic portrait. *Labor History* 43: 305–13.

Sutton, D. (2001). *Remembrance of repasts: An anthropology of food and memory*. Oxford: Berg.

————. (2005). Synesthesia, memory and the taste of home. In C. Korsmeyer, ed., *The taste culture reader: Experiencing food and drink*. New York: Berg. 304–16.

————. (2006). Cooking skill, the sense, and memory: The fate of practical knowledge. In Edwards, et al., eds., *Sensible objects: colonialism, museums and material culture*. New York: Berg. 87–120.

Swinbank, V. A. (2002). The sexual politics of cooking: A feminist analysis of culinary hierarchy in western culture. *Journal of Historical Sociology* 15, 4: 464–94.

Tangires, H. (2002). *Public markets and civic culture in nineteenth-century America*. Baltimore: Johns Hopkins University Press.

Tapinos, G. (1999). Migration, trade and development: The European Union and the Maghreb countries. In R. King, G. Lazaridis, and C. Tsardanidis, eds., *Eldorado or fortress? Migration in Southern Europe*. London: Macmillan. 277–97.

Tarrius, A. (1992). *Les fourmis d'Europe: Migrants riches, migrants pauvres et nouvelles villes*. Paris: Harmattan.

Testa, R. M. (2000). Fewer and older Italians, more problems? Looking for solutions to the demographic question. http://www.un.org/esa/population/publications/popdecline/Testa.pdf, accessed May 27, 2001.

Teti, V. (1978). *Il pane, la beffa e la festa: Cultura alimentare e ideologia dell'alimentazione nelle classi subalterne*. Firenze: Guaraldi.

————. (1999). *Il colore del cibo: Geografia, mito e realtà dell'alimentazione mediterranea*. Roma: Meltemi.

Thélamon, F. (1992). Sociabilité et conduites alimentaires. In M. Aurell, O. Dumoulin, and F. Thélamon, eds., *La sociabilité à table: Commensalité et convivialité à travers les âges: actes du [3e] Colloque de Rouen . . . 14–17 novembre 1990*. Rouen: Université de Rouen. 9–16.

Thompson, V. E. (1997). Urban renovation, moral regeneration: Domesticating the Halles in Second Empire Paris. *French Historical Studies* 20, 1: 87–109.

Trappolin, L. (2005). Gender victims and cultural borders: The globalization of prostitution in Italy. *Dialectical Anthropology* 29, 3–4: 335–48.

Triani, G. (1996). Dalla casa al supermercato e viceversa: Luoghi e percorsi del consumo. In G. Triani, ed., *Casa e supermercato*. Milan: Eleuthera.

Trubek, A. (2000). *Haute cuisine: How the French invented the culinary profession*. Philadelphia: University of Pennsylvania Press.

———. (2008). *The taste of place: A cultural journey into "terroir."* Berkeley: University of California Press.

Turner, V. (1967). *The Forest of symbols: Aspects of Ndembu ritual*. Ithaca, N.Y.: Cornell University Press.

Ufficio Statistica Comune di Torino. (2009). Residenti stranieri per nazionalità e circonscrizione, dati anagrafici al 31/12/2009. http://www.comune.torino.it/statistica/dati/pdf/nazionalitastranieriresidenticircoscrizione09.pdf, accessed August 20, 2011.

Varaldi, M., prod. and dir. (2006). *Quattro canti del mercato*. Torino: Kinoetika.

Venturi, R., D. Scott Brown, and S. Izenour. (1977). *Learning from Las Vegas: The forgotten symbolism of architectural form*. Cambridge, Mass.: MIT Press.

Villermet, J.-M. (1991). *Naissance de l'hypermarché*. Paris: A. Colin.

Ward, R. and R. Jenkins. (1984). *Ethnic communities in business: Strategies for economic survival*. Cambridge: Cambridge University Press.

Warnier, J.-P. (1994). *Le paradoxe de la marchandise authentique: Imaginaire et consommation de masse*. Paris: Harmattan.

Warnier, J.-P., C. Rosselin. (1996). *Authentifier la marchandise: Anthropologie critique de la quête d'authenticité*. Paris: Harmattan.

Warren, C. and J. K. Hackney. (2000). *Gender issues in ethnography*. London: Sage.

Watson, J. L. and M. L. Caldwell. (2005). *The cultural politics of food and eating: A reader*. Malden, Mass.: Blackwell.

Whellan, A., N. Wrigley, D. Warm, and E. Cannings. (2002). Life in a food desert. *Urban Studies* 39, 11: 2083–2100.

Whitehead, T. L. and M. E. Conaway, eds. (1986). *Self, sex and gender in cross-cultural fieldwork*. Urbana: University of Illinois Press.

Wilk, R. (1993). Beauty and the feast: Official and visceral nationalism in Belize. *Ethnos* 58: 294–316.

———. 2006. *Home cooking in the global village: Caribbean food from buccaneers to ecotourists*. New York: Berg.

Williams, R. H. (1982). *Dream worlds: Mass consumption in late nineteenth-century France*. Berkeley: University of California Press.

Wilson, M. (2005). Indulgence. In D. Kulick and A. Meneley, eds., *Fat: The anthropology of an obsession*. New York: Penguin: 153–67.

Wilson, T., ed. (2005). *Drinking cultures: Alcohol and the expression of national identity*. Oxford: Berg.

Wolff, K. H., ed. (1959). *Georg Simmel, 1858–1918: A collection of essays, with translations and a bibliography*. Columbus: Ohio State University Press.

Woodward, K. (1997). *Identity and difference*. London: Sage

Yom, S. L. (2005). Islam and globalization: Secularism, religion and radicalism. In A. Pfaller and M. Lerch, eds., *Challenges of globalization: New trends in international politics and society*. Edison, N.J.: Transaction Books. 27–46.

Zincone, G. (2000). *Primo rapporto sull'integrazione degli immigrati in Italia*. Bologna: Mulino.

Zola, E. (1888). *Le ventre de Paris*. Paris: Charpentier.

Zukin, S. (1989). *Loft living: Culture and capital in urban change*. New Brunswick, N.J.: Rutgers University Press.

———. (1991). *Landscapes of power: From Detroit to Disney World*. Berkeley: University of California Press.

———. (1995). *The cultures of cities*. Cambridge, Mass.: Blackwell.

INDEX

ACKNOWLEDGMENTS

This book began back in 2001, and many people have helped and encouraged me along the way. The people who shop, work and live at Porta Palazzo made my experience there possible; they let me into their world, shared their bread and stories with me. Thank you Rosella, Luigi, Andrea, Piero, Antonella, Andrea, Pier, Said, Luca, Davide, Naima, Paolo, Bruna, Alberto, Mohamed, Marco, Irene and Walter. Alberto without you, I would never have come to live in Italy and know your wonderful city. I would like to thank Carole Counihan for many years of mentorship, advice and encouragement. Her work in the anthropology of food has been an inspiration to me throughout my career. Many thanks are due to Paolo Viazzo at the University of Turin for his patience and support during my fieldwork, and to Francesco Remotti and others in the in the Anthropology Department. You offered constant intellectual stimulation and you pushed me to think of the world in new ways. Through the numerous rewrites of this manuscript, my husband Doug Cook encouraged and reassured me. Thank you to the students in my Anthropology of Food graduate class at Boston University, Katie Dolph, Michael Kostyo, Michelle Hastings, Lara Zelman, and Jennifer Logan, for their feedback on my manuscript. Thank you to Alex Galimberti for his help with indexing. I appreciated the opportunity to share a chapter in progress with Heather Paxson and her graduate class at MIT. Thank you to the reviewers who took the time to give me the constructive feedback that helped me shape this project into a book. I was fortunate to have insightful and encouraging comments and input from Kirin Narayan and Alma Gottlieb, the Contemporary Ethnography Series editors.

The writing of this book was made possible thanks to fellowship support from the International School of Advanced Studies at the University of Turin and from the University of Gastronomic Sciences.

CPSIA information can be obtained
at www.ICGtesting.com
Printed in the USA
JSHW030440121220
10199JS00002B/30

9 780812 2231